2/56

# Nothing to Lose

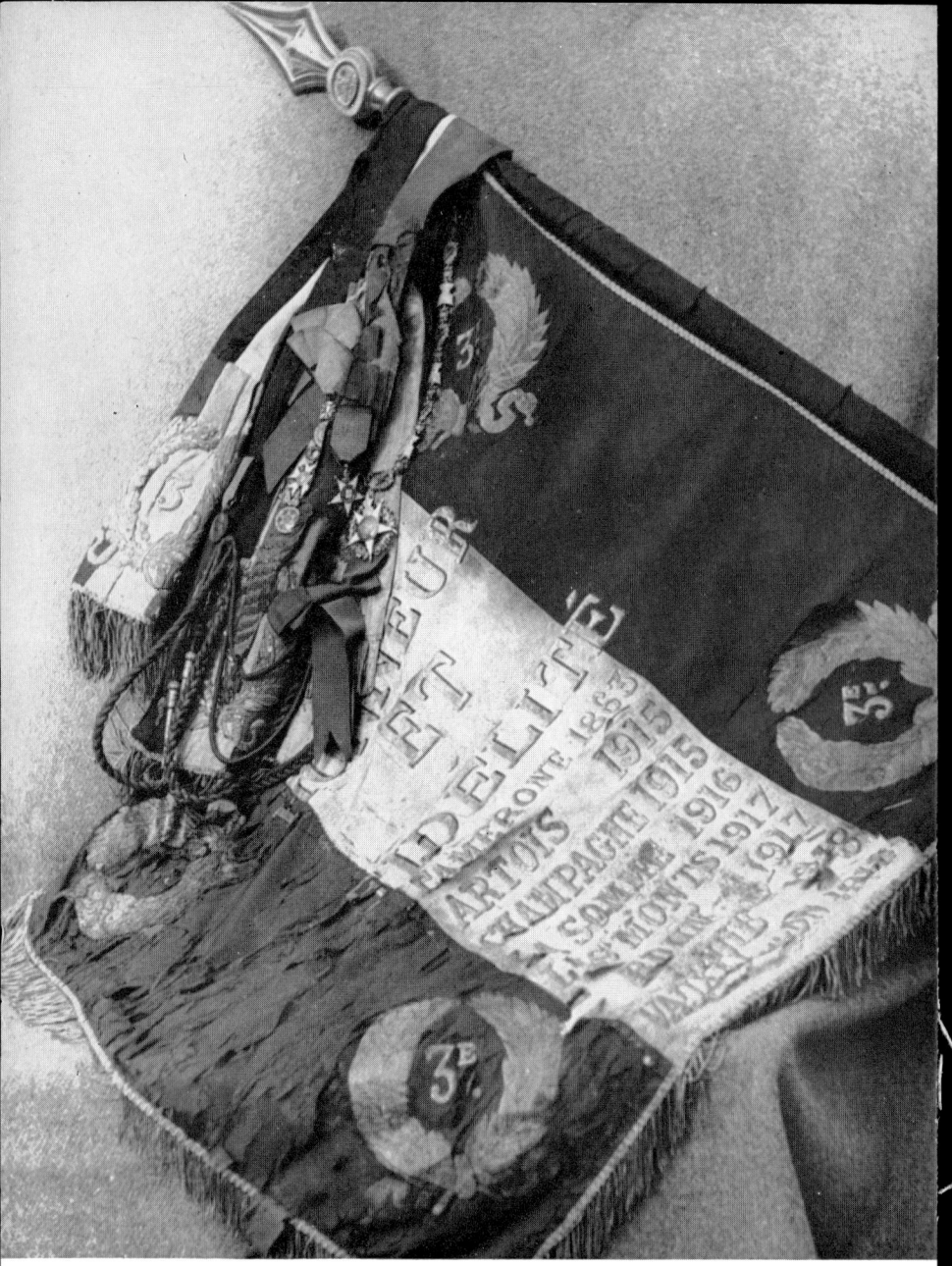

HONNEUR ET FIDÉLITÉ

The Regimental Colour of the 3rd Infantry Regiment, Foreign Legion

COLIN JOHN

# NOTHING TO LOSE

Andrew S. Thomas Memorial Library
Morris Harvey College, Charleston, W. Va.

**CASSELL & COMPANY LTD**
LONDON

CASSELL & COMPANY LTD
37/38 St. Andrew's Hill, Queen Victoria Street,
London. E.C.4

*and at*

31/34 George IV Bridge, Edinburgh
210 Queen Street, Melbourne
26/30 Clarence Street, Sydney
C.P.O. 3031, Auckland, N.Z.
1068 Broadview Avenue, Toronto 6
P.O. Box 275, Cape Town
P.O. Box 1386, Salisbury, S. Rhodesia
Munsoor Building, Main Street, Colombo 11
Haroon Chambers, South Napier Road, Karachi
13/14 Ajmeri Gate Extension, New Delhi 1
15 Graham Road, Ballard Estate, Bombay 1
17 Chittaranjan Avenue, Calcutta 13
Avenida 9 de Julho 1138, São Paulo
Galeria Güemes, Escritorio 518/520, Florida 165, Buenos Aires
P.O. Box 959, Accra, Gold Coast
25 rue Henri Barbusse, Paris 5e
Islands Brygge 5, Copenhagen

Copyright, 1955, by Colin John

FIRST PUBLISHED 1955

SET IN 12 PT. BEMBO TYPE AND
PRINTED AND BOUND IN ENGLAND BY
HAZELL WATSON AND VINEY LTD
AYLESBURY AND LONDON
F. 655

Au
TROISIEME REGIMENT ETRANGER
D'INFANTERIE

*'Mes amis, remplissex les verres!*
*Attention à la poussière!*
*Envoyez! Et vive la Légion!'*

# ILLUSTRATIONS

Honneur et Fidélité. The Regimental Colour of the 3rd
Infantry Regiment, Foreign Legion — *Frontispiece*

|  | FACING PAGE |
|---|---|
| Sidi Bel-Abbès, the handiwork of legionnaires | 48 |
| Camerone: Music, pomp and ceremony | 49 |
| Camerone: The march-past, with the pioneer company in their traditional parade uniform | 49 |
| Tongking in the heat of the summer | 64 |
| Hanoi—with the Transport Company | 64 |
| Legionnaires improving their quarters at Nam-Dinh | 65 |
| The road to Nam-Dinh | 65 |
| Nam-Dinh. The sentry outside the rear-base | 144 |
| Fixed defences overlooking the Red River | 145 |
| Ancient and modern in Indo-China | 160 |
| Legionnaires with American equipment | 160 |
| 'At the risk of losing boots and blood' | 161 |
| 'Go to ground and fire back' | 161 |
| The concentration camp by the church | 240 |
| Captured ammunition | 240 |
| Dropping-ground for supplies in Laos | 241 |
| 'Isabelle' | 256 |
| The men who had nothing to lose | 257 |

# FOREWORD

WITH the exception of the last chapter, the contents of this book represent my own experiences during five and a half years in the French Foreign Legion. Names of persons have been changed, and in many cases place-names as well. Sometimes I have even grouped two or more real persons or incidents together in order to make more interesting characters and situations for the narrative; but I have invented nothing. Everything in this account has a real basis of truth.

The last chapter, which describes the death agony of 'Isabelle', the Legion strong-point at Dien Bien Phu, is based on the story told me by a *sous-officier* who was severely wounded during the break-out, and was afterwards evacuated according to the terms of the agreement reached at Geneva. I visited him in the Val de Grace Military Hospital in Paris, and he gave me the details. They merely confirmed how I had imagined things to have been when I heard the news.

I have said some pretty harsh things about the French in these pages, and particularly about French officers serving in Indo-China. I am not the least bit anti-French. I love France and I like and admire the French people, but their greatest faults are precisely the ones which they usually attribute to us, the British. They are conservative, insular, and pig-headed. The consequence is that for them whatever is, is right, and so they go on using the most outmoded system of army administration in the world. It was invented by Napoleon, and has scarcely been changed since. It is slow, cumbersome, and leaves the road wide open to corruption, but—it was good enough for Napoleon!

FOREWORD

The call of the Legion, like Masefield's call of the sea, is a 'wild call and a clear call that may not be denied'. I might very possibly go back and sign on for another spell. So, with this book published, I shall perhaps spend a few years collecting material for another one—on the subject of Cayenne!

C. J.

# 1

I WAS leaning against the wall, my elbows on the parapet, my chin cupped in my hands, and was gazing out over the blue waters of the harbour. With the exception of that pair of red socks, I was wearing the same clothes I had worn for the previous month: a pair of brown shoes, very much down at heel, an old grey suit, frayed between the legs by the action of those same kilometres which had deprived the shoes of their heels, a shirt which had been cream in colour but was now almost as grey as the suit, and a red silk scarf. The socks had been given me by the wife of the *patron* of the *auberge* in the little village of Palette, just outside Aix-en-Provence. I left my overcoat there to pay for my night's lodging, so she hadn't done too badly out of the exchange.

The red socks, I suppose, came out of her husband's wardrobe and were a little too small for me; but they were better than no socks at all, and I had walked over two hundred miles since the last pair had fallen to pieces. One pair on the feet and one in the pocket is not a sufficient supply for a march of six hundred miles, I had discovered.

The contents of my pockets were not very much more exciting than my clothes: a tooth-brush, now used with water only, since the tube of toothpaste gave out six days before, a couple of handkerchiefs, and a wallet containing the fifty francs I had miraculously managed to save out of the thousand with which I had started from Strasbourg. Not a bad result, I thought, as I smiled wryly at the inside of my wallet. Six hundred miles on foot with a total outlay of nine hundred and fifty francs—less than one pound sterling!

I felt in my left-hand breast-pocket, but that, of course, was empty since the passport which it usually contained had been handed to the authorities at my first interview. But no, not quite empty! My fingers groped down to the bottom and found there three cigarettes—genuine Players, not the evil-tasting Gauloises I had been smoking, whenever I had a chance, since my supply of English cigarettes was exhausted. I remembered that before leaving the hotel at Strasbourg, I had stuffed all my pockets with packets of cigarettes from the carton I had in my suitcase. These three must have fallen out of the one which I was carrying in my breast-pocket. I took out my three treasures and laid them carefully upon the parapet before me.

The man beside me coughed.

We had already exchanged a few words, for we had walked in through the gates of the Fort at practically the same time. I had been hesitating outside, trying to make up my mind, but, when he came up from the direction of the Vieux Port, crossed the swing-bridge, and walked resolutely into the Fort, I plucked up courage and followed him in.

The result was that we waited together to be interviewed, lounging about with our hands in our pockets with the rest of them in that gloomy corridor, listening to a babel of conversation in all the languages of Europe. Three of the men waiting there were talking in German, two in French, and two in Italian. The others were speaking in a variety of tongues which I thought might have been Hungarian, Rumanian, Polish, and Russian. I had asked the stocky little man beside me to give me a light for my cigarette. When he returned a blank stare, I had repeated the question in German, still without result.

'Na,' said one of the Germans, ''s ist ein Kroat. He's a Croat and doesn't understand any civilized language.'

What a mixture! I remember thinking. How on earth do they

manage to command, control, and administer this mob?

I did not have to wait long to find out, for at that instant a huge hulk of a sergeant appeared in the corridor.

'There's too much bloody noise going on here,' he yelled. He spoke French, but everyone must have understood, for there was immediate silence, except, that is, for one of the Germans who had been talking so loudly that he had not even noticed the arrival of the NCO. He went on talking just as before. The sergeant did not waste breath on repeating his observation. He launched a tremendous kick at the German's backside, and then he, too, understood. Say what you will, when it comes to a ready means of international understanding, a well-planted boot has all your Esperanto licked hollow.

The man beside me coughed again. I knew what he was after, and taking one of the cigarettes, I handed it to him, putting the other two carefully away in my pocket.

It hadn't taken him very long, during the half-hour we had waited together in that corridor, to discover my nationality. He spoke almost perfect English himself, and this, together with the coincidence that willed we should enter the gates at the same moment, threw us together quite a bit for the first day or two. I didn't care very much for him at the beginning. He was a well-built man of about my own age—thirty-seven or so—with thinning hair and a weak chin, and in his eyes was that expression compounded of dissipation and despair which is often to be seen on the faces of those who have left all hope behind them. Grease spots and drink stains covered the reasonably good-quality suit he was wearing. His hand shook violently as he lit the cigarette I had just given him.

He was Swiss and came from Geneva. Later on that morning, when I was in a more receptive mood, he began to tell me how he had come to join the Foreign Legion; but for the moment I was thinking my own thoughts, and all I wanted was to be left alone. I took a couple of puffs from his cigarette, handed it back to him, and then continued to look absently out over the harbour.

I don't know whether you have ever reached a point in your life where you have said to yourself: 'Now, or never, I must take stock of myself. Now, this minute, I must look myself in the face and tell myself the truth about myself.' Believe me, if and when you arrive at that stage, and if you then carry out the operation honestly and sincerely, it can be a very, very bitter moment. If you are absolutely honest, you can tell yourself things about yourself which certainly nobody else can. And, by God, they can hurt.

And the worst of it is that there is no escaping these truths. If somebody else tells me that I am a liar and a fool and a cheat, I can always escape by telling him—or myself—that he is prejudiced, unbalanced, or a prig. You cannot do that with yourself. When you look yourself squarely and unflinchingly in the eyes and tell yourself the truth, you know that it *is* the truth. And you don't like it.

That is what I found myself doing that night in Strasbourg. I had been out in the town, and had gulped down a few morose, lonely drinks. When I returned to my hotel, I was a little drunk, though certainly not in the least merry. I sat down on the chair in my bedroom and saw myself, full length, mirrored in the glass of the clothes cupboard. I looked at myself and said out loud and quite deliberately: 'You're no damned good!'

I stared at myself for fully two or three minutes, waiting for the accused to reply, and watching the look of hate spread all over the face in the mirror. Then I began ticking off some of the items in the indictment.

'Item one. You were a failure at school and university. You wasted time, with the result that you were ploughed in your finals. All you succeeded in doing at the university was getting heavily into debt. Even in those days you were too fond of a gay life without considering where the money was coming from to pay for it. Even then you were already afraid of good, solid work.

'Item two. You have always been a dabbler, darting from one enthusiasm to another, like a butterfly from flower to flower. You thought you were a singer and a pianist; you weren't either. Then you thought you were a writer; you weren't, by a long chalk. You wrote a play; it was no good. You tried to work as a journalist; you were too lazy even to learn shorthand.

'Item three. You more or less deserted your wife and children at the end of the war. Then you ran off to that woman in France, lived with her for a year or so, and finished up by deserting her, too. Then you started that ridiculous business in Holland, met Lisbeth, lived with her for nearly a year, and ran away from her because you dared not look your own failure in the eye. And a much longer list than that could be made of your cowardly back-slidings.

'Item four. You're a drunkard. Every time in the last two or three years that you've made a little money, you've ploughed through the whole lot in a few days of riotous living. You will do exactly the same when you've finished and been paid for this damned silly translation of a guide-book you're supposed to be working on.

'Result. You're no damned good, as I said before. The trouble with you is,' I continued, looking myself straight in the eyes, 'the trouble with you is that you've nothing to live for. That's why you always do things badly. The only thing you've ever done well in your whole damned life was to execute an artillery barrage and thus help win the war; and post-war events are proving even that to have been to very little purpose.'

When I had come to this devastating conclusion, I put on my overcoat again—it was the beginning of January—put into my various pockets my toilet kit, a change of socks and underclothing, and all the cigarettes I had. Then I walked out of the hotel. I left all the rest of my things there, and never saw them again. For all I know they are still there.

I went out into the street and began walking. The night was frosty, and I walked fast. I haven't the faintest idea where I went that night, but I know that at dawn I was some twenty miles from the city and heading towards the snow-covered passes of the Vosges.

On the left-hand side of the road was a farm, and I saw a woman chopping up wood which she was taking from a pile of logs by the side of the path leading to the farm-house. Seeing her, I felt that I must, at all costs, do some physical work. With a '*permettez-moi, Madame*', I seized the axe and began chopping. The woman, frightened at first, soon began laughing at my clumsy handling of the chopper. When I had finished, she invited me into the house for some coffee. She turned out to be a Belgian, and had married the farmer two years before. We talked a little of Brussels. She enjoyed this, for she was obviously very homesick, planted there in the wilds of Alsace. She asked me what I was doing, wandering about on foot in the bitterly cold weather, and I told her I was walking for the good of my soul. She interpreted this in a somewhat material way by offering me some money, which I refused, and, although I'm sure she would have been prepared to have me stay the whole day and talk about her beloved Brussels, her husband having gone off to market, I pleaded the necessity for continuing my journey, and left her. As I went out of the door, she insisted on my accepting a packet of sandwiches which she had prepared for me. Only when I had left the farm did I look for the first time into my wallet to see how much money I had. There were precisely one thousand francs, about enough to buy two meals in an average restaurant.

I had thoughts of returning to Strasbourg and continuing with my work, but those snow-capped mountains fascinated me, and I plodded on towards them. Unconsciously, I was following the Route Nationale towards the south-west.

In the late afternoon I came to a small village nestling at the foot of the mountains and surrounded by the huge trees of the immense forest. I spoke to a labourer at one of the numerous sawmills dotted along the roadside, and he offered me a bed for the night. When he had finished work for the day, he took me off to his half-timbered cottage, and made me sit down to the evening *soupe* with his wife and their four small children. They must have been miserably poor, the woodman and his family, but, if ever I saw happy people, it was the six of them crowded together there in that tiny cottage, eating their thin, watery soup round the smoky wood fire burning in the hearth.

The man asked me what I did for a living and, as I wasn't very sure myself, I told him that I was by way of being a writer. I had already explained to him that I was walking through France with very little money in my pocket. He gave me a very shrewd piece of advice.

'When you come to a village,' he said, 'you may not always find somebody willing to put you up for the night. In that case you just go along to *Monsieur le Maire* and tell him that you're a writer. He'll see that you're looked after all right.' In the weeks that ensued I followed this counsel on more than one occasion. It always worked like a charm.

The bed I slept on that night was little more than a pile of sacking stretched out before the fire, but I was so tired that I think I could have slept on a bare stone floor. The next morning I was up with the family at half-past five. They gave me coffee, and by six I was on my way, ever southwards.

At midday I topped the crest of the mountains by the pass at Schirmeck and looked down the south-western slopes of the

Vosges towards Saint-Dié. At the top of the ridge there is an hotel which does a lively trade with tourists in the summer, though at that time of the year it was looking empty and forlorn. It is, however, the only house for miles around, and as I was feeling very hungry after my six hours' walk, I decided to eat my sandwiches there. I went in and ordered *café au lait*. Although it was mid-winter, the *patron* had lost nothing of his holiday season habits: he charged a hundred francs for the coffee and a cover charge of thirty francs because I was eating my sandwiches off his tablecloth.

I do not clearly remember what succession of confused thoughts raced through my mind as I made my way down the southern slopes of the mountains towards Saint-Dié. I did not know where I was going, and for the time being I did not very much care. I rather think that I toyed with the idea of suicide, and probably came to the conclusion that it was far too cold for a comfortable death. I remember that periods of blank despair were succeeded by other periods of wild, light-hearted exhilaration, when I would stride out manfully along the tarmac road, swinging my arms and whistling, full of *joie de vivre*.

That night I slept in a Jesuit seminary which was intended to be used for the training of missionaries. The first batch of students had not yet arrived, and I was given the use of a bed in the vast empty dormitory. I dined with one of the Fathers, a highly intelligent and very *sympathique* person of about fifty. We talked of books. He was chiefly interested, I remember, in Cronin and Graham Greene. During the two hours' conversation we had, he never once mentioned religion; but he sent me to bed with a pamphlet on the life of Sainte Thérèse de Lisieux. I read about half of it, but was not very much impressed. My reflections on *la petite Carmelite de l'Enfant Jésu* were distinctly Freudian in character.

Onwards, ever onwards. My period of black depression had

now almost passed, and was being succeeded by a desire, a physical desire, to live. I began to feel that what I most needed, in order to be at peace with myself, was hard, back-breaking, physical work. From time to time, on my way through Franche Comté, I chanced on a farmer who would let me chop a few logs or clean out a stable in return for a meal and a night's lodging. Sometimes, however, they were suspicious. I suppose I was still looking a bit too respectable for the part I was playing. On such occasions I followed my woodman's advice and went to see *Monsieur le Maire*.

The effect on these worthy local dignitaries, when I had made my little speech, was surprising. There was nothing they would not do for me. In one village the mayor turned his daughter out of her bedroom, despite my protests, so as to make a place for me. At another I was given a room in the best hotel and a magnificent supper with two bottles of wine. As I still had a few francs left, I ordered a packet of cigarettes, but, when I attempted to pay for them, the *patron* refused my money, saying that, on the mayor's strict orders, everything I consumed was to be put down to the account of the *commune*. I could only conclude that the officials concerned thought that I was making a *reportage* on French hospitality, and were afraid of having a black mark recorded against their respective villages.

The tenth day after my departure from Strasbourg was a bad one. I was approaching Bourg, having spent the previous night at another seminary to the south of Lons-le-Saulnier. In the late afternoon I found myself on a deserted stretch of road with not a village nor even a house in sight. The town of Bourg was still some fifteen miles off. I went on and on. Dusk fell, and I was shy of knocking at the doors of any of the few isolated houses, from behind whose curtained windows lights were already shining. On I went, and soon there were no more lights, for the country people were going to bed. When I arrived in the town, it was already half-past ten, and the only lights showing were those of the cafés which were still doing business.

In spite of the gnawing pangs of hunger, my innate self-consciousness would not allow me to enter a café when I had not even the price of a glass of beer in my pocket. So I just walked on, and very soon found myself leaving the town by the main road towards Lyons. I went on throughout that night, often trotting for a hundred yards or so to keep my circulation going, for it was bitterly cold.

When dawn came, I saw to my left the mist-enshrouded slopes of the Jura foothills. I got into conversation with a farm labourer on his way to work, and he told me that five miles farther on was the Trappe of Notre Dame des Dombes. 'Eight kilometres,' he had said. But it proved to be more than eighteen, and it was well on into the afternoon before I arrived, almost too exhausted to stand up.

I tugged at the chain which was attached to the swinging bell in the little cupola. After waiting for half a minute, I saw a little trap-door open and a face appeared. I stated my business, and the door was opened. 'Come in, my son,' said the *Père Hôtelier*. 'I will show you to your room. Supper will be ready in half an hour. Perhaps, after you have washed, you would like to attend the evening office.' He led me by the arm and requested me to sign the visitors' book. Then he showed me the room in which I was to sleep, the refectory, and the corridor leading to the visitors' gallery. After I had sluiced some of the dirt from my face and hands, I made my way along the passage, pushed open the oak door, and slid into a pew in the balcony.

'*Kyrie Eleison*,' sang the cantors. '*Kyrie Eleison*,' answered the descant. The monks, each facing his individual lectern on which was placed the enormous, heavily bound volume of Gregorian chants, bowed, genuflected, and prostrated themselves in the prescribed fashion as they chanted. With arms folded and hands concealed in the sleeves of their habits, they looked straight ahead, and sang to the glory of God, who, apart from myself, was the only witness to their devotion.

For I was alone in the visitors' gallery of that monastery chapel. Before me was one of the most beautiful stained-glass windows I had ever seen, and only the monks and a handful of pilgrims or wanderers like myself ever saw it. The office I was listening to was perhaps one of the finest of its kind existent in Europe, and only about a hundred people a year ever heard it. Such, I thought, was the measure of the Trappists' isolation. All day and every day spent in utter silence, never to be allowed to open their mouths except to eat, pray, or chant. A day made up of eight hours' hard manual labour at which any modern workman would balk, four hours' sleep on a hard bed in a cold bare cell, two hours' devotions, two hours for meals, taken standing and always in complete silence except for the voice of the Brother whose turn it was to read the Meditation, and eight hours' chanting of religious offices to which scarcely anybody ever listened.

'Was this the answer?' I asked myself, but I knew that it was not. If only I could have believed, yes; but I could not believe. I admired the monks, most of them great, strapping fellows. More, I envied them. But I could not follow them. I would stay a day or two watching them, listening to their chants, steeping myself in the calm of their austere self-discipline; but tomorrow, or the day after tomorrow at the latest, I would be on my way southward—along the Route Nationale, I knew not whither.

How far away now seemed England, the series of petty little jobs, silly week-ends in the country, the petty schemes for making money, and the idiotic ways of spending it. Even the outbreak of war and my commissioning as an officer in the Army seemed unreal to me as I sat in the gallery of the Cistercian monastery listening to None in the early evening of a cold day in January.

My hasty, ill-considered marriage seemed such a very childish and unimportant business viewed from the detached, calm seclusion of Notre Dame des Dombes. And what, I asked myself, would these white-robed, black-hooded Trappists know of the mental struggle which had taken place within me before I decided to desert my family rather than tell them of the disaster which had befallen me, and face the dismal prospect of struggling to earn a living for them?

What could they know of the motives which had made me run away from Amsterdam two years later, leaving Lisbeth to fend for herself. Lisbeth, who had worked her fingers to the bone to support me while I was writing that book. And Lisbeth had only been one of a very long series.

There are perhaps ways of obtaining a little happiness in this life, I thought, as I left the monastery the next morning and plodded down the lane which would lead me back to the Route Nationale. One of them is to have a nice little house, with a nice little wife and family, and a nice little job to support them with. Then you shut the door and turn the key and forget about the futility of the world outside, living in the smug comfort of your own satisfaction. I have thrown away that chance for ever. Another way is the monks' way. They also have shut and barred the door on the outside world, and I suppose in their way they are undoubtedly happy. But then, they believe and I don't.

About the middle of February, dirty, unshaven, with shabby clothes and no heels to my shoes, I arrived in the village of Palette, and went to the *Relai Bleu*. I had stayed for a fortnight in this delightful little pub just over a year before and, despite my bedraggled appearance, Robert the *patron* recognized me and stood me a drink. Then he told the maid to get my room ready.

'Robert,' I said, '*je n'ai pas le sou*. I'm broke to the wide.' And I told him as much as was necessary to give him some idea of my situation, material and moral.

'*Mon vieux*,' said Robert, when I had finished, 'Marseilles is only thirty-five kilometres from here. In Marseilles is the recruiting station of the Legion. If I have diagnosed your illness aright, that's going to be the best place for you for the next five years.'

Madame slipped the pair of red socks into my hand as I was going up to bed. She must have noticed that I wasn't wearing any.

'Put those on tomorrow,' she said.

The next morning I put on the socks and followed Robert's advice. As I leaned over the parapet and looked at the shipping in the harbour, I wondered whether I was going to regret it.

# 2

Very little had happened to us thus far. We had waited for about half an hour in that gloomy corridor smelling of stale urine and unwashed bodies, and I had time to look around me at my companions in distress. I was not very proud of my company. Such a crowd, I thought, as might have been seen hanging about outside a Labour Exchange or creeping furtively along the Victoria Embankment at midnight. Then I had looked at myself, reflecting that, after all, I was not in very much better shape.

Despite the look of gloomy despair in the eyes of most of the men in that, as I thought, degenerate mob, they were nearly all laughing and talking merrily enough. This, I soon discovered, was just superficial. They were trying to put on a bold front.

There were about a dozen of us, and we represented the day's intake at Marseilles; for volunteers are only admitted between eight and nine in the morning, and nine had already struck. This seemed to me to be an insufficient average to maintain the strength of the Legion but, as the Swiss explained to me later on, there are recruiting stations all over France, to say nothing of those in the French-occupied zones of Austria and Germany. Recruits from these other stations arrive at Marseilles in organized detachments and have already completed the preliminary formalities. The dozen or so of us waiting there to be interviewed were merely the volunteers who had applied to join directly at Marseilles.

At last my turn came. I went into a small, stuffy office, and found myself face to face with a sergeant. He told me to empty my pockets. I was so surprised that I did so without demur. He then proceeded to run his hands over me, from shoulders to feet. It was the first time in my life such a thing had ever happened to me, and I did not find it very pleasant.

*Tout comprendre, c'est tout pardonner.* I know now that he was merely looking for the blunt, or sharp, instrument which might have served to inflict bodily harm on other volunteers or, more probably, upon the person of its owner. Murder or suicide. The first three or four days of the volunteer's presence in the Transit Camp are a very dangerous period. He is, almost invariably, in a highly excited or depressed mental condition, and, in the past, so many cases have occurred of recruits running amok or ending their sufferings with a knife plunged into the heart, that nowadays the Legion authorities take no risks.

Having 'flushed' me—that is, I believe, the technical term—the sergeant examined the contents of my wallet and handed it back to me. He then asked me for my name, date and place of birth, nationality and profession, and compared my replies with the details given in my passport. I asked to have this document returned to me.

'No,' he replied. 'We keep that. You'll get it back in five years, if you're still alive.'

He looked at me from under his bushy eyebrows.

'Do you want to serve under your own name?' he asked.

I replied that I preferred to be simple John Smith.

'Good,' said the sergeant, and he gave me a new date and place of birth, which made me two years younger, and an Irishman, though what on earth an Irishman would be doing with a name like Smith I couldn't imagine.

'*Très bien*,' concluded the sergeant. 'You will be summoned for interrogation in a few hours.'

And that was all! I left the office and joined the remainder of the group waiting outside.

'Bad organization,' I said to myself. 'He would have saved time by interrogating me then and there.'

What I did not know at that time was that those few hours' interval were going to be used in checking up with the French police whether a man answering to my description was wanted for any crime committed on French territory.

When all had been interviewed, a legionnaire marched us off to the barrack-room where we were to sleep. I call it a barrack-room, but it was in fact a sort of dungeon encased in the massive stone wall of the fort. Four small, barred windows, placed high up near the roof, looked out over the harbour, but in order to reach them you had to perform a spectacular, and even dangerous, acrobatic feat. On either side of a central passage was a row of about a dozen double-tier beds made of wood, many of them in a dilapidated, rickety condition. On each bed was a doubtful looking, straw-filled paillasse and two blankets. One had the impression of entering a prison.

The legionnaire who had conducted us there handed us over to a colleague who was apparently the *chef de chambre*, responsible for the organization and discipline of the barrack-room. His name, I believe, was Brunner, and he had only one arm. After making a list of our names, he ordered us to stand each at the foot of the bed assigned to him, and explained, in French and in German, the few simple rules and regulations which he wanted us to observe. Then, ordering us to take our blankets under our arms, he marched us out into the open air and, telling us off in pairs, set us to shaking the well-worn coverings in which we were to sleep.

The clouds of dust which we shook from those blankets would have done justice to a sandstorm in Egypt at the height of the khamsin. I had picked up a bad cold during the last days of my walk from Strasbourg, and the fine particles found their way into my bronchial tubes and made me cough most painfully. I had a slight headache and, when I swallowed, I could feel that my tonsils were beginning to swell. 'However,' I said to myself, 'this is not the moment to be ill.' So I caught up my two blankets, and returned with the rest of the detachment to the barrack-room.

We had not been there two minutes when a gust of wind came howling through the door (it was mid-February and the mistral was doing its hateful worst). As it came, it brought a mist of minute particles of sand from the worn, century-old, sandstone floor. Although we shook our blankets every morning during my stay in Marseilles, the clouds of dust which emanated from them remained undiminished.

When we had finished installing ourselves, Brunner told us that we were free until the parade for the midday meal at half-past eleven. As we thus had half an hour to waste, the Swiss and I strolled up to the ramparts and, leaning our elbows on the parapet, looked out over the harbour.

'What would you say that fellow Brunner is?' I asked the Swiss, when I had thought my own thoughts long enough to be disgusted with them.

'Nationality? German, almost certainly,' he replied. About half an inch of the precious cigarette remained, and he offered it to me, but I took one look at the saliva in which the stub was soaked, and refused.

'He speaks perfect German,' continued the Swiss, 'and only rather indifferent French. He might, of course, be an Alsatian, but most of them speak the *patois*. He lost his arm at Cao Bang, so he told me, and was offered a pension, which he refused, saying that he preferred to carry on in the service.'

'I can understand that,' I replied. 'For some of these fellows who've lived a life full of adventure, the idea of going back to the normal rut of civilian existence must be simply appalling.'

'Yes,' said the Swiss. He had stuck a pin through the quarter-inch of the cigarette which remained, and went on smoking it, although it must have been burning his lips. 'And what about the reverse case? Don't you think that, for a man who has led an utterly uneventful, monotonous life, the thought of the uncertain adventure of five years in the Legion must be a pretty terrifying one?'

'Are you referring to yourself?' I asked, half laughing. 'I shouldn't have thought that you, for one, had led an uneventful life.'

The Swiss was silent for a moment. 'Either,' he said at last, 'you are a bad judge of character, or my unkempt, bedraggled appearance bestows upon me a vagabond's air to which I can lay no honest claim. An ordinary life? A life without incident? A life as monotonous as an *autobahn?*'

He broke off and laughed mirthlessly.

'My God, if ever a man led such a life, it was I. Look at me. What sort of a man do you think I am? What sort of a man do you think my father was? A farm labourer? A bank robber? An artist?'

He laughed again. I did not attempt to reply to his rhetorical questions.

'My father,' the Swiss went on, 'was a Calvinistic parson. I was the only child. You might think that he would have been a friend to me. He wasn't. He was incapable of speaking to me except to preach, scold, warn, or threaten. Consequently, even from my earliest youth, I had a hankering after those very things against which he was always warning me—wine, women, and song, idleness and dissipation.

'I left school at eighteen and was entered at the Faculty of Law at Geneva University. I had wanted to go to Zurich, so as to get away from home, but my father wouldn't have it. So I lived with my parents at their house only about a mile from the university, and didn't even have the chance of knocking about in lodgings, as did many of my fellow students.'

Two tears glistened in his watery eyes and, for the first time, he looked me straight in the face.

'Isn't it amazing,' he continued, 'what a fellow can do at the age of nineteen? While continuing my law studies, I yet found time to read the best literature of a dozen European countries, much of it in the original language; to study archæology, philosophy, sociology, and I've forgotten what else; to attend debating societies, concerts, and be a member of a musical study group; to write a full-length play and stacks and stacks of poems. Ah me, in those days, of course, I didn't drink, or very little. My father kept me far too short of money. The play I wrote was no damned good, and the poems must have been dreadful, but they created for Marthe and myself the illusion that we were in love with each other.'

The Swiss coughed chestily and spat a great gob of phlegm over the wall into the harbour.

'I met Marthe during my second year,' he sniffed. 'She was a cow, and she adored me. Quite a nice, ripe figure, wavy black hair, and great big doting eyes. She was studying sociology, and one evening at a meeting of the debating society we both supported a motion for free love. She didn't really believe in free love, of course, as I discovered when I accompanied her home after the debate. It was six months before I succeeded in persuading her to put her theories into practice, and I wish to God I had failed.'

I was committed now, and had to go on listening. I am quite certain, by the way, that during the whole of his five years in the Legion, Sibley—that was the name of the Swiss—never told this story to anyone but me. Why he should have made me his confidant I do not know, but he was not, by any means, the only legionnaire who honoured me, exclusively, with such a confession. Indeed, as time went on I became more and more a sort of depository for my comrades' past troubles. This may have been due to the fact that I was rather older than most of them, though this was certainly not the case with regard to Sibley. Or it may perhaps have been due to my being the one Englishman among them. There were so few of my nationality in the Legion that right up to the end I was considered as a case apart—by some respected, by others detested, and by a few, including the authorities, viewed with a great deal of suspicion. Or it may have been due to my being a good listener.

The Swiss went on speaking in his dreary, monotonous undertone, and I went on listening because I had nothing better to do.

'Marthe's love for her Antoine must have sustained rather a rude shock at the end of that year, for I was ploughed in my first Law Exams, and she had to face the prospect of marrying a future bank clerk instead of a rising young lawyer.

'She stuck to me, however, and I was grateful to her for doing so. Ah, my friend, what a hideous thing is gratitude, and what a hateful thing loyalty can be, when you are grateful for the loyal attitude of someone whose opinions you no longer respect and whose personality you no longer value. And I couldn't respect Marthe's opinions any more. She hadn't any: she got them all out of books she had read.

'As for her personality, how could I respect or value the personality of someone who was always cringing adoringly at my feet. For after a month or two I knew quite well I did not really love Marthe. All I wanted was her body. And so, like millions of other damned fools in this world, I was planning marriage. I was preparing to tie myself to a pin-headed nonentity in order to have a cheap permanent whore.'

I sacrificed one of my two remaining cigarettes, so as to interrupt, if only for a moment, this naked flow of self-revelation.

'Do you know,' continued Sibley, as he inhaled deeply and

was further interrupted by a fit of coughing and spitting. 'Do you know how military service goes in our country? Every able-bodied man from twenty to sixty years of age is considered a reservist. He keeps his uniform, arms, and equipment at home, and all that has to be done in the event of mobilization is to issue ammunition. The initial military training, which only lasts four months, is usually carried out between the ages of nineteen and twenty. When it became known that I had failed in my examinations, I left the university and went off to do my four months, at the end of which period I was to start a job in the bank of which Marthe's father was manager.

'The training took place at a camp on the south bank of Lake Zurich at the end of the summer of 1934. I must say that I enjoyed those four months, in spite of the gruelling exercise. Swiss military service consists almost entirely of intensive infantry training, and about half of it is spent on the rifle-ranges. I became a first-class shot. I also became a first-class drinker.'

He sighed and studied his nicotine-stained finger-nails.

'Towards the end of the four months Marthe came down and spent the week-end at an hotel near the camp. The inevitable happened. I only spent one night with her, but three months later she told me she was pregnant.'

Sibley threw away with regret the last quarter-inch of his cigarette and, leaning over the parapet, gazed with unseeing eyes into the blue of the harbour.

'My God,' he continued after a pause, and tears once more glistened in his eyes. 'She never made the slightest attempt to force me to marry her. I was already working in the bank, and earning two hundred francs a month, which wasn't bad for a start. In fact, I was doing rather well and was earmarked for rapid promotion, which was not entirely due to the fact that the manager, besides being Marthe's father, was a member of my own father's congregation. For some reason or other I found it very easy to do quickly the sort of simple calculations which the other bloody fools found difficult.

'Anyhow, Marthe telephoned me one morning and asked me to meet her for lunch. I had been avoiding her for some time, but as it was getting towards the end of the month and I was nearly broke, I accepted her invitation. Over the steak and chips she told me quite simply what had happened, gazing at me all the while with her loyal, affectionate, cow-like eyes. "I am so proud, Antoine," she said. Hell! If only she had made the slightest attempt to force my hand, I might have kicked over the traces and gone off to be a man somewhere. As it was, I just felt sorry for her. And, damn and blast it, I went on being sorry for her for another fifteen years. . . .'

'Come and have a drink,' I interrupted. It wasn't that I particularly wanted to drink with the Swiss. I had, in any case, only those fifty francs left. But I did desperately want to cut his story short, and could think of no other polite way of doing it.

Sibley accepted eagerly, and we strolled slowly past huddled groups of fellow scarecrows to the little canteen which was situated at the north-west corner of the parade-ground. There were only a few customers, and the two glasses of *vin rosé* which I ordered were quickly served.

'What do you make of this outfit?' I asked, after taking a sip. 'The Legion, I mean.'

'Well, it's ghastly at first,' replied the Swiss. 'But it's supposed to get better as time goes on—or, at least, so I've heard from some of those who came back. As you probably know, quite a lot of our people do their five years here. It's a sort of national tradition. There was a second cousin of my wife's, for instance, who was a legionnaire from 'thirty-eight to 'forty-six. He had originally signed on for five years like everybody else, but when the war broke out he volunteered to continue till the end of hostilities. He gave me quite a lot of inside information when he returned home.

'Incidentally, he had spent what must have been his last evening in Switzerland at our house, before going off to France to join, though he didn't tell us what he was going to do, of course. That night coincided, by the way, with the end of the first period of strained, though outwardly cordial, relations between my wife and myself. As I was saying just now. . . .'

It was evident that the Swiss was not to be side-tracked, and at this point, good manners or no, I could not stifle a yawn.

A pained look came into Sibley's eyes. I don't think he had realized that he was boring me. So hurt did he look that I covered up my rudeness with a white lie.

'Sorry, old man,' I said. 'Didn't mean to be rude. It's just that I didn't get much sleep last night. Do please carry on. How did you finally come to join the Legion?'

The Swiss looked at me doubtfully, scratching his unshaven chin with his filthy finger-nails. At last he decided to continue, though from thence onwards he cut his story short.

'There's not much more to tell,' he said. 'Where did I leave off? Oh yes, I remember. Well we got married, and so things went on until the beginning of the war. You probably know that my country carried out a partial mobilization during the war.'

I didn't know this, so I was interested.

'Yes,' said Sibley, 'on several occasions there were good reasons for believing that the Germans were about to violate our neutrality. We should, by the way, have been a pretty tough nut to crack, and that, I suppose, is why they never attempted it. Anyhow, volunteers for full-time service were called for, and I volunteered.

'I did so for one reason and one reason only: to get away from my wife. That sounds a pretty brutal thing to say, doesn't it? But, do you know, I honestly thought it was the best thing to do. Things were getting to the stage where I could no longer speak civilly to her. No two people live so much "on top of each other" or get so much in each other's way as a man and wife living in a small house in a narrow-minded town, especially in Switzerland. Far from loving her, I was not even fond of her any more. My attitude towards her was one of bored indifference, which often flared up into crises of fierce, illogical hatred. I was afraid of myself. I was afraid that one day, in one of these fits of unreasoning rage, I might strike her.

'And yet, you know, I was sorry for her most of the time. I dreaded hurting her. I did not want to see or feel her suffer. So much so that I kept up a pretence of loving her—yes, even in the physical sense.'

Sibley turned and watched a boat making its way towards Château d'If.

'Oh my God,' he continued in a half-strangled voice, his back still turned to me. 'Oh my God, those nights of hell, when she would turn towards me and begin caressing me, saying in a raucous, sexy voice . . .'

The Swiss broke off, coughed and spat into the sea.

'So I naturally leapt at the chance of getting away from all that,' he went on. 'I even hoped, poor fool that I was, that a long period of separation might restore some of the warmth to our relations.

'It didn't, of course. On the contrary, it made things worse, for, by the time I was demobilized towards the end of the war, I had got so used to freedom that I found it more difficult than ever to settle down to even a lodger-housekeeper association with Marthe, and, of course, she wanted far more than that.

'At the end of 'forty-seven I was summoned to the headquarters of the bank and given a new job as a kind of travelling inspector. I was also told that I would be employed later as a sort of liaison officer for exchange business with foreign banks, which would involve a certain amount of travelling outside Switzerland. I was pleased about this: strange though it may appear to you, I had never been abroad.

'I was given my first foreign mission about a month ago: Paris and London. Although the business to be done would necessitate only about five days' work, I took about three hundred pounds with me. My wife wanted to come with me, but I put my foot down and said we hadn't enough money.'

The Swiss turned round and faced me. 'It's a pretty rotten sort of story, isn't it?' he said. 'I honestly don't think at the outset I had the intention of running away, or at least not consciously. On my arrival in Paris I completed the first day's business. Then, in the evening, I set out to make the acquaintance of the Pigalle and Montmartre. What a debauch! I got so drunk that evening I hadn't the courage to go on with my business the next morning, so I got drunk again. I spent three weeks drowning my hangovers in the makings of their successors and leaping from bed to promiscuous bed. At the end of that time I was broke, I realized that I had fallen down on my job, and I knew that I could never go back to Marthe.

'From that situation to the gates of the Bas Fort Saint-Nicolas was a short, easy, and very logical step. I don't think I even hesitated. As I told you, we Swiss are traditional legionnaires.'

Sibley took a paper and a pinch of tobacco from his pocket, and began rolling a cigarette with his nervous, nicotine-stained fingers.

# 3

COLUMN of twenty by column of twenty, we filed into the refectory for the midday meal, the first four men in each column being directed to the cookhouse, where they would collect the pots of meat and vegetables and bring them to the tables.

As a meal it was not too bad. I had had many worse in the previous month. A chunk of meat swimming in a thick gravy, baked potatoes and green peas, green salad, very well prepared, and a hunk of yellow cheese. To drink; thin, watery beer. I had always understood that red wine formed an essential part of the French soldier's ration. What I did not then know was that, not yet having signed our contracts, we could not be included in the ration strength, so that the Transit Company at Marseilles had no credits for feeding us. The consequence was, for the authorities, that any of us who were eventually rejected as unfit for one reason or another represented a dead financial loss to them. Hence the intermediate ration scale.

The noise made by the men eating at our table was unbelievable. Some of them talked so much that it amazed me they found time to eat their dinners, though I must admit that the mere swallowing of a mouthful of food in no wise interrupted the flow of the most verbose amongst them. It is characteristic of a certain type of European that their conversation is no matter of give and take. The easy, back-and-forth exchange of opinion has no place in their conception of the gentle art. Their idea of conversation is to talk as long and loud, particularly loud, as possible, shouting all opposition down. About half the messmates at my table fell into this category. A Frenchman next to me began talking as soon as we sat down, and only finished when we stood up to file out again a quarter of an hour later. I heard the whole of his conversation: I couldn't help it. It was all about the correct way, or what he thought was the correct way, of baking potatoes; how his mother baked them, how his grandmother baked them, how Parisians and Corsicans baked them; the different sorts of fat you could use; how to time them, how to serve them, how to eat them. I am very fond of baked potatoes, but I left two on my plate in disgust.

Opposite me was an Italian, speaking fluent if not very elegant French, who put up quite a good show for about ten minutes on the subject of the smartness of Italian officers' uniforms. I lost the thread of his argument very soon, for my French neighbour outblasted him; but when I tuned in to him again just before we stood up, he was still ranting about gold braid. Nobody, apart from my unfortunate and unwilling self, had listened to either of them!

About half an hour after the meal we were paraded again, and the group of new arrivals to which I belonged was marched off for the interrogation. When we arrived once more at the block of offices where we had been interviewed that morning, two gendarmes were waiting with a Black Maria, and one of our number—the Frenchman with the trumpet-like voice who had destroyed my appetite for baked potatoes—was handcuffed and invited to take a seat in the interior of the van. I'm afraid I must admit to a certain vindictive satisfaction at seeing him go. This must have been a result of the check which the Legion authorities had made with the police during the morning. The Black Maria with the two gendarmes drove out of the gates to an accompaniment of hoots and derisive jeers from the legionnaires there assembled. They have no great love for the *flics*.

I was among the first to be summoned for interrogation. I

found myself in the presence of a very fat sergeant-major, who was sitting behind a desk in the corner of a badly lighted office. He invited me to take a seat opposite him. I was in the full light of the window, but he was in darkness. In fact, none of the little tricks, so dear to the hearts of makers of American crime films and writers of popular spy stories, was lacking: the bunch of keys swung to and fro at the end of a chain, the regular tapping on the desk with the butt of a pencil. My headache was getting worse; had I not felt so ill, I'm quite sure I should have burst out laughing.

He began his interrogation. Most of the pertinent details he already had before him. They were contained in my passport and my military papers from the British Army. What he wanted was background. He took me step by step over my past life: school, university, jobs before the war, activities since demobilization, always leading up to the question, 'And why do you want to join the Legion?'

I wasn't very clear on that point myself, but I said, 'I'm fed up with civilian life. I like Army life. I happened to be in France, and I was broke. So I came along here.'

The sergeant-major looked at me with a pained and incredulous air. '*Ce n'est pas très vraisemblable, ne trouvez-vous pas?*' This was a semi-polite way of saying that he didn't believe a word of it. He glanced at my military papers again in an absent way, waiting for me to offer further explanations. I should perhaps mention that he had started the interrogation in English, but had changed over to French when he discovered that I spoke his language better than he did mine.

'*Je n'ai pas l'habitude de mentir,*' I replied, very much on my dignity. 'I am not in the habit of telling lies.'

His fat face wreathed itself into a pained smile. After a moment he got to his feet.

'Excuse me a moment,' he said. 'Here, help yourself to a

cigarette.' He threw a packet on to the desk and left the room. I helped myself to several, reflecting ironically that it hadn't been my habit to pinch other people's cigarettes either.

He was back in about five minutes. 'Come with me, please,' he said. 'The captain wants to see you.'

The officer to whom I was presented received me very courteously, invited me to sit down, and began cross-examining me on certain details of the story I had already told the sergeant-major, whose notes were on the desk in front of him. There was one particular detail which seemed to worry him.

I should explain that at one period during the war I had performed the functions of Intelligence Officer in an artillery unit. Anybody acquainted with this employment will remember that the I.O. was merely a 'stooge' who collected and co-ordinated information from the observation-posts and dished it up in readable form for the colonel. He had nothing whatsoever to do with the Intelligence Service, and this appointment was not even an Intelligence appointment. This, however, the captain either could not or would not see. I had been an Intelligence Officer; therefore I was a member of the Intelligence Service. I was a spy, in other words. That was his reasoning.

In the end, by dint of careful and laborious explanation, I managed to plant a doubt in his mind, but even then he was far from being convinced. Indeed, all through those five years I served with the Legion, I was always viewed with a certain suspicion by officers, who thought I had been planted there by British Intelligence! The furtive little man with a black beard and a cloak stills looms large in the imagination of many French officers.

When the captain had done with me, I was taken to another office, where I had to repeat the story I had already told to yet another sergeant-major. This was part of their system—to make you repeat your history over and over again, in the hope of tripping you up. Altogether, during my first two months, I must have told my tale at least seven or eight times, but, as I always told the truth, there was no possibility of my making mistakes.

Worn out and feeling miserably ill, I left the offices at about six o'clock and went straight to bed.

'Hallo!' said Brunner, who was sitting at his table in the barrack-room. 'Bed already? What about the *soupe?*' (*Soupe* is colloquial French for a meal, and not for the liquid which normally precedes it.)

I told him that I was too ill to eat, and he very kindly went and scrounged me a can of broth, some of which I managed to get down. As all my comrades were at the refectory having their evening meal, I was then able to snuggle down in the blankets and lie for a while in peace.

But not for long! In about half an hour back they came, whooping and yelling, shouting and talking. There were about forty of us in that miserable cellar of a barrack-room, and the whole lot of them were talking at once at the tops of their voices.

Then they began singing. The Italians annoyed me the most those first nights. The Germans sang, too, but more softly. For the Italians—and it seemed to me in my jaundiced state that at least half of the men in that room must have come from Mussolini's peninsula—singing was not singing unless loud enough to burst the lungs of the performers and the ear-drums of those who were forced to listen. I moaned in my bed and longed for 'Lights Out'.

I suppose my view of conditions during those first two or three days was a biased one. I was feeling wretchedly ill and completely out of my element. After roll-call, when the lights had been dimmed, I lay awake for many hours listening to the whispered conversation of a group of Latins in the corner, and to the man sleeping in the next bunk to me, who was coughing and spitting on the floor.

# 4

I HAVE already mentioned the odd fact that many legionnaires recounted their life stories to me, mentioning intimate details which they probably never disclosed to anyone else. This privileged position in which I often found myself enabled me, at a very early stage, to form an idea of the principal reasons which caused men of different education, nationality, and upbringing to cut those five years out of their lives in order to serve a flag in which most of them had no interest, and which many of them even despised. But I will come to that later.

The little Frenchman from Marseilles never confided his story to me. He shouted it out loud, proudly and jubilantly, to all who cared to listen. His was certainly not a prevalent type in the Legion, though there were one or two like him. If I tell you his story, as he told it himself that morning, it is because I met him again right at the end of the five years and because during that time he changed a great deal. Indeed, those who knew Rousseau at the end would have found it difficult to believe that he was the same strutting little popinjay who had ranted and bragged in the Marseilles Transit Camp some five years before.

On the second morning we were paraded as usual, and our group of newcomers who had been interrogated the previous day was marched off to the Military Hospital to undergo X-ray examination. When we returned to the Fort, we were led straight off to a corner of the ramparts where a huge basket of potatoes and turnips was waiting to be peeled.

'*Corvée de peluches*,' said the legionnaire who had been put in charge of the fatigue, as he handed a knife to each of us. 'Spud peeling. Get on with it.'

Standing up, looking over the parapet across the harbour, we began grappling with the vegetables, and the Frenchman, pointing towards the town with his knife, began to speak.

'That,' he said, with an inclusive wave of the hand, 'is the Canebière.'

He proudly indicated, as though it were the centre of the world (which, indeed, of a certain world it is), the broad boulevard, flanked by tall buildings, which sweeps proudly down to the edge of the Vieux Port.

'The third turning to the right is the rue de Rome. That is where I was born.'

He gave the impression that there ought to be a brass plate commemorating this historic spot. He spoke with that sing-song, half Italian, Marseillais accent, which is so delightful when you hear it for the first time and so very irritating when you have heard it too much. He ran his fingers through his wavy, black hair, seized a potato, and went on.

'My name is Marius—between ourselves, of course—Marius Pantalone, though, *bien entendu*, I have given my name here as Jean-Jacques Rousseau.'

He carefully peeled off the skin of the half-rotten vegetable he was holding, and dropped the coiled mixture of dirt and decay over the parapet into the harbour. Huddled together around the basket, the rest of us, who had hitherto remained silent, began to show signs of animation. A Russian and a German, neither of whom had understood a word of what the Frenchman was saying, began to converse quietly in German.

'Yes, Jean-Jacques Rousseau,' repeated the Frenchman. 'A great French name that, though, of course, you foreigners wouldn't know that. He was an eminent French engineer in the eighteenth century.'

'What a surprise for the author of the *Nouvelle Héloïse!*' I whispered to Sibley, who was standing next to me.

'He got the century right, anyway,' he whispered back. 'Let's hear the rest of his story.'

'I have lived all my life in Marseilles,' the Frenchman was saying, when we once more concentrated our attention on him. 'It is a great city. The men how manly! And the women—oh, how kind. At sixteen years old I was already earning my living as a *garçon de café*. That is a fine life. Do you see that café down there by the water-front, the one with the blue-and-white striped sunshades? That's where I started. I didn't stay there, of course. The *patron* was too straight-laced. *Merde alors!* If a client is drunk, what the devil does it matter if you give him short change or take a few hundred francs out of his wallet as you are putting him into a taxi?'

'*Eh bien, merde!*' echoed the Belgian, a handsome, though somewhat dissolute looking, man of about thirty, to whom the Frenchman had been principally addressing himself.

'Moreover,' continued Marius Pantalone, alias J.-J. Rousseau, 'there weren't nearly enough unaccompanied women customers for my liking. . . .'

'*Attention! Achtung!*' whispered the legionnaire who was supervising the fatigue, and immediately silence, together with a considerable zeal for potato-peeling, fell upon us. An imposing figure with a silver-braided stripe on each shoulder-strap, three rows of medal ribbons, and a gold cross woven into the red top of his red and black *képi*, was approaching. Everywhere men stood to attention and saluted.

'*Adjutant de Compagnie*,' explained the legionnaire, when the menace had passed out of earshot. 'He's the company sergeant-major, and he's a holy terror. If he'd caught one of you not doing his share of potato-peeling, I should have got it in the neck. Then, of course, I should have had to take it out of you. *Alors, faites gaffe, les bleus.* So just you watch your step, you lot of raw rookies.'

'I was telling you'—the Frenchman had already taken up his tale again—'I was telling you how I was getting fed-up with my job in the café over there. *Y en avait marre à la fin.* Well, after a year or so, my luck turned. It was one day in spring. An old tart—she was at least fifty and a widow—who kept a *bistro* in the rue de Paradis, came into the place late in the evening. She had had a few drinks and was quite obviously on heat; and I flatter myself I was looking my very best that evening.'

Again the Frenchman ran his fingers through his long, wavy black hair and, as no one else spoke, he continued. '*J'ai plu à la vieille garce.* Oh yes, she wanted me all right. After we closed, she took me off to her place round the corner, where I gave her one hell of a good night. *Mais qu'est-ce je raconte-là?* One good night? I gave her a hundred good nights. And what does she do, the ungrateful bitch, after I'd been living with her for nearly a year? She throws me out, *comme un malpropre,* and just because I borrowed a thousand francs out of the till without asking her permission. I tell you all, this world is full of ungrateful people....'

'*Ne raconte pas ta vie, toi!*' a sergeant's voice boomed from twenty yards away. 'Stop telling your life story and get on with your work. Those potatoes are for today's dinner, not next Sunday's.'

There was a short silence, followed by a renewed activity around the vegetable basket; but as soon as the sergeant had turned the corner, Pantalone-Rousseau resumed his tale.

'... like a bit of dirt she threw me out. That was in nineteen-thirty-six. For a few months I earned a living on the boats, but that's frightfully rough work and it plays hell with your hands. You know how important soft hands are.'

He showed us his well-manicured fingers as he spoke, and my attention wandered to the hands of the other men in the group. Extraordinary, I thought! Out of the twenty of us, only two—

the little Spaniard who had already done ten years in the Legion and had come back for another five, and the Alsatian with the scar on his cheek—had hands which showed signs of having been used to hard manual work.

'Then,' Rousseau was saying, when I once more focused my attention on his autobiography, 'I made the acquaintance of Lucille. She was a platinum blonde who worked the upper end of the Canebière and the steps of the Gare Saint-Jacques. She was easily forty-five but, in the electric light, didn't look a day over thirty. She had a flat in the rue Salamanca, and did a pretty good business with commercial travellers and other strangers coming off the trains from Paris.

'They all need it, you know. The bravest, hip-swaying whore that ever went to bed with a drunken sailor cannot get on without a regular. If they try to steer their own ship, they go on the rocks sooner or later. They must have a man at the helm to keep 'em in order.

'When I took Lucille on, I did her a service really. And I wasn't, after all, such a bastard to her. I even let her keep ten per cent of her earnings, which is more than most do.

'What's more, I taught her the trick of regular hours. You know how it is. Some of these tarts work twenty-two hours out of the twenty-four, until they look so awful they finish up earning a living cleaning out the public lavatories. I made Lucille work from seven o'clock in the evening till midnight and from midday till three in the afternoon. She reported to me at three and at midnight with her takings, and even if she'd had a bad day, I never let her go on working outside those hours.

'*Naturellement*, if she brought in nothing at all, I used to beat her up. *Bordel de Dieu!* How she loved that! So much so that I more than once suspected her of spending the whole evening at the cinema, so that I should beat her up when she came home empty-handed. So then I promised to cane her the first time she came home with a thousand francs. A thousand francs of nineteen-thirty-eight, that was real money. Well, would you believe it? The very next night she came in at half-past eleven and spread ten one-hundred-franc notes before me on the table.

'I stripped off everything she was wearing except her silk panties and her stockings and caned her till my arm ached. She just yelled with pleasure, the silly bitch.'

The Belgian and a Pole were gazing at the Frenchman in rapt attention and admiration, and I noted with disgust that a trickle of saliva was flowing down the Belgian's lip.

'From then on,' Rousseau continued, 'I caned her whether she brought in the *felous* or not. After a while she got to preferring that to anything else, so I picked up another tart, who doubled my earnings.

'I was now well on my way to becoming a Jules, but unfortunately the good life was not to last. In November of 'thirty-eight I was called up for my military service, and as, during the first fifteen months, I did sixty-four days' prison and eight months' discipline, you can guess that, from then on, I didn't see much of the gay world.'

The last of the peeled potatoes had been thrown into the basket, and the private soldier who had been detailed to supervise told us that we could dismiss. The French-speaking members of the party remained huddled together at a corner of the ramparts. Leaning their elbows on the parapet, they gazed across the blue of the sunlit harbour below.

'And what did you do with yourself during the war?' I heard the Belgian asking. The Swiss and I had been about to leave, but I thought that Rousseau's war experiences might be worth listening to; so I stayed with the others. The Frenchman drew himself up to his full height and threw out his chest.

'*Ah ça, c'était ma vie, la guerre*. That was when life really started for me. Soon after the outbreak of war I was made a sergeant.

When the fun started, I was a sergeant-major commanding a platoon in the Vosges. I had come into my own, *voyez-vous?* I was decorated with the *Médaille Militaire* for my conduct during the attack of the nineteenth of May.

'The Boches attacked wave after wave, arm-in-arm, singing the Horst Wessel song and giving the Nazi salute. Supporting them were thousands of tanks, stretching away into the background for miles.

'What could we do? We shot down the first wave with our machine-guns, but the others came on. We mowed down the second wave, but by that time I had only two men left, and the third wave submerged us. After an heroic resistance I could do no more. I was taken prisoner.'

The Alsatian from Strasbourg, who had not said a word the whole morning, pursed up his lips and made a vulgar sound.

# 5

THAT afternoon occurred the incident I had been dreading ever since I entered the Bas Fort Saint-Nicolas. A trifling, unimportant matter it was, but there are times when trifles can assume vast proportions.

After the parade our group, which had no examinations or interrogations to undergo until the following morning, was detailed off as a fatigue party, for which purpose it was put under the orders of a sergeant. The fatigue consisted of dismantling a hut which stood in one corner of the parade-ground.

It very soon became evident that we were at least twice the number required for doing the work, with the result that had we all tried to lend a hand we should only have succeeded in getting in one another's way. Seeing how things were, I stood to one side and looked on.

This did not please the sergeant. He was a stupid-looking boor of about fifty, with a nose spread all over his face and a huge, gaping mouth. I learnt afterwards that he was accomplishing the last of twenty-five years' service, and the colonel had given him the rank 'out of pity' to ensure him a higher pension.

'You there,' he said in German, looking in my direction. 'Are you too high and mighty to work? Take your hands out of your pockets and get on with it.'

It was the first time anyone had ever addressed an order to me in German. Now, I understand German quite well. But I had just finished a war in which I had been fighting against Germans for six years. At the end of it I had helped to occupy their country for a further six months. So I wonder whether you can under-

Sidi Bel-Abbès, the handiwork of legionnaires

Music, pomp and ceremony

CAMERONE

The march-past, with the pioneer company in their traditional parade uniform

stand that I was not very pleased either to be taken for a German (if that was what he thought) or to be ordered about in the German language. A silly attitude, if you like, but that was how I felt. So I pretended not to understand what the sergeant had said.

'Ho!' he roared again, taking a step towards me. 'Did you hear what I said or are you deaf?'

'*Je n'ai pas compris*,' I replied with my most refined French accent, and hoping it was not too obvious that I was getting hot under the collar.

He then repeated the order in very poor French, and I complied, though my poor efforts did not have any great effect on the dispatch of the work in progress. The sergeant took himself off, mumbling, '*Ein verfluchter Franzose. Die konnen in iedem Fall nicht arbeiten.*'

When the work was finished, a few of us climbed the steps to the ramparts and began pacing up and down together. If I remember, there were three others with me: the Swiss, a very young Frenchman who usually walked alone, reading—rather ostentatiously—Pascal's *Pensées*, and the Alsatian.

'Smith,' said the Swiss. 'There's something I wanted to ask you. With regard to Rousseau's account of his heroic action in the Vosges, how could the Germans have been arm-in-arm, saluting, advancing to the attack and singing all at the same time, even if they had no arms to carry—which one supposes they had?'

'Oh that,' I sniffed contemptuously and probably a little haughtily. 'That, my dear fellow, was a story breathlessly told at that time by thousands of demoralized, badly frightened soldiers all the way from Dunkirk to the Alps, usually by men who'd been running too fast even to have seen a German.'

The young devotee of Pascal looked up at me in amazement. I'm afraid I had shattered one of his illusions. 'In any case,' he protested, 'Rousseau apparently had a very good record with the Resistance. He told me of some of his adventures.'

The Alsatian burst into roars of laughter. 'So, he's taken you in, too?' he asked. '*Ça, c'est le comble.*'

He was a well-built, clean-limbed young fellow of twenty-nine or thirty. From beneath a shock of chestnut hair and a broad forehead a pair of greenish-blue eyes looked out of an open face, which was marred by an enormous scar running from a point just above the left temple, across the chin to the lobe of the left ear.

'Listen,' he said, turning to me. 'I wouldn't normally do what I'm going to do now. I wouldn't normally blow the gaff on a fellow's past history. But Pantalone, or Rousseau as he now calls himself, shouted his version of it at the top of his voice to anybody who cared to listen, and I've noticed that there are far too many of my precious compatriots doing the same. First he tells us that nonsense about his magnificent stand during the Vosges battle, and now apparently he's been stuffing the young poet here with a lot of brag about his glorious deeds in the Underground. Underground Movement! Yes, they were underground all right, and they stayed underground, most of them, until they saw which way the cat was going to jump. Do you want to know what our fine friend Rousseau was really doing during the war? Here, read that.'

He took from his pocket a typed slip of paper and handed it to me.

'I got it from a pal of mine who works as a typist in the records department here,' he explained.

> *Légion Etrangère,*
> *Section Recrutement.*
> (Extract from dossier concerning Marius Pantalone, alias Jean-Jacques Rousseau, joined 20.2.49, Marseilles)
> *Para.* 7 (*verified*) War record. Vosges front with X Inf. Regt. from Sep. '39 to Jan. '40. Deserted 5th Jan. after being

detailed for night patrol. Recaptured 25th Feb. '40 living in concubinage with Marseilles prostitute. Sentenced 6th March Two Years' Imprisonment. Execution of sentence suspended at termination hostilities. Provisionally released from Mil. Service 6.6.41. From this time on Pantalone appears to have lived on immoral earnings of a number of known Marseilles prostitutes, for whom, after German occupation of Free Zone in '42, he acted as *rabatteur* among German troops stationed in town. Joined Resistance movement 15th Aug. 1944 (date of Allied landings in South of France).

I passed the paper to the young Frenchman who, having read it, passed it on to Sibley and went off to read some more *Pensées sur la Réligion*.

'Scheer,' said the Swiss, 'were you in the Resistance yourself?'

'Hell, no,' replied the Alsatian. 'I was more or less on the other side. I suppose you know,' he continued, turning to me, 'something of the recent history of Alsace. If I tell you that I was born in nineteen-seventeen, you will know that I was German at birth, French from nineteen-nineteen to nineteen-forty, German from then till nineteen-forty-four, and now French again. It's small wonder that so many of us find our way to the Legion; we never know for five minutes which side we're supposed to be on.'

I couldn't help thinking that we English do, after all, lead very sheltered lives. Here was a man who had had to change his nationality three times in twenty-five years, and his was by no means an extreme example. There are people in Central Europe who have had five or six nationalities, all different, in thirty or forty years. And there are many who have no nationality at all.

Scheer was the son of a small farmer, and was born just outside Strasbourg, he told us. His father, as a corporal in the German artillery, had been killed just before Scheer was born, and the son had led a miserable, poverty-stricken existence on the farm which his mother, who was consumptive, had worked alone since her husband's death, ruining what remained of her health in doing so. Scheer's mother died when he was fifteen, and he found employment in a printing office in Strasbourg.

He had been called up to do his military service in 1936, and found that army life suited him better than either the printing office or the drudgery of the miserable existence on the farm, so he signed on for the regular army. He was made a sergeant just after the outbreak of war, and in May of the following year was taken prisoner at Sedan.

Generally speaking, all French prisoners of Alsatian origin were incorporated directly into the *Wehrmacht*, retaining, in most cases, their previous ranks; but certain exceptions were made. On Scheer's military papers his civilian occupation was given as 'farmer' and, since the Germans considered food production as a reserved occupation, he was released in September and sent back home. He was put on half-pay for six months, which meant that he had to report to the barracks at Strasbourg twice a week. This left him plenty of time to go back to his old job at the printing office, which he did.

'I don't think,' he told us, 'that up to that time I had any very clear ideas about politics. My upbringing had been that of a peasant and, however wretched that upbringing may have been, you cannot put anarchist ideas into the head of a son of the soil. My trade might have been a good breeding-ground for such ideas, and in fact among the young fellows I met during the time I was working at the printer's, there were many who tried to indoctrinate me with their ideas, or rather with ideas they had picked up at second or third hand from others. Pro-German ideas, pan-German ideas, United Europe ideas, Marxian ideas, anti-British ideas, and so on. I was not very much impressed by any of them, chiefly because the raw young men who tried to preach them knew neither their subjects nor the historical background in which they tried to frame them.

'But, where the persuasive arguments of my fellow-workers failed, four years' service in the French Army succeeded. During those four years I had ample opportunity for observing the effect of Communist subversive activities within the framework of the Army itself. You know, there is a saying that the Alsatians are more French than the French. Well, I was a Frenchman and proud to be one. In spite of my German name and parentage, I considered France to be my country. And I can tell you that I was utterly disgusted by some of the acts of sabotage and treachery committed by Frenchmen of unmixed origin under the influence of a political dogma.'

The Alsatian turned aside and spat in disgust.

'By the end of nineteen-forty,' he went on, 'there wasn't a more convinced anti-Communist than me to be found in Strasbourg. When, in nineteen-forty-one, Germany attacked Russia, my only ambition was to be with the Germans fighting against what I then considered, and, for that matter, still do consider, to be the Red Menace. Other considerations didn't worry me. I wasn't particularly for or against England, and, when America came into the war at the end of that year, I wasn't particularly for or against her, but, as soon as Germany had attacked Russia, I was very definitely for Germany.'

By some means or other he got to Paris and enlisted, as a Frenchman, in the *Légion Volontaire Française*. Why he took all that trouble he did not make clear, for he could more easily have enlisted in the German Army directly from Strasbourg. He wasn't much pleased at having to change over from gunnery to foot-slogging—'as a *canonier* I had always been somewhat contemptuous of *le bif*'—but he was prepared to do even that so as to have a go at the Bolshevists.

He was in action for the first time on the Central Russian Front in March of 1942, with the German Army Group which was hammering at the gates of Moscow.

'But,' he said, 'I scarcely need to tell you the story of the war against Russia, do I? This,' he pointed to the enormous scar which disfigured the left side of his face, 'I got while we were defending the Dnieper crossings in 'forty-three. I was hospitalized at Spandau. At about the same time I learnt that I had become a member of the *Waffen-SS*. All the foreign units in the German Army became SS about that time.

'When I came out of hospital a year later, I was posted to garrison duties in Lindau in the Black Forest, where I was finally taken prisoner by the French Army. When I was released, I passed before a *Conseil de Guerre*, and was sentenced to two years' imprisonment and five years' loss of civil rights. I left prison three days ago and came straight here.'

'Bad luck,' said Sibley, 'or good luck; I'm not quite sure which. Consider. If you had been automatically transferred to the German Army in nineteen-forty with the rest of them, you wouldn't have had anything to fear from the French side, but there is a fair chance you would now be in the salt-mines in Siberia with all the other Alsatians who were taken prisoner.'

Legionnaire Brunner, our *chef de chambre*, was coming towards me.

'*Ho, l'Anglais!*' he shouted. 'You're wanted in the orderly-room.'

It appeared that the captain wished to see me again. I was escorted to his office.

'Sit down,' he said very politely. 'I have sent for you so as to give you a last chance to withdraw, if that is your wish. Consider a little.' He proceeded to paint me a most terrifying picture of life in the Legion, its toughness, its danger, and so on. 'You are going to sign a contract for five years of that,' he continued. 'In five years, even with your capabilities, you will only arrive, with luck, at the rank of *adjutant*. In exercising the most strict economy, you might be able to save two or three hundred thousand francs. Then you will come out—five years older. Is that really what you want?'

'I see no other future,' I replied stubbornly.

'Then you want to go on with it?'

'Yes.'

'Very good,' said the captain, standing up and offering me his hand. 'Then all I can say is to wish you good luck. I also apologize for the appalling conditions in which you have to live during your stay here. You will find that things are better over in North Africa.'

We shook hands and I left.

# 6

'*APOIL!*' shouted the corporal. 'Get your clothes off, there, and get 'em off in a hurry. *En vitesse!*'

Most of the men belonging to our group of new arrivals obeyed immediately. A few of us, however, were aware that the doctor had not even arrived at the fort, and that, as we were always passed through in alphabetical order, it would be at least an hour before we would be required to stand naked before him. So we merely made a pretence of unbuttoning our shirts and loosening our belts, while waiting for the corporal to go away and leave us. We were herded together in a room about twenty feet square, with benches all round the walls. In one corner was the door through which we would pass into the medical examination room. In the other was the one giving on to the paradeground; as soon as the coast was clear, the Swiss and I slipped through it, buttoning our clothes again as we went. The young German from the Rhineland followed us.

I looked around at the three or four hundred ragged, desperate, miserable human wrecks who were milling around the courtyard, talking, smoking, spitting, reading, writing, or just lounging.

'*La lie humaine,*' I said, half to myself. 'The dregs of humanity. That's what they are.'

The Swiss looked at me in some surprise. 'Do you really think so?' he asked. 'Do you, for example, consider yourself to be one of the dregs? I don't. No, my dear friend. I don't honestly think you know what the dregs of humanity are like. The dregs of humanity, the real dregs, wouldn't have the guts to come along here. And even if they did, they wouldn't be accepted. . . .'

'But, damn it, man,' I interrupted. 'Just look at that blasted Frenchman who was telling us his life story yesterday. Why, the fellow was nothing more nor less than a pimp.'

'Yes,' agreed the Swiss. 'Generally speaking, you'll find that the French are the worst elements here, simply because they have no valid reason for being here. . . .'

'Good morning!' The voice was that of the young Rhinelander who, having overheard our conversation in English, had decided to join in.

'Good morning,' he repeated. 'Excuse me. Allow me to present myself. Koch!' He drew himself up smartly to attention and clicked his heels. 'Hans Koch, formerly *Panzer-Grenadier-Leutnant* of the German Army, now second-class soldier of the French Foreign Legion. You're English, aren't you, sir?'

'How d'you do? Smith's the name,' I replied shortly. I did not offer to shake hands.

'*Guten Tag*, Kirsch,' said the Swiss, who appeared to know the German already.

'Good morning, Sibley,' replied the German. Was his name Kirsch or Koch?

'Excuse me,' I said. 'I didn't quite catch your name. Did you say Koch or Kirsch? I ask because I used to know a German family called Kirsch.'

'My real name is Koch,' volunteered the German. 'But when, yesterday, I signed the provisional contract for five years of this slavery, they told me that henceforward my name would be Kirsch.'

'Yes, didn't you know?' broke in the Swiss. 'They always make you change your name when you sign on here. For example, my real name is Antoine Zublik, but here I'm known as Tom Sibley.'

'Of course I knew it,' I replied impatiently. 'You don't suppose my real name is Smith, do you?'

'*Also*,' said the Rhinelander. 'Now would I like to ask a question. What is an Englishman doing in the French Foreign Legion?'

I was much tempted to advise the German to mind his own business, but I restrained myself and replied, 'I might very well ask the same question of a German.'

'But there is no parallel,' cried Kirsch. 'We lost the war. There is misery *bei uns*. We have not enough to eat. We are the slaves of the occupation powers. It is, of course, our fault, and we must pay. I, even I, must pay. We are many, very many, Germans here. We always have been ever since the Legion was formed and, after each of our national disasters during this century, the recruitment of Germans to the Legion has reached considerable proportions. It is our fault. It is our Fate. What we call *Schicksal*. Do you understand German?

'Yes,' he hurried on, without waiting for an answer. 'It is our Fate. But you, the English, the conquerors, living off the fat of our despoiled country, why is it to you necessary to sell your bodies for five years to this decadence?'

I laughed. 'The "fat" is rich.' I said. 'I wonder if you know what an Englishman's meat ration is in this fourth year after final victory. However, let's not be mundane.'

The man was annoying me, and I thought I would give him a run for his money.

'I'm here,' I continued in a very confidential manner, 'because I robbed a bank, a very big bank called the Bank of England. I got away with nearly a hundred million. The police chased me with armoured-cars, so I bought a squadron of tanks and fought them on Salisbury Plain. Then they called out the Army against me, so I bought a battleship on the quiet, and put out to sea. They turned out the fleet against me. There was quite a good battle in the Bay of Biscay, which I unfortunately lost, so I took to my heels—or boats, rather—and got to Lisbon. There I bought a Lockheed Lightning on the black market and flew off to Buenos Aires. Peron agreed to give me sanctuary—I still had nearly forty million, you see—but the Americans, to whom the English owed the forty million and a lot more besides, threatened to bomb B.A. with atomic bombs if the General didn't give me up. One dark night I took off with a Liberator which Eva had given me as a Christmas present. I had intended to head for Tangiers, but I must have missed the road, for at dawn I found myself over Marseilles.

'The French police were shooting at me with Sten guns and, even at fifty thousand feet, the result was not encouraging. The plane was riddled with bullets and the motors started backfiring, or doing something like that. So I took to my parachute and landed here in the parade-ground of the Legion's recruiting station. I threw my parachute over the wall into the harbour, and here I am.'

I paused for breath. The German was lost in thought for quite a time.

'Stens cannot fire up to fifty thousand feet,' he said.

At that moment a jeep drew up to the door of the medical inspection room, and an officer in the uniform of the French Army Medical Corps, his maroon-coloured velvet *képi* perched jauntily over the beaky nose of his wine-coloured face, alighted from it.

'The doctor,' exclaimed Kirsch, and hurried off to get himself undressed. I was about to follow, when I felt Sibley's restraining hand upon my arm.

'Smith,' he said, 'we're both towards the end of the alphabet, so there's no need for us to hurry. I'm going to ask you to allow me to give you a piece of advice. Don't do the sort of thing you've just done. You'll get yourself disliked. When Kirsch tumbles to it that you've been pulling his leg, he'll be frightfully hurt and probably very annoyed. Oh, I know you'll tell me that the

Germans ought to have more sense of humour, but there it is. So far as you know, you may have to live five years with Kirsch. Don't, for heaven's sake, start off by making an enemy of him.

'He was affronted right at the beginning because you didn't offer to shake hands with him when he introduced himself. I know you English don't go in much for handshaking, but in most continental countries they do, and, after all, when in Rome...

'You probably think I've got a hell of a nerve to lecture you in this way—me, a little man from little Switzerland. I do so precisely because I *am* Swiss. We are the traditional neutrals, and are, therefore, perhaps the only people in Europe who are capable of looking at Europe objectively. We're international, too. *Nous parlons français.* We speak English. *Wir sprechen Deutsch. Parlamo Italiano.* And, with an eye to possible future developments, a good many of us are learning Russian. I tell you, we're the traditional neutrals. You others, you couldn't even have a war without us, because there'd be nobody to act as the Protecting Power and run the International Red Cross. And you certainly couldn't make peace, for there'd be nowhere for you to hold a peace conference.

'But, seriously, that isn't the only reason why I interfere. You see, we Swiss, besides being traditional neutrals, are, as I've already told you, traditional legionnaires. You will remember that a number of the old mercenary regiments which fought all the way across Europe during the religious wars were levied in Switzerland. One might almost say that, when King Louis-Phillipe of France formed the Foreign Legion in eighteen-thirty-three, he merely took over where the mercenary regiments left off. A great many people I know in Switzerland have done their five years here. I may, therefore, claim to know, though admittedly at second-hand, a little bit more about that organization than you do. May I go on?'

'Of course,' I said. 'You are interesting me very much.' In fact

I liked the Swiss very much more in this forceful, argumentative mood than in his whining confession of the previous day.

'Very well,' continued Sibley. 'Now, first of all, try to forget nationality. In the course of time, during your five years, you will eventually do so automatically, but it will be much better for your own peace of mind if you begin straight away to look upon your comrades as men, and not as Germans, Poles, or Italians. And, for heaven's sake, never discriminate between nationalities. That is regarded as very nearly a crime in the Legion. Never ask a legionnaire about his previous life. If he tells you of his own free will, well and good, but never ask him. Wasn't there a Scottish poet who wrote, "A man's a man for a' that"? It could very well be a motto for the Legion.

'And remember that there are some very interesting men among them. Just now you scathingly referred to a crowd of ragged recruits as *la lie humaine*. It would perhaps surprise you to know that, among that human scum, was a professor of philology from a famous university, a pianist who was one of Béla Bartók's favourite pupils, and one of Warsaw's leading barristers. You can speak French and German, Smith. Why don't you get around and come to know these people? I cannot help noticing that, ever since you've been here, the only people you open your mouth to are those who can speak English. That—h'mm—wouldn't be an English failing, by any chance, would it?'

He glanced mischievously at me and I laughed uncomfortably, but, before I had time to reply, the corporal in charge of our group was shouting to us from the doorway of the waiting-room, telling us to hurry up and get ourselves undressed for the medical inspection.

'Next man!'

A sturdily built young fellow stepped naked into the inspection room.

'Forward march! About turn! Halt! Raise your heels and stand on your toes! Lower! Corporal, take his chest expansion. Four and a half inches? Fine, that'll do. Eye test. Ear test. Cough! Six teeth missing? H'mm. Well, he's a pretty good specimen otherwise. Let it go. All right, young man, go and get dressed. Next candidate!"

An Italian this time, covered from head to toe with curly, black hair.

'Forward march! About turn! Halt! Raise your heels and stand on your toes! *No capito?* Tell him in Italian, Bernucci.'

Bernucci did so. I could hear him through the open door.

'What? He can't do it? Flat feet. Candidate refused. Unfit for service. I see he has a varicose on his left leg, too. Call the next one!'

'About turn! Halt! Take his chest expansion! Only one and a half inches? Hand me my stethoscope. H'mm. Yes. No good, young fellow, we can't take you. Candidate refused. Unfit for service. Call the next one."

Next was Sibley. He was soon out again, passed as fit. Then came my turn.

'Forward march! About turn! Halt! Hallo! What's that?'

The doctor's eyes were fixed on my right leg, where there was a very small varicose vein, a mere half-inch long. I had had it for seven or eight years, and it had never got any worse.

'H'mm,' said the doctor, 'varicose on right leg.' He looked me up and down and then added, 'General condition feeble.'

'*Monsieur le medecin,*' I interrupted him. 'I have just walked here from Strasbourg in thirty-three days. I don't know if you consider that feeble.'

'*Celà se peut,*' he replied absently. Then briskly, 'No, sorry, *mon vieux*, it's no go.' Then to his secretary, 'Candidate refused. Unfit for service.'

If anything was required to make me absolutely determined

to do my five years, it was that. The idiocy, as I considered it, of rejecting for a mere trifle a man who had just walked six hundred miles in thirty-three days. I'd have liked to see that damned doctor doing it himself.

As soon as I had dressed myself, I walked out of the waiting-room in a flaring temper and stalked across to the block of offices where the interrogations had taken place. I demanded to see the captain.

'What's all this?' I stormed, when I was shown into his office. 'Do you want me for your Legion, or don't you? Your doctor has just rejected me as unfit for service because of a tiny varicose vein—*un rien du tout*—rejected me, who have just——' and I pulled out the argument of my thousand kilometres all over again.

The captain smiled, sat down at his desk, and wrote a short note.

'Go back to the doctor with that,' he said. 'It can probably be arranged.'

It was! The note worked like a charm. The doctor read it and passed me fit for service without even troubling to re-examine me!

# 7

'Do you know what?' cried Rousseau. 'There's a rumour going round that they're going to put us into uniform tomorrow and that the next day we embark for Oran.'

The group of hunched-up, forlorn, bedraggled men to whom he spoke included the majority of those of us who had come in through the gates four days before. The day's fatigues were over, we had eaten a good meal at midday, and were huddled together on the ramparts, looking out over the harbour, where divers were at work salvaging the wreck of some merchant ship sent to the bottom during an air-raid five years previously. We were forlorn because we had no money and nothing to smoke, and bedraggled because we were still in civilian clothes which were very much the worse for wear.

'Let's hope you're right,' said the Alsatian. 'Though I must say that all the information you've handed out thus far has turned out to be a lot of hot air.'

'*Toi, Scheer, ferme ta gueule!*' Rousseau's eyes sparkled with anger. 'Shut your trap and keep it shut, unless you want me to shut it for you.'

Scheer smiled contemptuously. It had been obvious for a day or two that there was going to be bad blood between these two.

'You may have been a hell of a guy with the tarts on the Canebière,' he said, 'but you don't cut any ice with me.'

'*Ah, tu me prends pour un con!*' Rousseau puffed out his chest like a little fighting-cock. 'All right. Take that!' And he swung a badly aimed, stiff-armed, right uppercut to the Alsatian's chin.

Scheer warded off the blow quite easily with his left hand and

Tongking in the heat of the summer

Hanoi—with the Transport Company

'*Légionnaire : démerd*
Legionnaires improvin
quarters at Nam-Dinh

(*Below*) The road to
Dinh. '*Quis custodiet . .*

pushed the other's face so hard with the open palm of his right that Rousseau staggered backwards and fell in a heap on the ground about four yards away. When he had recovered from the shock, he groaned a little and looked up at the Alsatian from under lowered brows.

'Get up and brush your clothes,' said Scheer, looking him straight in the eye. 'If I ever really started in to fight you, I should half kill you. I haven't lived the life of a Marseilles *maquereau*, as you have.'

'*Porco Dio!*' exclaimed the Italian. 'I hope he's right, all the same. It appears that once they've put us into uniform we sign our contracts, and then immediately draw our first pay and tobacco ration. *Inglese*,' he turned to me, 'haven't you a cigarette for me?'

'No,' I replied. 'I haven't even one for myself.'

'Why don't you buy some, *Inglese*?'

'Because I have no money, *Italiano*.'

'No money? Ho! ho! Do you hear that, Rousseau? The *Inglese* says he has no money. Why, Smitta, you have plenty money, ten thousand francs perhaps, on you. You don't believe? That silk scarf, *per esempio*, I get you four hundred francs or perhaps ten packets of cigarettes for it. What do you want with a silk scarf? You won't be needing it for another five years.'

I shrugged my shoulders. 'I don't *want* to sell my things,' I said pettishly. 'In any case, there's not a soul in this place who's got either four hundred francs or ten packets of cigarettes. They're all broke.'

The Italian winked. 'That's what you think,' he replied.

'Parade for all you lot in half an hour!' shouted a corporal who was coming towards us from the direction of the orderly office. 'Over there in front of the photographer's *atelier*. And wash your ugly mugs before then, so that the *flics* will be able to recognize you.'

We all laughed at this choice morsel of coarse humour. We were beginning to get used to well-intentioned insults. Even I laughed, though I was feeling like death; but I could not prevent myself from replying, 'That would be easier if they gave us some soap.'

'*Kaufen!*' laughed the corporal. 'Buy some.'

'*Kein Geld,*' said Kirsch. 'No money.'

'*Dann abstauben!*' shouted the corporal, as he walked away amid roars of laughter.

After only a few days we were already beginning to pick up some of the slang of the Legion. This is a mixture of French *argot* and German Army jargon, with a few words from Russian, Polish, Hungarian, Spanish, Italian, Arabic, and Annamite thrown in. The word '*abstauben*', for example, means acquiring anything by irregular means, but you won't find this use of the word in any German dictionary! This slang is further complicated by the fact that some of the German expressions used are not even recognized *Wehrmacht* jargon, but French *argot* translated literally, word for word, into German. If I say to a legionnaire '*Ich habe Suppe von Deinem Kopf,*' he knows that I mean I am fed up with the sight of his ugly face; but to a German who has never served in the ranks of the Legion the phrase has no meaning whatever.

The advantage of this medium of expression is that, since words from three or four languages are mixed up together in almost every sentence, everyone understands at least a part of what is being said, and so more or less follows the gist of the conversation.

'Ambrosio,' I said to the Italian, 'here, take the damned thing and see what you can get for it.' I handed over the scarf, and he darted away to a corner of the courtyard, towards a group of men with sun-tanned faces, who were looking rather awkward in the civilian clothes they were wearing for the first time in five years.

These were the *libérables*—legionnaires who had completed their five years and were on their way out to the battle for existence which is civilian life. For some of them there would be no problem; the little trouble which was the cause of their joining five years ago had long been settled. They had homes and jobs to go to, and would soon forget the hardships and tribulations, remembering only, from time to time, with a certain nostalgia, the pleasant and humorous episodes. Others would face the hard task of settling down in a new country which from then on would be their own (the legionnaire who has completed five years' service is entitled to apply for French nationality), with a newly acquired nationality and language. Some of these latter would succeed. Others would fail, and a month, three months, or a year later, back they would come to the Legion which is their home.

Ambrosio came back, stuffing a hundred-franc note into his pocket. He handed four others to me, and brought out a packet of cigarettes which he offered all round. He had obviously taken his cut out of the deal, and made no secret of it. He even invited three or four of us to come to the canteen, when it opened at six o'clock, to have a glass of *vino*.

'And by the way,' he said, 'if any of you has a good watch to sell, I can find a customer for it. Those fellows have plenty of money. They've most of them just come back from Indo-China.'

I turned to greet Sibley, who had just returned after having been called away for a further check on his life story. 'Hallo there, Sibley,' I cried. 'I've just been dealing in the local black market.' I explained what had happened and added, 'I feel rather mean about it, but at least I shall be able to buy a few fags.'

The Swiss smiled ironically. 'I don't know why you should feel mean,' he said, 'unless, of course, you intend to smoke all the cigarettes yourself. Good heavens, man, what's all the fuss about? These fellows who've just finished their five years have money and need clothes. You, on the other hand, need money and have clothes which you won't be allowed to wear again until nineteen-fifty-four, and if, by that time, you're sleeping with a little white cross over your head, you won't even be needing them then. The black market, as you call it—it isn't, of course, a black market at all—enables the demobilized man to obtain the things he needs at a quarter of the price he'd pay in the shops, and allows you to smoke and drink, while at the same time disposing of clothes which, if you left them in the stores, would be mouldy, moth-eaten, or lost by the time you come out again.'

'Yes, I suppose you're right enough there,' I answered slowly, 'but what I can't stomach is doing the business through the intermediary of a little cheating schemer like the Wop there, who makes a damn good thing out of it by taking a rake-off on every deal he puts through.'

'And why the hell shouldn't he? Would you have succeeded in finding or, when found, would you have approached the prospective customer yourself? No, my dear old Smith, he earns his rake-off just as the stockbroker, or whatever you call him, earns his percentage for selling the shares of the rich man who has neither the specialized knowledge nor the time and energy to find buyers for himself.'

He accepted the cigarette which Ambrosio offered him.

'And by the way,' he whispered, 'lay off the "Wop". You may have been chasing Italians across some battlefield or other a few years ago, but remember that here they're just as good as the next man; and you'll find out, if what I've been told is true, that in the Legion they make pretty good soldiers. Damn it, here I go, lecturing you again. Sorry!'

In fact, some of Sibley's pieces of advice did irritate me somewhat at the time, though I now know how right he was in most of what he said. Even with his sage counsels I managed to make quite a number of enemies. There was something about that atmosphere which provoked the aggressively 'British' side of my character, especially in the early days. If he had not been there to guide and warn me, I'm sure I should have made many more.

'Ha!' said Sibley, 'I see young Ambrosio is putting across another smart piece of business. I wonder what he was doing before he came here, to make him so quick on the uptake.'

Four years later, about six months before he was killed, Ambrosio told me. His story is typical of those of many young Italians who found their way into the Legion during the years immediately following the war. Here are the essentials of it.

He was thirty years younger than the century and lived with his mother in Florence. His father was a bomber pilot in the Italian Air Force and held the rank of captain. The captain was a simple soul and accustomed to obeying orders; neither is an uncommon characteristic in serving officers of any army. Because he was a simple soul, he thought that Italy, having entered the war on the side of Germany, should continue as her ally until the bitter end. Because he was accustomed to obeying orders, he executed those which he received at the end of September 1943.

He was told to place his squadron under the orders of a German colonel, and he did so. He was told to consider Badoglio as a traitor to his country, and he did so. He was ordered to fly his squadron from its airfield in Northern Italy and bomb the Allied positions around Naples, and he did so, and returned to his base with a shell splinter in his left lung which was going to make him a cripple for the little that remained of his life.

When the Allies occupied Florence a year later, he was still lying in the Military Hospital there; at the same time his pay was stopped, since he was now considered a traitor. This, of course, was the luck of the draw. Had he been stationed in Southern instead of in Northern Italy, he would have meekly surrendered with the rest of them during the autumn of the previous year, and would now have been treated as a hero.

Be that as it may, the fourteen-year-old Ambrosio was faced with a desperate situation. He was the only able-bodied member of the family of three, and his mother, an invalid whose health was worsening from day to day, hadn't a penny left in her purse. Young Ambrosio realized that he had to make money, and make it quickly. The means of doing so were at hand. There was a supply depôt of the American Fifth Army in the city. He found work there, loading sacks of flour, sugar, and coffee, and cases of bully-beef from the stores on to the waiting lorries.

It did not take him long to discover a means of exploiting the situation. He organized a gang of children of about his own age. Three of them worked inside the depôt and two outside. The civilian labour was very laxly supervised by the American sentries, and it was very easy for the three boys to slip one case or sack in every ten they handled, through the hole they had made in the wall, to their associates who were waiting outside in the street. There the stolen supplies were loaded on a handcart, covered with dirty old sacking, and wheeled off to a store which Ambrosio had organized in the cellar of a bombed-out house in the slum quarter of the town.

Ambrosio, whom the desperate state of his family's affairs had rendered precociously adult, was the unquestioned leader. When he discovered, after the first two or three days, that the merchandise was being filched from the cellar by the local inhabitants, he stole a tommy-gun and some ammunition, and put one of his subordinates on guard night and day to prevent further leakage.

After a time the sergeant responsible for the loading of supplies became suspicious. Ambrosio summoned to his headquarters the most beautiful and capable prostitute in Florence, and arranged to pay her a salary for becoming the gratuitous mistress of the sergeant. He very soon had the sergeant eating out of his hand, bought him into the racket, and paid him a salary, too, so that there was no longer any need for subterfuge, and he was able to take two sacks out of ten instead of one.

At the age of fifteen Ambrosio was making ten times as much money as his father had ever earned as a captain in the Air Force. Business slackened off a little in 1946, when the American depôt moved away from Florence, but the sixteen-year-old black-marketeer still had enormous stocks which he was keeping in a cave in the hills outside the city; and he was not long in discovering other sources of supply, though he had to organize a transport column between Florence and the ports of Leghorn and Spezia in order to exploit them.

That year his father came out of hospital, as the Italian authorities were tired of paying for his keep. He died within six months of his discharge. In Ambrosio's view, the Italian Government was entirely responsible for his death.

At the same time his mother's health changed for the worse, and her paralysis began developing into that madness which the doctor had always feared. By the beginning of 1948 the case had surpassed the competence of the doctor; the state health authorities intervened, and the wretched physical and mental wreck of a woman was sent by order to a mental asylum. Her eighteen-year-old son chalked up another score against the Italian Government.

With his mother being cared for at the expense of the state, Ambrosio no longer had any valid motive for continuing his black-market activities, but he had by now developed a considerable distaste for the idea of working for money.

For some time the stealing of goods from the Spezia and Leghorn dockyards had become more and more difficult. Ambrosio, therefore, embarked on a venture which he had been contemplating for months: the large-scale smuggling of wine, spirits, perfumes, and cosmetics between Italy and France.

Two of the youths he employed for this purpose were French

and had their homes in France near the Italian frontier. Ambrosio always made arrangements with them, as soon as a 'job' was finished, as to the rendezvous for the next.

One day one of the two Frenchmen got very drunk and talked too much. The French customs police, to whom the information was passed, were not slow to act, with the result that the next convoy fell into a strongly armed ambush. A week later Ambrosio, who had hidden in a mountain cave for two days and nights without food or drink, found himself at Marseilles, penniless and with a warrant out for his arrest in his own country.

He came quickly to a decision. He went to the gates of the Fort Saint-Nicolas and asked to be admitted. Inside he found two members of his gang who had also succeeded in escaping, and he immediately set to work with them to organize the marketing of all saleable and barterable commodities within the camp. He was young and gay, and everybody liked him. He was always singing and joking and laughing. I wonder what sort of deep, dumb despair there was in his heart, for at the age of nineteen he had no hope and certainly no illusions left.

# 8

WITH a blast of the whistle the corporal paraded us for the photographer. The moment was approaching when we would be told to sign our names at the bottom of a contract engaging us to serve for five years *avec honneur et fidélité* in defence of the French flag against all nations save our own individual countries of origin.

And thereby hangs a tale. I cannot guarantee its authenticity, but it struck me as amusing when I heard it a year or so later. In the event of France being at war with another people, the legionnaires who are nationals of that country are paraded and given the option of fighting against their own country (they have to sign an agreement stating they are willing to do so) or being interned. So it was that, in the autumn of 1939, a large number of legionnaires of German origin were interned at Sidi Bel-Abbès in North Africa. The internment was technical only; they were allowed to come and go as they liked, providing they did not leave the town. At the same time contingents of the Legion went off via France to Norway and, after Narvik, were evacuated to England, where they were re-formed, under British control, as the 13th Demi-Brigade.

Meanwhile France had been overrun, the Vichy Government had been installed, and the whole of the Foreign Legion in North Africa came under Vichy control. This story is concerned with the First Regiment of Cavalry of the Legion, which was on patrol duty in Syria and which, it soon became apparent, was to be used against the British Forces there. One of the legionnaires in this regiment was an Englishman and, as soon as he heard the news, he deserted and made his way by a variety of means towards Cairo, hoping to join up with the British Forces there. It took him a long time and, when at last he arrived, the first person he ran into was his platoon commander of the previous year, on leave from the 13th Demi-Brigade, which was now fighting with the Eighth Army in the desert. He was a sergeant-major of German origin who had opted to fight.

'Where are you off to?' he asked.

The Englishman told him.

'Oh no, you don't,' said the sergeant-major. 'I'll have no desertions on my conscience. You're coming along with me.'

And he cut his leave short, took the Englishman in tow and returned with him to the 13th Demi-Brigade, where the Englishman remained for the duration of the war.

The corporal told us to fall in in three ranks and, having numbered us off, stood us at ease.

'Smoke, if you want to,' he said.

'*Kein Zigaretten*,' came the reply.

'*Alors, crachez!*' There was a roar of laughter.

'Don't make too much damned noise,' cried the corporal, looking up apprehensively at the window of the sergeant-major's office. He told off two men to bring a table and chair and place them in position.

'After you've been photographed, that's where you'll go and sign on the dotted line,' he said.

'The photographs are for our identity-cards, I suppose,' I said to the Swiss, who was standing beside me. 'It seems to me that it would be more logical to take them after we've signed our contracts instead of before.'

Sibley nodded. 'Perhaps so,' he replied. 'Though it comes to exactly the same thing for, as you'll see, nobody will refuse to sign. Oh yes, I know, theoretically now is the moment to withdraw, but morally we all signed away those five years of our lives when we walked in through the gates four days ago. At the bottom of our hearts we know it, and the authorities know it, too. It was then that we took the decision. What we do here and now is a mere formality.'

'I don't think that they want the photos merely for our identity-cards,' said Kirsch. 'There's also the question of desertion.'

'Yes,' said Rousseau, who always knew everything. 'They make three copies; one for the identity-card, one for the records, and one to be held in readiness for the *gendarmerie* in case the fellow takes off.'

'Is there so very much desertion, then?' asked somebody else.

The Swiss nodded again. 'From what I've heard a large number try to run away during their first six months' service. They regret the decision they've taken, or they can't take the toughness of the preliminary training, or perhaps they receive news from home to say that their little bit of trouble is cleared up. Generally speaking, however, once they have got over the initial period, they settle down to make the best of a bad job.'

'And do you blame them for deserting?' asked Kirsch. 'I don't. Look at the conditions here. Look at the way we've been kept for five days without a penny in our pockets, eating bad food, being bullied and insulted without respect to our previous rank and status, doing fatigues which they have no right to make us do seeing that we haven't yet signed our contracts. I think it's disgusting. In fact, the whole business is disgusting. Why can't the French fight their own battles instead of having a mercenary army to fight for them?'

'If that's the way you feel,' countered Sibley, 'I suppose you will refuse to sign your contract.'

Kirsch did not reply.

'Well, I look at it this way,' I said, breaking the silence. 'Nobody forced us nor even asked us to come along here, did they?

I take the view that we came here of our own free will, and that a contract is a contract and should be respected as such. Then, again, we go into this thing with our eyes wide open, or should do. Ask the ordinary man in the street in any country what he knows about the Foreign Legion; the first thing, perhaps the only thing, that he knows about it is that it's supposed to be tough. That is so much common knowledge that it is useless for any of us to profess ignorance of it. If we weren't prepared to accept that toughness, we shouldn't have come along to the Bas Fort Saint-Nicolas in the first place.'

'And do you mean to say,' asked Kirsch incredulously, 'do you really mean to say that you, an Englishman, don't regret being here? Why, you'd be better off in an English prison.'

'I don't know whether I should,' I replied coldly. 'But I do know that I have no wish, nor, so far as I know, any reason to be in one.' Then I remembered the tale I had spun Kirsch the day before. I'd asked for that one, right enough.

'Well, Kirsch,' said Scheer the Alsatian, laughing, 'you're a fine one to talk about mercenary armies. Tell me, how many foreign divisions were there in the German Army at the end of the war?'

But before the Rhinelander had time to reply, the corporal called us up to attention and the formalities began. Half an hour later, by a stroke of the pen, I was a member of the French Foreign Legion until February 1954.

That night I was very ill. I don't know to this day what was really the matter with me, except that I had tonsilitis, bronchitis, and a shattering headache. At about eight o'clock in the evening Brunner, our *chef de chambre*, came along and looked at me and, despite my protests, went off to get a member of the infirmary staff. The medical orderly took my temperature, and I was immediately bundled off to the sick-bay. An hour later I learnt that a detachment was leaving for Oran the next day, and that my name figured on the list.

The infirmary was just a small room with six beds in it, not intended to be used as a permanent sick-room. When the doctor arrived the next morning, he took one look at me and gave some rapid instructions to the orderly.

'Ha! ha!' I expected him to say. 'So, my friend, I was right after all, eh? You're not strong enough to stand the tough life of the Legion. You're going to be more of a nuisance to us than you'll be worth. Out you go!'

How little I knew the Legion then!

'Well, old fellow,' was all he said. 'We'll have to pack you off to hospital this afternoon. Hurry up and get well, and come back to us in good form.'

I then began to perceive that once the Legion has embraced her sons she looks after them as a mother looks after her children—lovingly, jealously. I have already said something of the medical examinations designed to sort out weaklings and the interrogations designed to sort out criminals. But no system is infallible, and I have known both weaklings and criminals to be accepted in error. Yet once the Legion had taken in a volunteer of either category, she always took the responsibility for her mistakes. The weaklings might spend half their five years in sick-wards and hospitals: the Legion always stood by them. The police of a dozen nations might come hammering at the gates to claim the criminals: they always went empty away.

Towards midday I heard that the detachment of which I should have formed part was leaving at two o'clock in the afternoon. I thought dimly that I should have liked to say good-bye to Sibley and some of the others, wish them good luck, and so on. After a time I had a fit of coughing and thought no more about it. It was then that I had my second big surprise.

There was a subdued whispering and scuffling in the corridor. I heard the voice of the infirmary attendant, 'All right, then, but only five minutes and don't let the doctor see you.' And they all came trooping in: Sibley, Scheer, Pantalone-Rousseau, Ambrosio, the Pascal Frenchman, and half a dozen others whose names I did not even know. Every blessed one of the men who had joined at Marseilles on the same day as I was there. They had come to say good-bye!

They brought with them a sackful of oranges—each one of them must have forgone his dessert at dinner that day—and two packets of cigarettes. And the poor fellows hadn't two half-pennies to rub together! They stood about awkwardly for a few minutes, wishing me good luck and telling me to get well quickly. Then the orderly shooed them out.

Not one of them had I known for more than four days, and to some of them I had never addressed a single word!

# 9

I WILL not waste your time or mine by giving you a description of those fifteen days I spent in hospital. Still less will I disgust and revolt you by describing the hospital itself. Suffice it to say that, for lack of organization and hygiene, for dirtiness, callousness, and carelessness, it was unequalled—except by every other French Military Hospital I have ever known.

Unfortunately, apart from Unit Medical Officers and their assistants, the Legion has no *Service de Santé* of its own, so that once a legionnaire is hospitalized he falls to the tender mercies of the Regular Army Medical Service. We were six legionnaires in the hospital at Marseilles, and they put us all together in the same ward. This was a great advantage since it enabled us to maintain a sort of oasis of cleanliness amid the filth and disorder which reigned in the remainder of the building.

Of my five ward companions two, both raw recruits like myself, were discharged on the same day that I left and, as it turned out, we crossed to Oran in the same detachment and remained together for quite a time. They were a Pole and a Frenchman.

The Pole's name was Jaderny and, like Scheer the Alsatian, he had just come out of prison before joining the Legion. He told me a long and involved story about himself, which was chiefly interesting because he had been an eye-witness of the fall of Warsaw in 1939 and had taken a prominent part in the ill-fated Insurrection five years later.

When the Germans attacked Poland, Jaderny told me, he was twenty-eight years old and a sergeant-major. As peace-time promotion goes, he considered that he had climbed quickly in the ranks of the Polish Army. He had been ambitious then. Until the war had started, he had nourished high hopes of further promotion. Regimental sergeant-major, yes! Even the officer ranks might have been open to him, for he had a smattering of glib education and even some of what passed for the attributes of a gentleman in the cock-eyed, continental Europe of 1939.

When the invasion started, Jaderny had sincerely believed that his high merits would ensure his being posted to GHQ. Not a bit of it! He found himself in command of a simple infantry platoon, and in a forward position at that. And for twenty-five days he and his men had been bombarded, Stuka-ed, machine-gunned and overrun by tanks, from Ostrow to Kalisz, from Kalisz to Lodz, from Lodz to Lowicz. At last he came to Warsaw, his platoon reduced to half its original strength; and some very strange reports were being spread.

It was said, for example, that the shortage of food and ammunition was not entirely due to enemy bombardments, but that the inefficiency of the gentlemen with gold-braided shoulders who commanded, and of the other gentlemen with silver-braided ones who did their staff work, might also have something to do with it.

It was murmured that the order to counter-attack before Lodz had been a supreme folly of the commanding general, inspired by the effects of two bottles of champagne. 'This,' said Jaderny, 'was only a half-truth. For "two" read "six".'

It was whispered that the costly and quite unnecessary delaying action before Lowicz had been partly motivated by another general's desire to evacuate his wife and her valuables before the Germans took over. 'Again only a half-truth,' said Jaderny. 'For "partly" read "wholly", and for "wife" read "mistress", and since the latter was a German spy, she gave the general the slip and remained behind, anyway.'

But the most disturbing rumours of all were the ones about the Russians. They had come across the frontier on the seventeenth. They were said to have already crossed the River Bug in the north and to have taken Lwow on the twenty-third. Was it possible? And were they coming in to help Poland, to help Germany, or to help themselves?

'It was the thought of the Russians being in Lwow that worried me,' said Jaderny. 'My girl friend was there.' Then, with a wealth of intimate detail, he told me about the girl Nadja.

'I had been stationed in Lwow up till about a month before the war started, and Nadja was the manageress of a rather chic and very discreet café, the Nevsky Din. The establishment consisted of two salons. The first, which you entered from the street, contained the bar, several easy chairs, and a small floor space in the midst of them where it was just possible to dance to the tune of a gramophone operated by the barman. Behind a pair of red velvet curtains was the second room.'

The Pole told me about the first evening he had pushed open the door of the Nevsky Din. He was the only customer, for it was early. Nadja, a tall, slender blonde with high cheek-bones and very striking, greenish-blue eyes, was dressed in a scarlet evening gown which had a slit on the left side reaching to well above the knees. When she walked, she swung her hips so as to make the slit open and reveal her shapely legs. She was smoking a cigarette in a long jade holder.

'When I opened the door, she was scolding the barman. She halted in the middle of a sentence and looked at me. I removed my cap and returned her stare. She fixed me with the penetration of her extraordinary green-blue eyes. I held her eyes in mine, and I knew, without a shadow of doubt, that there would never be any other woman but her in my life. Neither of us spoke a word. We just stood there looking at one another.'

The barman placed a record on the turntable of the gramophone, and the strains of *The Blue Danube* crackled forth from the tinny horn. Then suddenly she was in his arms, whirling round in the confined space between the tables and chairs. There was not enough room to make steps, so they just turned on the one spot. After a while Jaderny forced his right leg between the legs of his partner. He soon found his knee in the vice-like grip of the girl's powerful thigh muscles. He trapped her right leg in the same way, and she pressed the whole of her body against his, 'until I could distinctly feel the sharp outline of her pelvis. My lips were caressing her perfumed hair, and our two bodies, as we whirled faster and faster to the rhythm of the Strauss waltz, could not have been more intimately locked together had we been buried in the same coffin.

'At last the music stopped, but we remained for a long time clinging to each other, and boring into the depths of one another's eyes. We were both giddy with the swiftness of the dance and the overwhelming suddenness of the sexual urge. Then I kissed her. Smiling, she returned my kiss, and I took her up in my arms and carried her into the room behind the velvet curtains.'

On another occasion Jaderny told me how he had been taken prisoner by the Russians. During those last twenty-four hours before the surrender he had seen Warsaw die. The German Air Force had bombed the city throughout the night, and continued with waves of Stukas during all the following day. With his company, he crossed the bridge to the east side of the Vistula and had marched towards the Bug, until finally, about thirty miles from the capital, too tired to resist, they had walked into a Russian prisoner-of-war camp.

'At least I had sense enough to tear off my badges of rank and get rid of my paybook before entering the enclosure,' said Jaderny. 'Among the three thousand Polish soldiers in the camp I found my captain who was also passing himself off as a private soldier. He told me that he thought we had both done the right thing. "As far as officers are concerned," he told me, "I don't suppose the Russians will ever let them go, at least not until the end of the war."

'Even at that he was optimistic,' continued Jaderny with a sigh. 'You know what happened at Katyn.'

He had invented a story for himself and stuck to it, with the result that, after seven months' captivity, he was released and sent back to Poland. There he became a member of the Resistance, and for four long years he existed in Warsaw by day, doing menial jobs in order to earn a living, and really living at night, when he attended secret meetings, organized acts of sabotage, and helped to run the Underground Press. And whatever he was doing, both night and day, he thought of Nadja.

From time to time he saw her, for, every time a liaison officer was required to go to Lwow, no matter how dangerous was the mission, Jaderny volunteered. Then one day she disappeared, leaving no address.

One evening, a couple of days before we left the hospital, he told me about the Warsaw Insurrection against the Germans in the autumn of 1944. When the uprising started, on the first of August, he was commanding a group whose objective was the south wing of the main post office. At that time the victorious Russian Armies under the command of Marshal Rokossowski were bearing down on Warsaw from the east, and there appeared to be no reason why they should not be in the city in a day or two and thus come to the relief of the insurgents.

Jaderny took his objective in the face of a fierce, though not very effective, resistance by the German occupation troops, and within the first few days of the uprising that and most of the other vital points in the capital were controlled by the Polish Underground Army. Even the main railway station, upon which the Germans relied for supplying their armies, was cut off from the outside world, and by the end of the first week it was impossible for the Germans to circulate in the main streets, for they were all covered by the fire from the insurgents' machine-guns.

The Germans had been taken by surprise and were not immediately in a position to react. Their salient on the east banks of the Vistula was in a most precarious position, and it was only with difficulty that they succeeded in maintaining control of one of the two bridges. Now was the moment for Rokossowski to attack, reduce the bridgehead, and march into the city.

'Rokossowski,' said Jaderny, and he was on the verge of tears as he told me. 'Rokossowski did nothing of the sort. Acting on orders received from Moscow, he left Warsaw to its fate. From my observation tower I could plainly see German soldiers in the salient walking about in broad daylight in full view of the enemy; the Russians did not even trouble to fire at them!'

When the Russians 'liberated' the city at the beginning of January, he was not alone in viewing their arrival with mixed feelings. For four years he and most of his fellow partisans had tried to look upon them as allies, but the events of the previous autumn had awoken them to reality. Again Poles were putting to themselves and to one another the question, 'Have they come to help us or to help themselves?' They did not have to wait long to find out.

'From the day of their arrival in Warsaw,' said Jaderny, 'the Political Commissars viewed all members, and in particular all leaders of the Polish Underground, with the deepest suspicion. They perhaps thought that those who had so well succeeded in resisting the Germans might be capable in the future of resisting them. In April, a month before the end of the war in Europe, the officer who had introduced me to the Resistance in the first place was deported to Russia to face a trumped-up charge of "sabotage in the rear of the Red Army". He never returned to Poland, and a few weeks later a dozen or more partisan leaders disappeared in the same way.

'One night at the end of May I heard a knock at my door. When I opened it I saw a boy who had acted as a messenger with us during the Insurrection and had an arm blown off for his pains. "Get out, Rottmistr Jaderny," he whispered. "Get out of Warsaw and out of Poland as quick as you can. They are coming to arrest you tomorrow morning." He handed over an envelope containing a wad of banknotes, and disappeared.

'I needed no further warning. I had suspected for some time that I was being watched. I quickly packed a few belongings into a sack, stuffed the money into my pocket and was on my way out of the city in less than an hour.'

For two years he wandered across Europe, doing a job here, engaging in a little black market there. He lived in Berlin, Bremen, Hamburg, Brussels, and Lille. At last, in the summer of 1947, he went for the first time to Paris, where he had arranged to meet a compatriot with whom he intended going into business. He arrived at the Gare du Nord at seven o'clock in the evening and, as his appointment was for the following morning, decided to see something of Paris night-life. He left his suit-case at the station and walked into the first bar that caught his eye. He walked into many bars that evening, and had a drink, if not two or three, in each one of them.

At midnight he walked into the seventeenth, somewhere in the rue Blanche it must have been, and ordered his twenty-eighth glass of cognac. The place was deserted except for the barman. There was a dim, shaded light over the bar, and a wireless-set was playing soft dance music. In one corner of the room was the door leading to the toilets, and in another an opening partitioned off by a pair of red-velvet curtains. Jaderny was tired and drunk. He took his glass and sat down on a settee in the corner opposite the velvet curtains. He began to nod and was very soon fast asleep.

'The opening of the street door,' said Jaderny, 'awoke me. A well-dressed, fattish man of about fifty had come into the bar.

At the same time the red curtains were parted by a tall, slender blonde with high cheek-bones and striking green-blue eyes. She was dressed in a scarlet evening gown and was smoking a cigarette in a long jade holder. She could not see me, for I was in semi-darkness, but she saw the new-comer, and she fixed him with her extraordinary, penetrating eyes. I remembered our first meeting and something snapped within my brain.'

The elderly man had returned her stare, the barman twisted the knob of the radio, and the strains of *The Blue Danube* came softly into the room. The man took the girl into his arms, and they danced together. When the music stopped she led the man away through the red velvet curtains. Twenty minutes later she called for a bottle of champagne, and at last the elderly man came back into the café, paid what he owed, and left.

'I staggered to my feet,' said Jaderny. He was telling me this the night before we left hospital, and tears were streaming down his cheeks as he spoke. 'I walked slowly and unsteadily towards the curtains. I hesitated with my face a few inches from their undulating, plush surface. Then I tore them apart. I found myself in a short corridor, at the end of which was a flight of stairs. I went up the stairs and tried the first door on the left. It was unlocked, so I wrenched it open.

'Nadja was sitting on the bed, naked except for a brassière which she was adjusting over her provocative, pointed breasts. Her lovely, ash-blonde hair fell in disordered masses over her perfectly shaped shoulders. She looked up with fear in her eyes when she saw me. She seized a slip which was hanging over the bedrail and held it in front of her. "*Tu as du culot, tout de même,*" she said, and her use of French told me she had not recognized me. "You've got a nerve to break into a girl's bedroom like this".'

He advanced a pace into the room, then another pace, placing one foot slowly and deliberately before the other, until his face was only six inches from hers.

'*Kurva!*' He spat the word, the most insulting a Pole can use to a woman, into her eyes, and in them he saw that she had recognized him. He placed his hands on her shoulders and shook her.

'*Kurva!*' he repeated. 'When I last saw you, you promised to be faithful to me. I have waited three years and more for you, and in that time I have been through hell. I have lost my parents, my home, my career, and my country. And now I have lost you.'

He slid his hands up to her beautifully shaped throat.

'I love you,' he continued. 'I have always loved you. That is why I am going to kill you. I am going to squeeze the breath out of your filthy whore of a body.'

Tears were streaming down his cheeks as he felt her go limp in his hands. Then came a crushing blow on the back of his head, and all went dark before him. Releasing his grip, he sank slowly to the floor and remained there.

He was sentenced to eighteen months' imprisonment for assault, the French being lenient towards *le crime passionel*. The *Juge d'Instruction* told him he was lucky to get away with only that. 'For,' he said, 'if the barman, who had followed you up the stairs, had been only two seconds later in knocking you over the head with the empty champagne bottle, the girl Nadja would have died.'

'When I came out of prison,' concluded Jaderny, 'the first thing I did was to get miserably drunk. I remained so until I had no money left, and then took the Metro to the Legion recruiting office at Fort Vincennes. I had nothing more to lose; nothing whatsoever.'

Poor old Jaderny. I thought, even at that time, that he was a wee bit off his rocker. Four years later, in Indo-China, when I saw him amusing himself by eating live lizards, I began to be convinced of it.

Of a very different type was the Frenchman who left the hospital with us the next day. Indeed, he was different from nearly all other Frenchmen I ever met in the Legion. In the first place, he was that almost indefinable something which can only be described by the word 'gentleman'. I learnt later, though never from his own lips, that in private life Legionnaire Blanc was the Vicomte de P——. He had been, and still was, a *blanc du midi*, and his royalist opinions had got him into trouble with the Government, expecially as, towards the end of the war, he was commanding a company of volunteers on the Russian front. That is all I know of his antecedents, for he was as secretive towards me concerning his past life as I was to him about mine.

He was a man of wide culture and easy good manners, and we spent many an hour together discussing music and literature. Occasionally the talk veered to politics. His views, although I'm quite sure he was intelligent enough to have worked them out for himself, were identical with those of Monsieur Charles Maurras. That is to say, he considered the great enemies of France to be England, the Jews, the Reformed Church, and International Freemasonry. The first named *bête noire* in no way prevented him, however, from becoming a very good friend of mine.

A few months later, in North Africa, he gave me a present which I have with me to this day—a copy of the 1947 edition of that magnificent little dictionary and encyclopædia, *Le Nouveau Petit Larousse Illustré*.

# 10

When the three of us left the hospital and walked back to the Fort Saint-Nicolas, I was feeling as fit as a fiddle. That was the one and only time I was ill during the whole of my five and a half years in the Legion. I think it must have been mainly due to my having overdone it in walking from Strasbourg, when I was certainly not in a physical condition for such a performance.

All three of us were in uniform. A corporal had visited me in the hospital ward and issued me with mine: to wit, a forage cap three sizes too small for me, which fell off every time I attempted to salute, a khaki shirt torn down the back, underclothing which really did merit the epithet 'indescribables', a pair of American Army trousers and a 1914 pattern British Army tunic complete with the buttons of the Queen's Royal West Surrey Regiment! These, with socks and a pair of down-at-heel boots, completed my uniform. In addition I had a *musette*, or knapsack, containing a *gamelle* (mess-tin), a 'housewife' with neither needle nor cotton, and a towel marked 'British Red Cross'. No other toilet necessities were given us, and I was getting thoroughly fed-up with borrowing other fellows' razors.

Jaderny, Blanc, and I started on our way back to the Fort. This was our chance to desert if we wanted to, but the idea didn't occur to any of us, and I am rather inclined to believe that, if one of us had made the attempt, the other two would have done their best to prevent him! As soon as we arrived at the Quai des Belges, Blanc invited us to have a drink at the *bistro* on the corner. He always had plenty of money so, although neither Jaderny nor I could afford to stand a round of drinks, we had no hesitation in accepting his offer. So we had a drink at the first *bistro*, then another at the second, and so on all the way up the hill to the gates of the Fort.

When we arrived, we discovered that a detachment was leaving for Oran that very afternoon, but it appeared that a rigid bureaucracy was incapable of adding our names to the list. Blanc knew how to deal with bureaucracy: two thousand francs to a corporal and a thousand to the clerk, and the affair was settled. At the midday parade we were all three detailed for the detachment leaving at three o'clock in the afternoon.

'What made you so certain that you could bribe them?' I asked Blanc later that evening, as we stood at the ship's rail and watched the narrow strip of Mediterranean which divided us from the Quai de la Joliette broadening into a purple expanse of rippling water, while Europe faded into the distance and the red rays of the setting sun mingled with the blue of the sea.

'They were both Frenchmen,' replied Blanc bitterly. The siren gave forth a despairing wail, and the ship turned her bows towards Africa.

When, in May of 1943, I left North Africa for the last time, after three years of chasing up and down the desert with the Eighth Army, I swore to myself that never in my life would I set foot in the place again. Only six years later, there I was, on my way back!

And in what conditions!

Never have I seen anything quite so filthy as that boat. When you touched the rail, your hand came away black with a mixture of grease and soot. The decks, at least the lower ones on which we had to walk, were thick with a slime that made walking a very dangerous business. The latrines—but no, let's leave it at that.

There were fifty of us in the detachment which left Marseilles that afternoon in early March. We were escorted by a sergeant and two corporals. The sergeant, who had just finished two months' leave in Paris, had spent the five hundred thousand francs he had saved during five years, and was going back to rejoin his comrades and save some more. One of the corporals was going back for the second, the other for the third time.

The remaining passengers on the boat were civilians either going back home or on their way to take up appointments in Algeria and Morocco. Even had they wanted to, they had no chance to mix with us, for we were travelling what is called fourth class on French boats. That is to say, we slept in the hold on the bare wooden floor, with our two blankets arranged about our persons in which ever way we thought the conflicting interests of warmth and comfort would best be served. We drew our meals from the galley in large pots, and distributed them among ourselves as fairly as possible. We were not, of course, allowed on the main decks, though we could observe them quite easily, and could see our sergeant, whose rank entitled him to travel second class, promenading a sweet young thing with blue-black hair and laughing eyes. We didn't envy him. We gazed up to his Olympian heights as though he were a god. I glanced at the two corporals, who were forced to remain with us, to see how they were taking it.

'*Il a le droit,*' said one of them philosophically. '*C'est un sous-officier.*'

As the boat approached the harbour of Oran the two corporals began shouting.

'*Alors, les bleus, qu'est-ce que vous attendez?* You lot of raw recruits, what the hell are you waiting for? Get your packs on and fall in there in three ranks. You there, the macaroni, what sort of a soldier do you call yourself? Look at those damned puttees! You, Stari, put your hat on straight.'

One of the corporals turned to the other with a gesture of

despair. 'What a bunch! Just look at Stari there. How the devil do these Poles manage to get drunk when they've nothing to drink and no money to buy drink with?'

The other corporal shrugged his shoulders. '*Je m'en fous*,' he replied. 'In any case, it's you who have to present the mob to the sergeant. You're senior.'

At that moment the *sous-officier* appeared on deck.

'*Garde-à-vous!*' yelled the senior corporal, bringing the detachment to attention and turning to salute the sergeant. But the sergeant ignored the salute.

'The fifth man from the left in the rear rank has a button undone,' he said.

The corporals had paraded us a good quarter of an hour too soon, and they spent the next ten minutes making last-minute adjustments to our uniforms, telling one to retie his bootlaces, another to put his collar straight, and so on. At last the ship nosed her way to her moorings and the gangway was lowered.

'Prepare to disembark,' shouted the sergeant. 'First rank, right turn, forward march.'

We filed down the gangway and were lined up on the quay, where the sergeant presented the detachment to an officer and, in his presence, called the roll—for the fifth time since Marseilles—to make sure there had been no desertions. Then we were marched up the hill to the Legion's depôt, a distance of about two and a half miles. The French civilians and the Arabs whom we passed on the way paid little or no attention to us. Apparently we were a sight to which they had long been accustomed.

The depôt consisted of a small barracks with accommodation for three or four hundred men, and there for the first time we saw *en masse* the proud wearers of the *képi blanc*. Some of the legionnaires spending a night or two there were going on leave, others returning from it. Others, again, were undergoing treatment at the hospital. A few were awaiting the decision of the *commission de reforme*, which was going to decide whether or not they were to be released from service on medical grounds before the expiration of their contract. And there was also a small permanent staff. There was about nearly all of them, whether they were walking out through the gates for an evening in town, going about their duties within the barracks, or merely standing about in groups chatting and joking, an air of determined self-confidence which made it difficult for me to believe that, two or three years before, they had walked into that same depôt as members of a detachment similar to the one with which I had just arrived.

The final destination of our group of fifty *bleus*, as recruits are called, was Sidi Bel-Abbès, the home of the Legion, which is situated about sixty miles south of Oran. We were to take the train at seven o'clock the following morning, and orders were given us to parade at five-thirty sharp, ready to march to the station.

The barrack-room in which we spent the night was about fifty feet long by thirty-five wide. Straw had been spread on the floor, but not in very liberal quantities. However, most of us were so tired that we had very little difficulty in getting to sleep. I had bedded down at eight o'clock and was asleep almost immediately, but I woke again round about nine to the sound of singing.

'*Am Brunnen vor dem Thore da steht ein Lindenbaum,*' a dozen German voices were murmuring. 'Schubert in North Africa,' I said to myself, and smiled. This was vastly different from the raucous shouting which had prevented me from sleeping in the barrack-room at Marseilles. The music, for music it certainly was, came, not from our sleeping quarters, but from somewhere outside in the barracks. The singers were obviously old stagers and not new recruits. The Germans were singing very softly, and there was a hint of nostalgia in their voices. This was a song of their homeland, and in singing it they were perhaps thinking of the dear ones they had left and whom they might never see again.

The song came to an end. There was no applause and no comment. Then, from another corner of the barracks, another chorus broke the stillness of the night. This time the singers were even farther from home, for they were chanting a folk-song from the banks of the Volga, not the well-known one, though the tune was not unknown to me, and I once more had that impression of homesickness in the hearts of the men who were chanting the deep-throated chorus. When the Russians had finished, the Italians took over with a Neapolitan folk-song. Then the bugler sounded 'Lights Out', and all was silence.

As the years went by, I came more and more to love those national songs. I have heard them on desert marches and around camp-fires. I have felt them stir new life into a beleaguered and decimated garrison which was hanging on like grim death to a hilltop in Tongking. And now I know that, before the tattered remnants of the Legion battalions defending Dien Bien Phu went out to meet their death on that last, mad, magnificent bayonet charge, the strains of *Westerwald*, *Mama Mia*, and a dozen other popular songs of Europe were wafted across the barbed wire to the waiting Viets.

For that is the only way in which a legionnaire ever openly expresses his nostalgia.

# 11

THE next morning we were duly paraded and marched off to the station, but if any of us thought we were going to travel in the luxury of passenger compartments, we were doomed to disappointment. A goods train was waiting at a siding, and two cattle wagons were earmarked for the detachment. The wagons bore the ominous inscription, '*Hommes* 40. *Chevaux—en long*—8.' The British Tommy's First World War joke was a joke no more. It had come true!

Luckily there were only sixty of us—ten legionnaires returning from leave having joined us at Oran for the journey to Sidi Bel-Abbès—so that we would be only thirty to a wagon instead of forty. We thought that we might, after all, have a little room to stretch our legs. And what, we asked ourselves, is sixty miles? A mere nothing.

Well, sixty miles in a passenger train represents, at the most, two hours' running; but in a goods train in North Africa it means a little over twelve, with innumerable jolts, shakings, and jerkings as trucks are shunted into sidings all the way along the line. At midday we had only covered half the distance and, as the locomotive was making an hour's halt for the purpose of taking in water, we were allowed to get out and make a meal with the rations we had been given at Oran.

The two corporals organized the distribution of rations. This appeared at first sight to be a complicated business. There was, for example, a loaf of bread for five men, a tin of sardines for four, and a tin of potted meat for six, to say nothing of a jerry-can full of wine for the entire detachment. The method employed was simplicity itself—for the corporals. They paraded us in four ranks and handed a tin of sardines to each front-rank man. Then they formed five ranks and repeated the operation for the bread, and so on, six ranks for the potted meat. All we had to do was to memorize three faces and associate each face with a type of food. When we scrambled back into the wagons an hour later some of the fellows were still searching for the front-rank man who should have given them a fifth of a loaf.

When it came to the wine, the corporals asked the sergeant for a decision. The great man made a rapid calculation. The jerry-can contained just over nineteen litres, and each man was entitled to a quarter of a litre. 'Serve a *quart* to each man,' he ordered. (The *quart* is the regulation French Army mug containing exactly a quarter of a litre.) The corporals executed the order and, when all sixty of us had been served, divided the remaining four litres between themselves and the sergeant.

One of the old hands who had joined the train at Oran came towards us. We could easily distinguish the old stagers because of the comparative smartness of their uniforms, the white *képi* on their heads, and a general air of alertness and awareness which had nothing to do with the way they were dressed.

'*Wollt Ihr Zigaretten?*' he asked of the company in general. 'Do you want cigarettes? If so, don't touch your *pinard*.'

There was a chorus of *Jawohls* from the Germans and any others who had understood. He turned to one of them.

'I'll give you six cigarettes for your *quart*,' he said.

'Done,' replied the recruit, handing over his mug. The *képi blanc* drained it at one gulp and handed over the six cigarettes. He then concluded a similar contract with a second German, but the next man was an Italian, a business-man who knew his market.

It was an amusing scene. The fully-fledged legionnaire, a German, could speak no Italian, whilst the Italian knew no German and only a few words of French. Moreover, the German had now quenched his thirst and his own *quart de pinard* was still waiting for him, whilst the Italian happened to have his pockets full of cigarettes and money to buy them with. They were both, therefore, conducting the transaction from a purely technical point of view and not out of interest.

'*Io* want *diece zigaretten—dix*,' said the Italian, holding up the fingers of both hands.

'Seven,' replied the German in English, taking a packet of *Troupe* from his pocket and beginning to count them out.

The Italian looked at the packet with an air of dismay.

'*Ces cigarettes nicht bon*,' he said. 'They *dreissig franc le paquet*. Seven *cigarettes çà vaut* ten *franc; quart de pinard venti franc. Io no marche dans la combine*.'

The German felt he was losing the battle. He added another cigarette to the seven.

'*Voilà!*' he said. '*Und* I let you *boire un petit coup zuerst*.'

The light of victory shone in the Italian's eyes. He took up his *quart* and drained off half of it, snatched the eight cigarettes out of the German's hand and proffered the half-empty mug. The German took it with a laugh.

'*Ach, Du Jude, Du*,' he said, as he emptied it.

One of us asked him how long he had been in the Legion.

'Five years,' he replied. 'And now I've signed on for another five. I did three years in Indo-China out of the first lot, and I'm hoping to go back there again; but I want to do my *peloton* before I go.'

'What's that?' I asked.

'The *peloton*? Well, that's the course you have to do in order to be promoted corporal. There's a *Peloton One* for corporals and a *Peloton Two* for sergeants. The second *peloton's* pretty difficult, and you have to be able to speak French pretty well. I don't suppose I'll get that far. Corporal will do for me.'

'And how do you like life in the Legion?' asked one of the Germans who had bartered his wine for six cigarettes.

'Not too bad. The first year is pretty awful, as you're on the small pay—only about four hundred and fifty francs a month—and also because you're undergoing instruction. But once you get over the first year, or when they send you to Indo-China, which is generally sooner, you go up to the full rate of pay, and then conditions aren't any better or any worse than they were in our army.'

The legionnaire had broken into German.

'Of course,' he continued, 'there are sometimes things that make you pretty sick. The material you have to work with is often putrid, the stuff that's made in France, that is.' He dropped his voice a tone or two. 'And often the higher-ups don't seem to know what they're doing, but then the higher-ups are French too, aren't they? But what the hell! There's no German Army now, and I can't go back home—I'm from Breslau, by the way—so I'm carrying on here. Well, I'll be off to eat my *casse-croûte* before the train starts again.'

When we arrived at Sidi Bel-Abbès just after seven that evening, most of us were surprised to find that it was quite a large town. As we marched from the station to the barracks, we noticed a theatre, two or three cinemas, and streets full of modern, well-lighted shops. On every side could be seen the white *képis* of legionnaires walking out after duty. Some of them had a girl walking beside them, and there were some very pretty girls, too.

Five abreast we marched into the emplacement reserved for us. This was an enclosure within the barracks, and was walled off from the remainder, with barbed-wire entanglements all round the top of the walls. A sentry at the gate saluted the sergeant, who brought the column to a halt and ordered the gates to be closed.

Five legionnaires, each with a little bag in one hand and a stool in the other, came forward and stood to attention in front of the detachment commander, who directed them to place themselves, one at the head of each of the five columns of recruits. The five legionnaires put down their stools, ordered the first five men to sit on them, and produced from their bags a pair of barber's clippers. I was the first man in the left-hand column, and I felt the clippers sweep over my head from back to front. Then I saw a mass of greyish black hair fall to the paving-stones before my eyes. There was another sweep of the clippers, this time over the right ear, and another bunch of hair fell to the ground. I reflected that I needed a haircut, anyway, and put up my hand to feel my scalp. Only a tiny tuft on the top of my head remained.

'Clean,' the hairdresser reported to the sergeant. 'Next man!'

I rose from the stool, and my place was taken by Jaderny the Pole.

A corporal directed me to a building on the left-hand side of the parade-ground. I opened the door; a legionnaire told me to get undressed and leave my clothes and belongings against the wall. Before I had time to take off my tunic and shirt I was joined by Jaderny, but a Jaderny whose bony head was now surmounted by a single tuft of yellow hair about the size of an apricot. We both laughed at the sight of each other.

'I hope I don't look as funny as you do,' said I.

'I was just hoping the same thing,' said Jaderny.

'Get your clothes off there, *maulen*,' shouted the legionnaire. 'Hurry along there and take a douche.'

We undressed and passed into the shower-room. The showers were, of course, icy cold; but our disappointment at the lack of hot water was alleviated by our each receiving a bar of soap—the first most of us had seen for several days—before taking our bath.

As soon as we were dressed again and while we were still shivering, another order was bawled at us.

'The first ten men to finish, take all your belongings and go in through the door on the other side of the parade-ground.'

'Perhaps,' whispered Jaderny through his chattering teeth. 'Perhaps they're going to give us something to eat. I'm starving.'

The door indicated opened into a room where were seated four NCOs, each one behind a desk. Jaderny, who was the first to enter, saluted and looked around him.

'You don't know how to salute yet, so don't try,' shouted two sergeants simultaneously, one in French and one in German. 'Just take off your cap and come here.'

The Pole removed the nondescript forage cap he had been given at Marseilles and advanced towards the first table. The effeminate German who had followed him into the room took the hint and merely doffed his hat without attempting to salute.

'Come here, pretty boy,' said the sergeant at the second table. 'What's your name?'

When all ten of us were inside the office, the NCOs began.

'You have said that you were at Besançon on such and such a date. Point out Besançon to me on this map.'

'So you're the woman strangler, are you? You didn't think we knew that, did you?'

'You say your mother's name was Pattinini. Where was she born?'

'You have stated that you were never in France before that date. How comes it, then, that we found in the pocket of your civilian suit a railway ticket from Dijon to Paris dated the fourteenth of April?'

'Now just tell me all that happened between April and October of last year.' This was the question addressed to me, and I protested. 'Yes,' continued the sergeant imperturbably. 'I know you've told it all before. I want to hear it again.'

And so on and so on. The idea, of course, was to shock us into contradicting our previous statements by interrogating us at a moment when we were ravenously hungry, tired from the journey, demoralized by the loss of our curly locks, and still shivering from the cold showers. They made me laugh.

When the interrogation was finished, we left the room and were directed to the refectory where a hot meal was awaiting us. We were also told where we were to sleep—in the ten beds along one side of a barrack-room on the first floor. It appeared that we would remain together as a group for several days, and the sergeant detailed one of us—a German named Kargel—as our chief.

'There's no particular reason why I pick on you,' he said, 'except that you speak both French and German, and that you've obviously had previous military experience. There may be men here who've had far more experience than you, but that doesn't matter. Once I've designated you as chief of the group, you act with my authority, and your orders are to be obeyed. Is that understood, everybody? If you have any trouble, Kargel, either report to me straightway, or knock the fellow down first and report to me afterwards.'

The sergeant then told Kargel to translate into German what he had said thus far, and continued.

'Now, I want you to keep this room clean, your half of it, anyhow. There will be a chief appointed out of the men who will occupy the other ten beds, and you will both be responsible to a corporal who will act as *chef de chambre*. You will detail one man per day as barrack-room orderly. His job will be to sweep the room morning and night, your half of it, that is, to go and fetch the coffee and *casse-croûte* in the morning and distribute it, and to present the strength state to the roll-call sergeant in the evening at nine-thirty. You'll probably have to give most of them a hand to show them how to do that. Blankets will be folded and placed at the head of the bed for early morning inspection at seven-thirty and beds are not to be made up before three in the afternoon. Names of men reporting sick are to be handed in at early morning inspection: sick parade at eight. Is all that clear?'

'*Jawohl, Herr Feldwebel!*'

'Answer in French. *Oui, Sergent!*'

'*Oui, Sergent!*'

'Good. That's all for tonight, then.'

As soon as the sergeant had left the room, a babel of comment and speculation broke out.

'Kargel is already nearly a corporal.'

'I wonder why he chose Kargel. Why not Smith? He speaks French and German, and English, too. Besides, he's an educated man.'

'Well, so's Kargel, and Kargel could easily knock out anybody who was being a nuisance, whereas Smith couldn't.'

'Yes, and Kargel was an SS man. The SS run this outfit.' This from a Frenchman.

'*Ta gueule, Roger*,' shouted another. 'Shut your bloody trap and don't talk nonsense. If you knew as much about the French Army as you claim to do, you'd know that one of the medal ribbons that sergeant was wearing was the *Croix de la Libération*. Just work out how *he* could have been an SS man if he was wearing that.'

Kargel took advantage of the silence which followed this remark to begin making a list of the names of the men in the group. He took from his pocket a pencil and a notebook.

'Now look here, all of you,' he said. 'You all heard the orders given by the sergeant. I'm going to make a list of your names alphabetically, and you will go on duty in the order of that list. In that way there'll be no favouritism. Now, who has a name beginning with A? Nobody? B? Ah yes, Bordelais. Funny, I thought there was an A somewhere. Hey, Macaroni, what's your name?'

'Aminardi, *Chef*. Sorry. I didn't hear you first time.'

'Why don't you keep your ears open? Right. Aminardi, Bordelais. *Jetzt kommt der Berliner. Wie heisst Du?*'

'Felden,' replied the man from Berlin, the one who was always grinning.

'*Ach ja*, Felden. Now the Stari. How do you spell your name, Stari?'

Jaderny spelt out his name. He was looking ill at ease, had a black eye and his nose had been bleeding. The interrogators had given him a rough passage when he refused at first to admit the story of his attempted murder of the girl Nadja, and his subsequent imprisonment. When he had finally confessed, they told him he was a damned fool not to have told the truth in the first place since, the crime having been expiated, it made no difference to his standing with regard to the Legion authorities.

'After Jaderny,' continued Kargel, 'we have myself. Then Roger, Smith, and who else? Ah yes, Vogel. Is that all? One, two, three. . . . Hallo! That makes only nine. We've missed one out. Oh yes, it's you, young fellow. Why didn't you speak up when your turn came? What letter does your name begin with?'

The recruit whom Kargel addressed was a smallish, stockily built young fellow, with broad shoulders and a deep chest. In the moon-shaped face under what, until the barber shaved most of it off, had been his curly black hair, was set a pair of soft eyes rather like those of a young doe. He had very rarely spoken to any of us, but was always gazing at us with eyes full of wonder. You might have said that he was seeing all the strange things going on about him for the first time in his life. He had given his age to the Legion authorities as nineteen, but, in fact, he was only sixteen. And you had the impression that he would have been happier folded in his mother's arms, or at least clinging to her apron-strings.

To Kargel's question he returned a blank stare. He spoke no

French at all, and only a few words of very broken German. Kargel repeated his question.

'You there, what letter does your name begin with?' he asked in German.

The young fellow still did not seem to understand. His gentle eyes searched those of Kargel, his lips were slightly parted, and he rubbed the tips of his fingers together nervously. It hurt me to feel him straining every nerve in his body in order to try to understand what Kargel was saying. I stepped to his side and tried a new line of approach.

'*Komm her*,' I asked persuasively, '*wie ist Dein Name?* Come now, young fellow, tell the *chef de chambre* what your name is.'

The boy looked from Kargel to me, and then back to Kargel again, and suddenly a noise like an explosive sneeze escaped from his lips. All the others were looking at him and, despite the fact that they had been together for eight or nine days, you would have said that most of them were seeing him for the first time, so insignificant had he been. And with unintentional mental cruelty we formed a half-circle round him and stared at the nervous, self-conscious little fellow.

'Well, that's fine,' said Kargel, 'if that sound like an eighty-one-millimetre mortar firing charge two really is your name. But how do you spell it?' He repeated the question more slowly. '*Wie schreibst Du ihn?*'

'I can't spell,' replied the embarrassed boy. 'I have never learnt to read or write.' But he did quite an intelligent thing. He took from his pocket the temporary identity-card they had given him at Marseilles, and handed it to Kargel.

The German wrote down the name—Czsabo—and handed the card back. He told the boy that his name began with a C.

'All right,' he continued. 'You'll do your turn of duty after Bordelais here. Don't worry about the business of the roll-call. I'll give you a hand with that. Now, Aminardi, your turn first.

You have half an hour in which to clean up our half of the room in time for roll-call. The rest of you can get to bed. We'll sleep from left to right in the order of this list. Aminardi, you in the left-hand corner there, then Bordelais, Czsabo, and so on until we reach Vogel in the right-hand corner.'

'I think I'd rather sleep next to Bordelais,' said Roger. 'After all, we're the only two Frenchmen here, so I don't see why we shouldn't be together. Besides, Smith snores and——'

'I certainly have no desire for you to sleep next to me,' I interrupted him. This was a gross calumny. I'm perfectly certain I don't snore.

'Nor I,' added Bordelais. 'Nor do I take any particular pride in your claim to share a common nationality with me.' The Frenchmen in the Legion were always squabbling amongst themselves.

'You'll all sleep where you've been told to sleep,' said Kargel trenchantly and raising his voice a little. 'So let there be no more argument about it.'

As all the rest of us had already occupied the places allotted us, Roger had no alternative but to take the bed next to mine, which he did with a bad grace, muttering under his breath, 'We won the war, didn't we?'

Now this was more than I could stand, especially as I was still smarting under his recent libel.

'That strikes me as being something of an over-statement,' I remarked.

'*Ah toi, l'Anglais, la ferme!*' shouted Roger angrily. 'We all know about Dunkirk and Mers-el-Kebir. We also know that the English fight to the last Frenchman.'

Roger, like many Frenchmen of his type, was stuffed full of catch-phrases which he had learnt by heart and which, as he was incapable of thinking for himself, he employed as the basis of his conversation.

'They certainly didn't during this last war,' I retorted.

'*Messieurs les Anglais, tirez le premiers,*' countered Roger quite inconsequently, simply because it was the first catch-phrase which came into his head. And since I failed to grasp the pertinence of the quotation, I was quite at a loss for a reply.

'*Silence à l'appel!*' roared Kargel. 'Silence for roll-call.' He must have learnt the stock French Army phrase in a prisoner-of-war camp. The roll-call sergeant came into the dormitory, followed by the ten recruits who were to occupy the ten beds on the opposite side of the room. Having counted us, he told the others to get to bed quickly and quietly. Shortly afterwards the bugler sounded 'Lights Out', and the silence was broken only by the soft whimpering of little Czsabo.

Poor little Czsabo! He had been so ashamed when he had to confess before all his newly found comrades that he was illiterate. Not to be able, in the middle of the twentieth century, to read and write! And yet Czsabo had been to school, as he told me later. Yes, from the age of six until he was eight and a half, he had attended the tiny village school about a mile and a half from where his father was a poor, struggling, Hungarian smallholder. Then the school had been closed. There were no teachers left, for they had gone off to the wars, both of them. Czsabo remembered dimly that German, Russian, and Romanian troops had successively camped in the neighbourhood of their farm. Then the Romanians had gone and the Germans came again. In talking to them—there was one soldier who had carved a wooden dagger for him and another who had taught him how to fly a kite—he had first begun to pick up a few words of the German language.

And then, many years later it seemed, the Russians had come again, and they pillaged the farm, and Czsabo's father, who had attempted to prevent his property from being plundered, had been shot out of hand.

Czsabo told me that he thought he must have been about twelve years old at that time. He remembered sitting on the family bed with his mother's arms tightly round him. His father was lying on the far side against the wall. There was three of four days' growth of beard on his lifeless chin, and Czsabo's mother was plucking up courage to shave him before she went for the priest.

She had closed all the shutters and barred the door, for the noise of guns going off could be heard all around, and even closer was the shouting of drunken soldiers. Mother and son had been sitting thus for many hours, and little Czsabo was hungry; but he dared not tell his mother so, for she was shivering with fright. And because she was frightened, Czsabo was frightened, too.

After a long time his mother rose and lit the lamp. Then came a heavy knock at the door and, when neither of them made a move to open it, a rifle butt pounded the frail woodwork till it flew open with a noise of rending timber, and a man staggered into the room.

Czsabo saw his mother carried screaming to the bed. He saw half her clothes ripped from her body, while the soldier struggled and grunted over her, his bestial mouth breathing the fumes of vodka into her panic-stricken eyes. The sobbing boy began beating with his childish hands upon the man's back and head, until he, furious, sent his enormous fist crashing into the lad's face, so hard that the bones cracked.

And little Czsabo had never learnt to read and write. That was why he wept on his hard bed in the barrack-room.

# 12

At Sidi Bel-Abbès the round of interrogations and interviews began all over again. The medical examinations were repeated. We discovered to our surprise that not even yet were we definitely accepted and, as it turned out, one man from our detachment was rejected and sent back to France. I must admit I discovered later that this was exceptional and that the man in question was largely indemnified. During the three or four days occupied by these formalities we were not allowed outside our enclosure, except in organized groups of a dozen or so under escort as fatigue parties.

We were paraded twice a day under the orders of the company sergeant-major—a curly haired, ruddy complexioned, very fat Alsatian with a wooden leg. Lists of names of those required to undergo the various interrogations and examinations were read, and those named had to run out and parade in their respective groups under a legionnaire detailed to escort them, If any recruit did not jump to it quickly enough, the sergeant-major aimed a flying kick at him, as he passed, with his dummy leg.

We never saw an officer on parade, although it was known that the company—*Compagnie de Passage No. 3*—was commanded by a captain assisted by a lieutenant. In fact, during the whole of my service in the Legion, I rarely saw officers attending routine parades, the whole of the normal running of the company being generally entrusted to the NCOs. The impression I gained during those early days was that this system gave the NCOs far too much power, and led to abuse or at least risked leading to abuse. I changed my opinion later.

During our occasional sorties as fatigue parties, we had an opportunity of seeing something of the town. Eighty years ago, they told us, when the Foreign Legion settled upon the place as her future home, Sidi Bel-Abbès was nothing more than a desert oasis surrounded by a few Arab huts. Today it is a flourishing town, with a civilian population of about a hundred thousand.

There is a rather vulgar French saying, '*Tu es légionnaire: démerde-toi!*' Freely translated, this means, 'You're a legionnaire? All right, fend for yourself. Get yourself out of the mess, and don't expect us or anyone else to give you a helping hand.'

During the whole of his five years' service, the legionnaire is a victim of this principle. It is nothing out of the ordinary for a packet of legionnaires to be dumped on a piece of waste ground and told to build a house. Nobody gives them any tools or materials. No one gives them any advice. And, lo and behold, one fine day the house is built. Nobody quite knows how, or cares very much either.

And this is precisely the attitude adopted towards the Legion by the French Government. Knowing full well that the Legion is very capable of fending for itself, they have rarely, if ever, granted credits for the purpose of construction. They did not even do so when they ordered the Legion to settle in Sidi Bel-Abbès. Consequently it is quite safe to say that the two vast groups of barracks, the thousand-seater military cinema, and the military swimming-pool, reputed to be the finest in North Africa, are all entirely the handiwork of legionnaires, and that no penny of French Government money was spent on the materials necessary to their construction.

Nowadays, though this was by no means always the case, the Legion as a corporation is a very wealthy body, and is, for example, one of the biggest landowners in Algeria. On the many farms owned by the Legion, which supply meat and vegetables to the units in their districts, are employed superannuated and partially disabled legionnaires, many of whom have married and settled down to a rural life with their families. And if ever, one day, you should be touring through North Africa and should happen to see, on the slopes of the Atlas Mountains, a flock of sheep tended by a tall, bearded shepherd wearing military uniform with a white *képi* on his head, you will know that the sheep belong to the Legion and that the shepherd probably fought against Abd-el-Krim during the Riff War of 1926.

But all these were things we recruits had yet to learn. For the moment we were awaiting impatiently our release from what appeared to us to be something not very different from a concentration camp.

On the fourth morning after our arrival there was great excitement. First of all, it appeared that little Vandewelde, a Belgian who had joined, so he said, because of family troubles, had taken to his heels. He had been absent from roll-call the night before, and was nowhere to be found in the morning. The previous afternoon he had been with a fatigue party which went to clean up the cinema, but he did not come back with the party, although this was discovered later. It was known that the legionnaire in charge of the fatigue was now *en taule*—in prison—awaiting trial on a charge of negligence, for he omitted to count the recruits who had been confided to him before returning to barracks. It was also known that a car full of Belgian tourists had been in the town during the afternoon, and it was supposed that Vandewelde had persuaded the driver to take him along with them.

The second cause for excitement was the news that those of us who were now accepted as fit for service would be issued with a complete kit during the morning, and leave the following day for the various instruction centres to which we would be posted after having been interviewed by the captain. At last, after periods of waiting varying from ten days to six weeks, we were about to begin the life of legionnaires.

Many of the details of my early months in the Legion are beginning to grow dim in my memory, but that last morning in the CP3 at Sidi Bel-Abbès stands out very clearly, and I think, always will.

At ten o'clock a fatigue party was called for by the vast kitchens which did the cooking for the two thousand inmates of the block of barracks in which our enclosure was situated. Volunteers were never lacking for fatigues at the cookhouse, for, in return for the peeling of a few potatoes or carrots, you were certain to be treated to an extra *casse-croûte* and a drop of wine. I volunteered with the others.

About thirty of us were marched off, but when we arrived at the flagged courtyard in front of the kitchens, instead of the usual baskets of vegetables, all we could see were hundreds and hundreds of live chickens, tied together in bunches of twenty by their legs. The job to be done was to kill and pluck them.

Volunteers were now called for to do the killing. Six were required, and I remember to this day how those six volunteers were made up: one Italian, two Spaniards, and three Frenchmen, of whom two were from Corsica. To this day do I remember the bestial look on their faces as they took their knives and prepared for the bloodthirsty work, and the Frenchman who said, 'This knife is too sharp; give me a blunt one. I like chopping 'em off slowly.' The sparkle that came into the eyes deep set in his crafty face will remain with me till I die.

Never shall I forget that scene of carnage. The butchers started, and off came the heads. Soon the courtyard was covered with staring, bloodstained beaks, while headless bodies with flapping wings were walking blindly about in all directions. Blood was spurting all over the place.

Two men had the task of retrieving the dying, but still active, bodies and dropping them into a vat full of boiling water, which was designed to soften the skin and make the feathers come out more easily. The rest of us had merely to take out the corpses and pluck them.

Blanc was working next to me.

'Not a very pleasant job, this,' he said. Apart from a mumbled '*Non*,' I was far too miserable and disgusted to reply.

'I don't care for eating chickens which have been tended by Arabs,' he continued, and explained why. I was very nearly sick, and grabbed clumsily at a chicken which I had just pulled out of the water. The headless neck emitted a cheerful 'Cock-a-doodle-doo!' and I dropped it, horror-stricken, to the intense amusement of some of those standing near by.

Call it squeamishness if you like. I have seen blood before and since, plenty of it. But never have I seen anything to equal the sadistic cruelty of those six Latin butchers.

Back at the company, we were paraded for the issue of uniform: battle-dress, much the same as in the British Army, boots of French manufacture, gaiters from surplus American stocks and, at last, the famous *képi*—the hallmark of the legionnaire. We were shown how to fit the white *couvre-képi* over it, so that there were no creases and so that the seam coincided exactly with the circumference of the crown. Then we were given an hour's saluting drill and told that we must salute all officers and *sous-officiers*, on or off duty.

The next thing they taught us was how we should present ourselves to an officer.

'You open the door and enter the office. You march smartly up to a point six paces in front of the officer's desk, salute, and then remove your *képi* with your left hand. You then present yourself in the following form, "Legionnaire so-and-so. So many months of service. *A vos ordres, mon capitaine*".'

That was the theory, but for me, at least, it didn't quite work out like that. When my turn came for interview, I opened the door and, as directed, marched smartly to a point which I estimated to be six paces in front of the desk. Then, as I had entered from a door on the officer's right, I did a smart left turn and saluted, but I didn't get any further.

'Well, I'll be damned,' said the captain in English.

I looked at him and blinked. He was a dapper little fellow of about thirty, with an elfin face and smiling brown eyes. I opened my mouth to say my little piece. He laughed.

'You don't have to introduce yourself to me,' he said, standing up and stretching out his hand. 'We had lunch together seven years ago.'

If that was so, I didn't remember it. I didn't even remember his face, but then, I have a shockingly bad memory for faces. I realized then, by no means for the last time, that many French officers have extraordinarily good ones, not only for faces but for names, too. He must have noticed my perplexity.

'Why, Captain ——,' he said, using my real name. 'Don't you remember? The Café de France, wasn't it? In the Sharia Kasr el Nil?'

Then it came back to me. My meeting in Cairo with a cousin who was doing French liaison work; his introducing me to a French *commandant* and a rather insignificant little second-lieutenant, both survivors from Bir Hacheim. The *commandant* had invited us all to lunch, I remembered. The captain sitting at the desk in front of me must have been the second-lieutenant of 1942. The captain invited me to sit down and have a cigarette.

'Listen,' he said, still speaking English. 'I'm not going to ask why you are here. That doesn't concern me. It doesn't even surprise me. I've been commanding this company, through which all recruits must pass on their way into the Legion, for nearly a year, and nothing can surprise me any more.

'The main thing is that you are here. It's a pity you didn't arrive a month or two earlier. I could have pulled a few strings and pushed you up in rank fairly quickly, a thing we've been doing in exceptional cases since the war. But now a new colonel has taken over the instruction, and he has insisted that we revert to the old methods of the Legion: no promotion on the grounds of previous service. In other words, I'm afraid you'll have to go through the grind of the *peloton*. A *peloton* is a course of three or four months with examinations at the end of it. There's a *Peloton One* for the formation of corporals and a *Peloton Two* for sergeants. So I'm afraid that the first thing you'll have to do is to undergo three months' instruction to fit yourself for the rank of corporal. Silly, isn't it?'

His eyes twinkled and he puffed for a moment at his cigarette.

'Though not quite so silly as it sounds,' he continued. 'In some ways it is more difficult to be a corporal in the Legion than a colonel in any other army. You'll see for yourself.'

He laughed.

'You'll be all right, though,' he chuckled. 'With any luck, you can be a sergeant in seven months from now, and then you'll find that life in the Legion is a much more pleasant affair. Now, let's see.'

He consulted some typed sheets which he took from a folder on the desk.

'There's a *Peloton One* starting at Saida ten days from now. Normally you'd have to do five weeks' preliminary recruit training before going there, but I think that can be fixed.'

He picked up the telephone and had a short but rapid conversation.

'That's all right, then,' he concluded, when he had replaced the receiver. 'I'll send you off with the detachment for Saida tomorrow. You'll have just a week's recruit training to do, and then you'll start the *peloton*.'

I stood up, put on my *képi*, and saluted. The captain laughed.

'Don't be so damned British,' he said. 'Good luck!'

# 13

'LEGIONNAIRES, in the name of the *Commandant*, I welcome you to Saida. Stand at ease!'

The officer paused a few seconds, to allow the shuffling of feet to subside, before continuing.

'Before you ever thought of joining the Foreign Legion, you knew that it was reputed to be tough. In fact, it is not half so tough today as it used to be, more's the pity; but it so happens that you have been sent for your preliminary training to a place where the traditional toughness of the Legion is more or less maintained. For Saida is tough still; you're going to find that out.'

Having uttered these encouraging words, the officer, a tall, slim lieutenant with straight black hair and piercing black eyes, embraced with a sweeping glance the detachment of thirty men with which I had arrived, so that each of us had the impression that he had been appraised individually. He clenched his right fist and looked at it intently for a moment or two.

'The training you will undergo here,' he continued, 'lasts six weeks. It is the preliminary instruction to which every recruit, no matter what his specialities, antecedents, or capabilities may be, submits. There may be, there certainly are, among you men who have held rank in the French or another European army. That makes no difference. In the Legion a man has to prove his worth, no matter what his previous history may be. At the end of this period of initial training, those who are recommended for advancement will join the *Peloton One*, others will be sent to do their specialist training, others again, who have no less honour for that, will be drafted to infantry units, mostly in Indo-China. A certain number of volunteers for the parachute battalions will also be called for.'

The officer was speaking, slowly and deliberately, in French; but he paused a few seconds at the end of each sentence to allow the sergeant time to translate into German. There was a slight stir, a sort of ripple of enthusiasm, as soon as parachute troops were mentioned. I could feel, by the atmosphere, that volunteers would not be lacking.

'During these first six weeks,' the lieutenant went on, 'I want you, over and above assimilating the instruction, to do three things. First, I want you to inculcate in yourselves the Legion's motto—*Honneur et Fidélité*. Be honest and faithful with yourselves, with your comrades, and towards the Legion. And remember that other saying, *Legio Patria Nostra*. The Legion *is* your home, at least for five years. Many of you have, alas, no other homes to go to. Try, then, to make the best of what the Legion has to offer you. Play the game, and we will play the game with you.

'The second thing I want you to do is to learn French. Whether you like it or not, the official, administrative language of the Legion is the French language. In the course of time you will find yourselves forced to learn some rudiments of it in order to carry on your normal daily life. Even the most unwilling of legionnaires soon learns that *argent* is *Geld* and *soupe* means *essen*. But it will be much better for you if you set to with a will to learn French, rather than wait until you are forced to do so because of the opportunities you are losing. At various times we have made attempts at the organized teaching of French as part of the training, but it doesn't work out very well. We found we were wasting too much time for too little result. So now we merely say, "*Légionnaire, démerde-toi!*" In order to keep yourselves out of trouble and profit from the advantages offered you, learn French as quickly as possible.

'Finally, I want you all to become first-class shots. The Legion's job is fighting, and a fighter who is a first-class shot stands a better chance of remaining alive than a poor one. Experience in Indo-China has abundantly proved it.'

The lieutenant sank his chin on to his breast, clutched his hands nervously together, and remained deep in thought for several seconds. Outside, a noise like two pieces of wood being knocked against one another announced that the cranes had come back to their summer quarters on the chimney-tops and were calling for mates to help them build their nests. One of the recruits blew his nose, and the sergeant slew him with a glance. The lieutenant drew a deep breath and continued.

'Having told you of some of the things I want you to do, I will now tell you of things I don't want you to do. First, I will talk about desertion. Now, let's get one or two things straight. Nobody asked you to come here. You came of your own free will and, having come, you signed a contract binding you to serve *avec honneur et fidélité* for five years. Now, the recruit who, having signed that contract, attempts to run away from its consequences, is not a man, but just a coward, a good-for-nothing yellow dog.

'He creates trouble for the Legion authorities, for his comrades, and for himself; trouble for the authorities by causing unnecessary work, trouble for his comrades, because they are usually confined to barracks when a desertion takes place, and trouble for himself, because he is always caught. Your friend Vandewelde, by the way, who deserted from Bel-Abbès two days ago, has already been caught. I may tell you that he was not a pretty sight when he was handed over to the prison.

'You perhaps do not know that there is a reward of fifty thousand francs for the capture of a legionnaire who has deserted. Now, for an Arab, fifty thousand francs is a veritable fortune, and he will do anything short of, and even including, murder to lay his hands on that reward. Moreover, by some uncanny instinct, he can smell out a deserting legionnaire from a distance of about two kilometres. So believe me, even if you are yellow enough to desert, you cannot get away with it, and when you are caught the punishment is very severe.'

The officer paused for a minute to let this sink in, and I reflected that the views he had expressed on the moral aspect of desertion were exactly those which I myself had voiced at Marseilles about three weeks before.

'Another crime which is frowned upon here,' he continued in his harsh, somewhat nasal voice, 'is that of selling army material and equipment. I know very well that you are not paid very much during your first year's service; but do not make the mistake of attempting to augment your pay by selling a shirt or a pair of boots to the Arab tradesman in the market. Let me warn you once again that you cannot get away with it. There will be frequent kit inspections, and the excuse, "I've lost it," will not be accepted. Items missing from your kit will be charged against you at ten times their value and, in addition, you will go to prison for fifteen days.

'One last word. Forty different nationalities are represented in the Legion, but the men from all these nations are legionnaires first, and Poles, Frenchmen, Turks, or Argentinians afterwards. Do not make the mistake of trying to reverse that situation. Whether you come from Hamburg, Odessa, Madrid, or Chicago, you are all in the same boat; so try to pull together. I will not have national or racial discrimination from my staff of NCO instructors, and I certainly won't have it from you. Any cases which come to my notice will be very harshly dealt with. That is all. Sergeant, you may dismiss the parade.'

It appeared that our detachment was to be split into two groups of fifteen for the purpose of instruction, each under a sergeant with three corporals to assist him. I found myself in the same group as Blanc and Jaderny, together with one or two of the others with whom I had shared the barrack-room at Sidi Bel-Abbès. We had arrived at Saida at four o'clock in the afternoon, after thirty-six hours' confinement to cattle wagons and, having dumped our kit in the dormitory assigned to us, had been paraded in a lecture-hall for the lieutenant's speech of welcome.

At the early parade the next morning our sergeant introduced himself to us.

'I am Lopez,' he said, and drew himself up to his full height, so that there should be no mistake about it. 'Manuel Lopez. Or, if you prefer my full name, Manuel Lopez y Garcia de la Fuerte, sergeant in the French Foreign Legion. Don't forget it. I will stand no nonsense from any of you, for you are dealing with Manuel Lopez y Garcia, and Lopez y Garcia is a name to be obeyed.'

He was tall for a Spaniard, very nearly six feet, and very thin and wiry. He had close-cropped, wavy, blue-black hair and green eyes, and there was about him that proud, aristocratic air peculiar to Spaniards of good family. The sensitive nostrils over his clipped, black moustache quivered, as he continued.

'Now to begin with, your barrack-room was a pigsty when I looked in there this morning; so, just to remind you that I prefer it to be clean and in good order, you will all be in *tenue de campagne* for roll-call this evening. The corporals will now explain to you what that means.'

The corporals explained, one in French and one in German. *Tenue de campagne*—Field Service Marching Order—was a collective punishment. At the time of roll-call all the legionnaires included in the punishment were to stand at the foot of their respective beds dressed as follows: complete uniform with boots and gaiters, great-coat, with epaulettes—the enormous red epaulettes of the Legion—fixed in position on the shoulder-straps, pack containing complete kit on back, water-bottle full of water slung at the belt, needle and cotton stuck into the lining of the *képi*. In the pocket, paper, pencil, and five francs. . . .

'And supposing we haven't got five francs?' asked Jaderny.

'*Tu es légionnaire; démerde-toi*,' came the inevitable reply. 'You're a legionnaire, aren't you? Work it out for yourself.'

The next item on the programme for that morning was the drawing of arms and equipment. One of the corporals marched us off to the armoury, where we awaited the storeman, who had not yet arrived. When the legionnaire responsible finally condescended to put in an appearance, he issued to each of us a museum piece of 1893 pattern which was to serve for our initial instruction. These rifles were about five feet long and weighed about twelve pounds. They were the standard equipment of the French infantryman at the beginning of the First World War, but were now a little out of date. We also drew a complete set of leather equipment, including a scabbard for the twenty-inch-long bayonet, four enormous ammunition pouches, and a four-inch-wide leather belt. We were then told to spend an hour cleaning our rifles and equipment, and for this purpose were allowed to go up again to our barrack-room on the second floor.

We learnt many things that first day, although most of it was spent in cleaning things; cleaning our rifles, our boots, and our buttons; cleaning our beds and the floor under our beds; cleaning the windows, the doors, and the stairway. We learnt how to arrange our kits on the shelves at the head of our beds in a neat square, with no loose ends hanging out. We learnt the regulation way to make our beds. We learnt that when a *sous-officier* entered the room, the first man to see him had to cry, '*Garde-à-vous!*' and everybody had to come to attention. Or, if an officer appeared, '*Fixe!*' was the cry, and everybody had to remove his *képi*.

We learnt that, if you held out long and firmly enough, the old sweats would give you ten cigarettes for your cup of *pinard*. We learnt that it paid to be a volunteer for fetching the wine ration from the *ordinaire*, for the man who fetched it had the right to distribute it, and there was always half a litre left over after each man had received his *quart*. I noticed that Jaderny never sold his wine ration. I suppose, like Omar, he wondered 'what the vintners buy one half so precious'. When he needed cigarettes, he scrounged them, usually from me. One day I refused him, and he went into a sulk that lasted for twenty-four hours.

We also learnt the meaning of the word *pelote*. There had been some indiscipline in the other section of recruits, and their sergeant had ordered the whole lot on parade in the courtyard below. They were in fatigue dress with full packs on their backs. A corporal commanded the punishment; it was far beneath a sergeant's dignity to do so.

'Attention! Right turn! Forward—march! Double march! Left, right, left, right. . . . Halt! On all fours—down! Forward—march! Double march! Halt! On the feet—up!'

And so on for nearly an hour, round and round the parade-ground, marching, double-marching, and crawling went the fifteen men, each with a forty-pound pack on his back, who were being punished for the fault of one or two of them. These collective punishments were used extensively during the training period, the theory being that it was psychologically sound to make it apparent that the majority always suffer for the faults of the few, which is certainly a fact under combat conditions, though the application of the principle in barracks tended to create a feeling of resentment among the majority who were suffering for no fault of their own.

We had all crowded to the window to watch this exhibition, and it was just the moment that Lopez chose to come along and see how the rifle cleaning was getting on. One of the corporals shouted '*Garde-à-vous!*' and the sergeant ordered us to continue with our work. He did not even remonstrate with us for our lack of application, but he dealt out four days' CB to the senior corporal. Later we heard that this punishment had been confirmed and increased to eight days by the company commander.

Sergeant Lopez had a few words to say to us.

'Tomorrow,' he announced, 'we shall start our training in real earnest. Parade at six-thirty in fatigue dress with rifles and full equipment. Stick your PT kit into one pocket, and I should advise you to put your *casse-croûte* in the other, so you can eat it during the half-hour break at eight o'clock. Otherwise you will be very hungry before we return to barracks at half-past eleven for dinner. Oh, by the way, if any of you have boots that don't fit too well, give your names to Corporal Stein here, and I'll try to get them changed.'

Having given these orders, Lopez stayed to have a little chat with us. We were all surprised to discover that he already knew each one of us by name. He had under his arm a packet of yellow-covered booklets, the *livrets matricules*, or individual records, of the fifteen men in his section. These booklets were normally kept in the company office, but he had brought them along in order to fill in the paragraph—'Name and address of next of kin, or other person to whom the death or dangerous illness of the legionnaire should be communicated'.

Lopez had very little writing to do. Of the fifteen men in his section, one gave the address of a girl in Vienna. The rest of us replied, 'Nobody!'

# 14

IT is difficult to describe accurately the initial training we underwent at Saida. I know it was rough, but I can now remember but few of the details. I know that I found it boring and unpleasant, but I cannot now distinctly remember why, except that, I suppose, sloping and presenting arms for hours on end must be boring for the recruits of any army.

The Legion has developed a method of instruction which involves a minimum of talking and a maximum of demonstration and imitation. Such a method is very necessary where recruits, to most of whom words mean nothing, are concerned, but is boring in the extreme for those who would have understood the words had they been spoken. The instruction was, of course, scaled down to the standard of the least capable member of the section. More than half of our crowd had previous military experience, but we had to learn how to march in step and execute left and right turns for the benefit of those who had never done either.

The marching rhythm of the Legion is very slow—sixty-eight paces to the minute—and the stride is long to compensate for it. I found it very tiring at the beginning, though, once I had got used to it, I discovered that it was very well adapted to long marches over uneven ground, especially in hot weather.

We swung out of the barrack gates on the first morning and marched to a space of open ground about a mile away. There we changed into shorts and tennis shoes and did half an hour's physical training. Having changed back into uniform, we had a short breather and then began our instruction. For this purpose we were divided into three groups, each group under a corporal. One group learnt how to stand at attention, the second how to stand at attention with the rifle, and the third how to salute. Each corporal had his speciality, and we changed round at regular intervals.

On our way back to barracks at eleven o'clock, we sang—by order. The Legion has a great number of marching songs. They are nearly all of German origin, with French words adapted, and some of them are very fine indeed. The Legion authorities regard the melodious, rhythmic, vigorous, and unanimous execution of these songs by detachments on the march as of the first importance. It is considered that singing in chorus does a great deal towards the inculcation of an *esprit de corps* in men who have no other universal way of communing together. As I said, the songs of German origin have French translations of the words, but the Germans could sing the original words if they wanted to. All that was required was a unanimous and rhythmic execution of the melody. I know now that this was, not only a traditional, but psychologically, an essential part of the legionnaire's training; but at the time of which I am writing I did not know it, and this singing to order—or 'song fatigue' as I called it—annoyed me, especially on the way back from exercise, when I was tired and out of breath.

When we arrived in the barracks, we had fifteen minutes to wait until the company parade for daily orders at eleven-forty-five, so I walked round the parade-ground and located the various amenities—the canteen, the library, the reading-room, the showers —and the prison. I was surveying the door of this last, and wondering how long it would be before I found myself the other side of it, when a voice hailed me. 'Smith!' Then another and another. I turned round, and saw a group of three legionnaires running towards me.

'So you've arrived at last,' exclaimed Sibley, Kirsch, and Scheer all together. 'What section are you in?'

'We're all going to the *peloton* at the end of next week,' said Kirsch.

'We've nearly completed our five weeks' preliminary training,' said Scheer.

'What a pity you won't be coming to the *peloton* with us,' said Sibley.

'I might be joining you there,' I replied, though without telling them why I was certain of it. 'How are you finding the training?'

'Tough,' said Sibley. 'I cough my guts up about three times a day, and I've twice had to do the *pelote* for answering back to a corporal.'

'I've already been in *taule*,' said Kirsch proudly. 'Eight days for being thirty seconds late on parade.'

'I haven't found it so tough up to the present,' I said. 'But then I only started this morning.'

'Wait till you do the *parcours du combattant*,' cried Sibley. 'They've got hold of a damned silly idea—I believe they copied it from the English commandos, by the way—of making everybody do a sort of combat course, an obstacle race over mountains, up and down trees, and through rivers. It not only half kills you, but it's damned dangerous. However, I don't suppose that worries 'em. What's one legionnaire more or less? How long did you stay in hospital, Smith?'

I told them, airing my views on French Army medical arrangements at the same time.

'Where are the others?' I asked. 'Ambrosio and the rest?'

'Oh, they all got sent to Mascara for their training,' said Scheer. 'Only four out of our lot came to Saida. Us three and the poet.'

'And where's the poet?' I asked. Sibley jerked a thumb towards the prison door behind him. 'In there,' he said. 'Forty-five days. That's why we're waiting here. The prisoners come out to get their meal in a moment, and we want to slip him a few cigarettes.'

'How on earth did he manage to get forty-five days?' I asked. I could not imagine anyone less capable of the sort of indiscipline which would normally merit such a punishment than the quiet, Pascal-reading Frenchman.

'It was like this,' Sibley explained. 'When we arrived here, we were all drafted into the same section, and, there being no sergeant available at the time, we were commanded by a corporal, a half-Polish German from somewhere on the Silesian border. The man was an ignorant, half-educated fool, but very ambitious. Apparently he had been told that, if he made a success of commanding the section, he would be promoted sergeant without having to go through the *peloton*.

'The corporal's idea of commanding the section successfully was to brutalize us. The man was, of course, an utter sadist. He was always inflicting collective punishments for no reason at all; it was easy to see that he enjoyed doing so. From time to time, when the look on one of the recruits' faces didn't please him, he would walk up to the man in question and punch his jaw, and, like the lot of sheep we were, we just went on taking it.

'Then, one day at the end of our second week, we were sitting on our bunks in the barrack-room on the first floor there, when the corporal came in. Although it was outside working hours, he said, "Take a pencil and paper, each of you, and write down the characteristics of the machine-gun we were studying this morning." Everybody did so except the poet, and he was just finishing the third stanza of some epic or other.

' "Hey, you," shouted the corporal, "read out what you've written!" The poet did so; it was a very witty and cruel lampoon on the corporal. I don't think he could have understood all of it, but what he did annoyed him very much, for he walked up to the poet and slapped his face. Then things happened very quickly. There was a short scuffle and before you could say "Knife!" there was a tinkling of broken glass and a splintering of woodwork.

The corporal had disappeared through the window! Luckily he didn't fall on his head or he would have broken his neck. As it is, he had both legs broken. So that's why the poet's in clink. You wouldn't have thought he had it in him, would you? Here they come. Scheer, slip him the fags!'

A bugle sounded.

'*Eheu*,' said Kirsch. '*Rassemblement pour le rapport*. Parade for daily orders. Let's get a move on.'

To the insistent accompaniment of the bugle we trotted to our appointed places. The orderly sergeant called the parade to attention and handed over to the company sergeant-major. The latter was a Russian, who rejoiced in the nickname of Timoshenko, because of his exact resemblance to the famous field-marshal. He spoke French fluently, but with an appalling accent which made it quite impossible to understand half of what he said. Fortunately, during recruit training, orders were always read both in French and German, so that, when the sergeant took over and read the German version, at least those of us who understood that language knew what was going on and were able to translate the orders back again into French for the benefit of those who understood no German.

I got to know Timoshenko very well later on, after I became a sergeant. He was a fine fellow, with a heart of gold. His only failing was that he thought he could play chess and was always furious if he lost, because he considered it to be a slight on his national honour. It became known as a sort of good deed for the day among *sous-officiers* to play chess with Timo and let him win. Then he would be in a good temper for the rest of the evening. In one mess I knew there was even a secret duty roster drawn up for the fatigue of losing to Timoshenko!

There was nothing very much in orders that morning: a few practices which were to cease forthwith, the announcement that a certain café was out of bounds until further orders, and the distribution of a few days' prison and CB for minor offences. In five minutes the parade was over, and we went off to our midday meal.

The food at Saida was excellent. In fact, I must say that the catering throughout the Legion was always maintained at a very high standard, especially in North Africa, where units could draw on the produce of the Legion-owned farms. The kitchens, which I had occasion to visit every time I was a member of a spud-peeling fatigue, were, although years out of date, of a spotless cleanliness, and the cooks were specialists who knew their job. They were nearly always Germans and Poles, by the way. Why, I don't know, unless it be that the Germans are fond of eating and the Poles of drinking.

At two o'clock in the afternoon we were paraded again for exercise. This time it was to be weapon training, and we took along with us a few of the 1929 pattern French light machine-guns. On the way out of barracks, two or three of the men in our section began talking while we were still marching at attention. Sergeant Lopez immediately halted the column.

'Halt! On the hands—down! Lie flat on the ground, and place the rifle across the arms, lodged in the crook of the elbows! In that position, forward—crawl! If I see a single rifle touch the ground, the holder will go to prison for fifteen days. Keep those arses down and don't bend your knees. Pull yourselves forward with your elbows. Get a move on there, the second man in the left-hand column!'

After we had progressed for about a hundred yards in this hideously painful and fatiguing way, the sergeant halted us.

'Halt! When you march at attention, you march in silence. I am now going to command you to get up on your feet. Before I do so, however, I warn you that, the next time any one breaks silence during *la marche en cadence*, you will march the remainder of the way to the place of exercise *en rampant*, just in the same way as you have now done for a few yards. The distance to the place of exercise is about two kilometres. On the feet up! Forward—march!'

We had not gone more than ten paces when there was a murmur from somewhere in the ranks.

'*J'en ai marre*,' we heard someone say quite plainly.

Lopez again halted the column; but this time, fortunately for the rest of us, his quick ear had detected the offender.

'Fall out, Blanc,' he said. 'Corporal, escort him to *les Palmiers*.'

The section arrived at the group of palm trees under whose shade we were to pass the afternoon at two forty-five. Ten minutes before we left again at half-past five, the Vicomte arrived, still dragging himself along by his elbows. He stood up, weary, but smiling haughtily, and asked the sergeant if he might smoke a cigarette. The sleeves of his battle-dress blouse were in rags and his shirt beneath it was soaked in blood. He seemed to enjoy that cigarette.

As soon as we had returned to the barracks and deposited our arms and equipment, we were told to take soap and towels, and were marched off to the showers. The same procedure was adopted every evening during our training after the return from exercise, and this leads me to speak of the subject of cleanliness in the Legion.

Everything at Saida was scrupulously clean—within the limits of possibility. Barrack-rooms were inspected twice daily, kit, both for completeness and cleanliness, once a week. The douche was enforced after the afternoon exercise and encouraged first thing in the morning. A man unshaven on parade was liable to eight days' prison. Blankets were shaken every day and mattresses and pillows taken out for airing every two days. Bedsteads were rubbed over once a week with insect repellent. This was the Legion's effort at cleanliness. It was, alas, but one side of the picture.

Now let us look at the other side. In the first place, the fool who had designed the barracks some sixty years before had placed the latrines only ten yards from the cookhouse, so that the kitchen staff waged a constant war against flies. Then again, the blocks of buildings were so old that the walls were infested with bugs which, despite all efforts to exterminate them, sooner or later found their way into the bedding. Then there were the drains, as old and outmoded as the buildings, and which functioned when they thought they would, which was not often. The general result was a continual feud between parsimonious, inefficient planning and Legion efficiency, energy, and enterprise.

And not only in the matter of hygiene did this strife exist. The undeclared war between the 'authorities' and the Legion was ubiquitous and continuous. I saw all this very much more clearly later on in Indo-China, and I will speak of it more fully in its proper time and place.

# 15

'COMPAGNIE, *garde-à-vous!*' The orderly sergeant called the company up to attention and presented it to the sergeant-major for daily orders.

'*Au rapport!*' shouted Timoshenko. 'Orders! The legionnaires whose names follow will proceed to the *Peloton One* for corporals at two o'clock this afternoon. Parade with full kit ready to march to the *Camp des Chasseurs.*' He read a list of some sixty names. Scheer, Sibley, and Kirsch had all been selected, and my name was also read out. As the captain at Sidi Bel-Abbès had promised, I was being sent to the *peloton* after only about ten days of recruit training; and very thankful I was, for those ten days had certainly been tough.

We had run the combat course three times. We started off in full uniform with rifles and equipment. First came a flat run of about two hundred yards, at the end of which was a river which we had to cross by climbing a tree on one side of it, leaping from branch to branch to a tree on the other side, and then climbing down. After a further run of about fifty yards, we came to a sheer perpendicular rock face fifty feet in height, which we had to climb by means of a rope suspended from a stake at the top and a number of uncertain footholds. Here it was to your advantage to be among the first; otherwise you found yourself hanging at the end of a rope which was swinging like the pendulum of some mighty clock.

Once at the top, we started on an obstacle race of five hundred yards, leaping over crevasses, jumping from boulder to boulder, to arrive eventually by a steep and perilous descent at a mountain stream about twelve feet wide, which we had to leap—or get our feet wet.

After another flat run of four hundred yards, we arrived at my own particular horror, a horizontal barbed-wire panel some twenty feet long and about fourteen inches from the ground, under which we had to crawl. I had about an inch too much diameter, and I never managed to come through without leaving a portion of my pants, and usually a strip of skin as well, hanging on the wire. For some reason or other, this seemed to amuse everybody.

When Company Orders were finished and the parade had been dismissed, Sergeant Lopez called to me.

'Come and have a drink,' he said, and led me off to the canteen. It was the end of the month and we had just drawn our pay, so I wasn't surprised to find my old friends Sibley, Scheer, and Kirsch already at the bar, celebrating the good news. Lopez stood all four of us a drink.

'I shall be seeing quite a lot of you fellows,' he said, with assumed ferocity. 'Don't imagine you're going to give me the slip. I've been posted to the *peloton* as an instructor, so I shall be coming along with you.'

'And what's going to happen to the rest of us, the ones who haven't been selected for the *peloton*?' asked a legionnaire who had been in the same section as Scheer.

'You're the lucky ones, really,' said Lopez. 'You'll probably hang about here for another week or so, and then you'll be off to Indo-China. And I wish to hell I were coming with you. I'm fed up to the back teeth with being an instructor. I've already done two years in Tongking, but I'm quite prepared to go back for another two. Then I might get married and settle down.'

'Are legionnaires allowed to marry, then?' asked Kirsch.

'Of course,' said Lopez, offering his cigarettes all round. 'But you have to be a *sous-officier* with more than five years' service to get married officially, and there's not much sense in marrying otherwise, because you wouldn't get either a married allowance or free quarters.'

'And how much service have you, Sergeant?' asked Scheer.

'Ten years. *Prosit!*' He lifted his glass in acknowledgment of Kirsch's toast. 'Yes, ten years. You'll find a lot of us Spaniards with ten years' service. Ten years ago was the end of the Civil War in Spain and, as you may know, a lot of us came over the Pyrenees into France."

'You were fighting on the Republican side, of course,' I said.

'Hell, no! I was with Franco. There are a lot of Spaniards here in the Legion who were with Franco, almost as many as there are of those who were fighting on the other side. What so many people who are not Spanish fail to understand is that the Civil War was not just a clear-cut issue between Fascists and Communists. The Russians on the one hand, and the Germans and Italians on the other, tried to make it so, with England poking her little blue nose in on both sides in a thoroughly amateurish and interfering way. No offence meant, Smith. It *was* like that, you know.

'But for those of us who were with Franco it was a rebellion of Law and Order against Anarchy, and of the Catholics against the persecution of their Church. Unfortunately, you cannot start a rebellion without creating further anarchy, especially if a lot of uninvited ideologists get mixed up with it. The consequence was that when Franco started in to clean up the mess in nineteen thirty-nine, he found, among those who had been fighting with him, the very kind of troublesome elements he had fought the war to eliminate.

'Then again, there was a lot of jealousy created on our side, because he allowed some of the more honest Republican officials to remain in office; and jealousy in Spain at that time almost inevitably resulted in murder. A number of members of my family had to take to their heels in order to escape from the police, and I took off with them. On arriving in France, I joined the Legion, and a year later I was at Narvik, fighting side by side with men I'd been doing my best to kill for three years. It's a funny world, isn't it?'

'Were you in England, then, after Norway?' I asked.

'Yes, of course. I was with the Thirteenth Demi-Brigade of the Legion. You probably know that we were re-formed in England after the evacuation of Narvik, and later went out to the Middle East, where we became part of the First Free French Division and served with the British Eighth Army. The Thirteenth Demi-Brigade, which, by the way, still exists—I was with them in Indo-China—is the only regiment of the Legion which is allowed, under active service conditions, to wear the khaki beret of the British Army.'

'Good God!' I ejaculated. 'Then you were at Bir Hacheim. I was only five miles away, at Bir Belifa, with the artillery which was supporting you. We were overrun by a German tank brigade, and I was lucky to get out alive. Why, we must have been within a stone's throw of each other.'

'Pooh! There's nothing very surprising about that,' said Lopez. 'For example, I wonder if you can remember the name of the German Armoured Division which attacked us.'

'Naturally. It was the Twenty-first Panzer.'

'Right! Tell me—Kirsch is your name, isn't it?—with which Division were you serving in North Africa?'

'Twenty-first Panzer,' replied Kirsch.

I must admit that I looked at the Rhinelander with a new light in my eyes; the light of that respect, which often ripens into friendship, between men who have fought on opposing sides of the same battlefield.

Kirsch seized on the opportunity to break into the conversation.

'Sergeant,' he said to Lopez, 'there is a thing I don't understand. How does it come about that legionnaires fight so well—and from all accounts they do fight well—in support of the French? I know that we Germans had what amounted to a Foreign Legion during the war; but then all the foreigners serving with the German Army had a common aim—the fight against Bolshevism. It seems to me that such a common cause is lacking here. For example, units of the Legion fought on different sides during the last war: the Thirteenth Demi-Brigade with the British in Libya and the First Foreign Regiment of Cavalry against the British in Syria. And yet it appears that they both fought well. How do you explain that, Sergeant?'

'I can give you an explanation,' said Lopez slowly. 'But I want you to remember that what I tell you is my own opinion and is not to be taken as the official view. My ten years of service have taught me that legionnaires don't really fight for France at all. They fight—for the Legion, which is its own ideal. Oh yes, I know that nominally the Legion fights under the French flag. It is, of course, equally true that the legionnaires' pay, food, clothing, and equipment are provided by the French Government, but they'd probably serve any other government which paid, fed, and clothed them, and serve it with equal zeal. What do you think of that theory, Scheer?'

'I'm quite sure you're right,' replied the Alsatian. 'I would go even further, and say that most of the Frenchmen among us would follow suit. We also are legionnaires first and Frenchmen afterwards.'

'D'you hear that, Kirsch?' asked Lopez. 'That's the opinion of a Frenchman. *Non, mon vieux*, please don't imagine that the Legion fights for *Liberté, Egalité et Fraternité*, or any other such worn-out nonsense. The Legion fights well—and they *can* fight, by God, the legionnaires. I can tell you that from my own experience—for the same reason that any collection of men thrown together by the same sort of misfortune will fight, and they need no catchwords or ideologies to bolster up their courage. Ask yourself why you joined the Legion—no, no, don't tell me; I don't want to know—and then ask yourself whether all your comrades here had not, basically, the same sort of motive for doing so.'

The Spaniard turned to face the rest of us.

'*Mes amis*,' he continued, 'men who have nothing to lose no more need courage to confront danger than a man who has lost all hope needs courage to commit suicide. I have seen legionnaires in Indo-China go out and face death cheerfully, almost eagerly. And when they had had it, and the *toubib* was feeling their pulse as they lay in the ditch and telling them their number was up, I have heard them say "Thank God" as they died with a smile on their lips. That is the sort of thing which makes the strength of the Legion.'

Lopez broke off, and I could almost have sworn that there were tears in his eyes. Then he pulled himself together.

'What the hell!' he said. 'We're getting too damned serious. Come on, let's have another drink.'

I had already ordered another round, but Lopez insisted on paying for it, and, as I knew that his pay was about fifty or sixty times as much as mine, I allowed him to do so.

The pay system in the Legion, by the way, is now essentially the same as in the rest of the French Army, though at one time legionnaires were paid at a very much lower rate. Up till the end of his first year's service, or until he goes to a theatre of operations, such as Indo-China, the legionnaire receives exactly the same meagre pittance as a young Frenchman doing his military service year—round about four hundred and fifty francs, say nine shillings, a month. The theory is that, since the recruit is being trained, he is of no value to the Government; which is all very well for the young Frenchman who probably receives money from home, but is very little consolation to the legionnaire, to whom, in any case, the theory scarcely applies, since nearly all have previous military service. Even promotion has very little influence on this miserable rate of pay. When I became a sergeant after eight months, I earned only about twelve shillings a month until the anniversary of my joining date came round.

So much for the first year. Thereafter a legionnaire second-class (private soldier) was paid between three and six thousand francs a month, according to his length of service and the specialist's pay to which he might be entitled. A corporal with similar qualifications would make about a thousand francs extra. Then came an enormous jump between corporal and sergeant. The latter could earn anything between twenty and thirty-five thousand francs a month according to qualifications. Considering that a glass of wine in the canteen cost ten francs and a packet of smokeable cigarettes sixty, this was not bad pay. It paled into insignificance when compared with the Indo-China rates, but of those latter I will speak in due course.

This very wide divergence between the pay of a *sous-officier* and that of other ranks is explained by the anomaly that all NCO ranks from sergeant upwards are not only soldiers but *fonctionnaires*, or Government officials. The consequence is that every time a certain grade of employee in the post office or the railways goes on strike for more pay and gets it, up go the salaries of *sous-officiers* in the army, those of the Legion with the rest.

Ironical, is it not, that a sergeant of the Legion should benefit, directly and materially, from the agitations, very possibly Communist inspired, of some band of *petit bourgeois* grouped together in a trade union?

# 16

BEFORE we had finished the first week of the *peloton* we discovered that it was going to be even more strenuous than the recruit training. The combat course, which I had only run three times during the ten days, was now to be completed every morning before breakfast; and if the instructors were not satisfied with the speed at which it was run, they often sent us round the course for a second tour.

Not all the candidates were recruits, I discovered; a great many of them were legionnaires of two or three years' service. The prize at the end of the four month's training would be the rank of corporal; but it was by no means certain that all would be accepted. Among the sixty legionnaires competing were twelve who had been officers in various European armies; one, it was said, had even held the rank of colonel in the *Wehrmacht*.

Sibley, Kirsch, Scheer, and I found ourselves in the same section for the purpose of instruction, and the section was commanded by Lopez, who went up to the rank of *sergent-chef* shortly after the beginning of the course. We four kept very much together and had very little to do with the other members of the section, of whom I think it interesting to mention only one. He represented a class of legionnaire which was extremely rare but which has been exaggerated out of all proportion by certain writers. He was a Frenchman who, having committed a series of crimes at a very early age, had been sent to the French equivalent of a Borstal institution and thence incorporated into one of the *Bataillons d'Afrique*, or *Bats d'Af*, as they are familiarly known.

These labour battalions, which are employed on road construction and other heavy manual work in French North Africa, recruit their private soldiers from the prisons and reformatories and their cadre from NCOs expelled as a disciplinary measure from regular units. It may well be imagined what sort of character is produced by such an environment. If the recruits to the *Bats d'Af* are not criminals at heart when they join, they certainly are when they are released.

Legionnaire M—— was no exception. Some time or another he had visited a tattooist, and printed indelibly in letters an inch high across his right hand was the one word '*Merde*'! This had somehow escaped notice at his medical examination, and later created quite a bit of embarrassment. He was ordered to wear a glove on his right hand so as to avoid giving offence to officers when saluting. As he liked nothing better than giving offence, he was constantly losing the glove, and each time he was sent to prison for fifteen days. He was thrown out of the *peloton* after a week or so, and the last I heard of him was that he had been ejected from the Legion with ignominy. He should never have been accepted.

But I am wandering away from my subject, which was the *peloton* and its toughness. The fact is that I was a good bit older than most of my fellow candidates and had not led the sort of life best calculated to maintain me at the top of my physical form, so that whereas the youngsters of twenty or so had no difficulty in running a mile or two before breakfast, for me it was sheer agony. I can honestly say that there were moments during those first few weeks at the Camp des Chasseurs, the hutted camp where we lived for the duration of the course, when I felt like throwing up the sponge and reporting sick. Why didn't I? You will probably think the reason idiotic, but I didn't think it so at the time.

Consciously or unconsciously—I do not now clearly remember which—I would say to myself: 'Smith, my lad, you are the only Englishman in this *peloton*. In fact, you're probably the only

Englishman for miles around, and in the eyes of a lot of Germans, Poles, Frenchmen, and what not, you represent England.'

So I just gritted my teeth and stuck it. I honestly don't think I worried very much as to what sort of a figure John Smith was cutting; but I did very much care what sort of showing England, as represented by John Smith, was getting in the eyes of the rest of the world, as represented by the remainder of the *peloton*. In the obstacle races and other endurance tests, I was physically incapable of coming in first; but, even though I had to half-kill myself in the effort, I made very certain that I never came in last.

Sergeant Lopez had told us that legionnaires made good fighters because they had nothing to lose. I thought I was beginning to be aware of another factor which contributed: purely and simply, the mixture of nationalities. For do not imagine that I was alone in thus upholding my national honour. I spoke to several of the others, and each told me that he had been doing precisely the same from his own national point of view.

I suspected then that what was true as regarded physical exertion during training might hold good for courage under combat conditions. I was not wrong. Not even their best friends will claim that Italians, for example, fighting in their own national army, are good fighters. If they are honest about it, they don't even claim it themselves. An Italian surrounded by his Bersaglieri or Alpini colleagues tends to follow the movement, which is generally a rearward one. But an Italian legionnaire with a German on one side of him and a Czech on the other was a very different kettle of fish. I have seen them fight like wildcats.

What surprised me was that, as well as the physical effort demanded, a fair mental effort was also required of the *peloton*. Without going into too many details, I can perhaps give some idea of the professional knowledge required of a Legion corporal by saying that, at the final examinations, questions were put on the characteristics and functioning of all French, British, and

American small arms in current use, and that a thorough knowledge of the handling of 60-mm. mortars and heavy machine-guns was considered essential. If a candidate was not well acquainted with the mysteries of map-reading and orientation, he might just as well stay away from the examinations at the end of the course. The rank of corporal was by no means given away!

Towards the end of April, when we had been at the Camp des Chasseurs for about three weeks, all training was suddenly stopped and the whole of the following three days was devoted to preparation for the parade and march past which were to take place on April 30th, the anniversary of Camerone.

The battle of Camerone, in Mexico, took place in 1863 during Napoleon III's ill-fated expedition there. The story goes that a Foreign Legion company, with a total strength of only sixty-three officers and men, was besieged in a *hacienda* by two thousand Mexican soldiers. After having resisted for several hours, only twelve legionnaires remained, among them the captain who, although mortally wounded, was still directing operations. The Mexicans had set fire to the farmhouse and the defenders had very little ammunition left; but in spite of their desperate situation, the dying captain made the eleven other survivors swear that they would defend their position to the last and would not surrender. The Mexican commander called upon them repeatedly to capitulate, but they refused. At last, when the captain was dead and all the ammunition was expended, the five men who remained alive, commanded by a corporal, fixed bayonets and charged the besiegers. Three were taken prisoner by force and were subsequently, in recognition of their bravery, allowed to retain their arms and rejoin the French ranks. It is said that to this day units of the Mexican Army halt and present arms whenever they pass the *hacienda* of Camerone.

This battle, unimportant in itself and in its material consequences, has been commemorated ever since by the Legion as the supreme example of bravery, sacrifice, and fidelity to the sworn word. It is marked every year, wherever units of the Legion happen to be, by massive parades, with music and all the usual pomp and ceremony, the awarding of decorations, speeches by high-ranking officers, and all the gaudy display and pageantry dear to the hearts of the military-minded.

Our *peloton* was to take a leading part in the parade; so we spent the three days before the 30th in marching, counter-marching, presenting arms, and executing eyes left and eyes right, so that we should give a faultless performance on The Day. Our gaiters had to be painted a perfect white, and we were shown how to put on the blue waist-sash and the huge red epaulettes which are the traditional parade dress of the Legion. We washed and re-washed our white *couvre-képis*. And, for the first time, we heard the *Boudin*—the march of the Legion—played by one of the military bands, with its peculiar refrain:

> *Tiens, voilà du boudin, voilà du boudin, voilà du boudin!*
> *Pour les Alsaciens, les Suisses et les Lorrains.*
> *Pour les Belges n'y en a plus; pour les Belges n'y en a plus!*
> *Ce sont des tireurs au cul.*

Look, here's some sausage, here's some sausage, here's some sausage,
For the Swiss and the lads from Alsace-Lorraine.
But there's no more for the Belgians, there's no more for the Belgians,
Because they're just a lot of shirkers.

It is not known what the Belgians did at some remote period in the history of the Legion thus to bring down upon themselves the wrath and scorn of their comrades. What is certain is that the tune is a very stirring one, and that the military band which executed it was one of the finest I had ever heard. It should have been, for nearly half the instrumentalists were professional musicians, some of them from famous orchestras, and one or two even camouflaged names of European renown behind their Legion incogniti.

After the ceremony at the main barracks on the morning of the 30th, we marched the two kilometres back to the Camp des Chasseurs, where a huge meal was awaiting us, together with wine in abundance.

Sibley, who drank something like four litres between midday and three o'clock in the afternoon, was the first to begin making a nuisance of himself. He started by singing. There was no harm in that, of course, except that he had not a very pleasant voice and was tone deaf. When he had made himself thoroughly hoarse and unpopular by singing for half an hour without a break, Sibley drank another litre. He then decided that he was going into town, and shambled towards the gate, dressed as he was in a pair of shorts, sandals, no shirt, and no hat. The guard sergeant ordered him to return to his room.

'What?' exclaimed Sibley, to whom his libations had given an unwonted self-confidence, which expressed itself in the stridency of his raucous tones. 'What? Me? A citizen of the free and neutral republic of Switzerland, to be ordered about by a little whippersnapper of a sergeant with bow-legs. Stand aside, young fellow!'

The sergeant repeated the order, less patiently. He did have bow-legs, and it was a sore point with him. Sibley took no notice, but continued to walk out of the gate; whereupon the sergeant launched a straight left to his nose and a right uppercut to the chin. The Swiss sank down in a heap on the ground, and was carried off to the cells by two members of the guard. The sergeant brushed his hands and turned round to wait for the next candidate.

The principle applied was that we could get as drunk as we liked and do what we liked, short of causing material damage, so long as we remained inside the camp. If we wanted to go into town, we had to be properly dressed and reasonably steady on our legs.

At about four o'clock Kirsch, who had somehow managed to steal an Arab's donkey from outside the gates, was giving a wild display of horsemanship up and down the alleys between the huts, when suddenly the animal stumbled and Kirsch disappeared through a window. Kirsch himself escaped serious injury, but the window did not; and all this, unfortunately, happened at the very moment the company sergeant-major had chosen to make a round of inspection. He ordered Kirsch to prepare himself for spending a night in prison. To Scheer, who was standing by and who had also freely partaken of the *vin rosé* of Mascara, this seemed most unfair, and he attempted to explain his point of view to the sergeant-major, with the result that he spent the ensuing fourteen hours in Kirsch's company.

Of the four of us, I was the only one who now remained at liberty. I had drunk very little. I had been suffering all day from *le cafard*.

*Cafard*, in case you don't know it, is a state of mental depression in which all the sins and tragedies of your past life loom up like mountains before you and the future looks very black indeed. Nearly all legionnaires suffer from *le cafard*, particularly during their first six months or year of service. Many of them drink heavily in order to get away from their depressing thoughts. Others merely retire into themselves and work out their problems, to the extent that it is possible to work them out, in a stony and impenetrable silence.

I had sat silently brooding ever since we had returned to the camp at midday, not even troubling to reply when I was spoken to. I had scarcely pecked at the excellent meal which had been

Nam-Dinh. The sentry outside the rear-base

Fixed defences overlooking the Red River

provided and, although it was not my turn, I took away all the plates and dishes, washed and returned them to the cookhouse, all without saying a word. My comrades, recognizing my state of mind as one to which they were only too accustomed themselves, had left me strictly alone.

Now that all my friends were in prison, I decided that I would get myself dressed and walk down to town alone. Best khaki shirt with the green tie of the Legion, neatly pressed khaki-drill trousers, *képi* with newly washed *couvre-képi*, and I was ready. I went alone because I wanted to, apart from the fact that I had made no other friends in the *peloton*, beyond the three who were now under lock and key. The guard sergeant, who knew who and where my friends were, looked me up and down suspiciously as I went out of the gate; but he said nothing.

As I was passing the entrance to the main barracks, out came Jaderny, who was still there with the recruits doing his initial training. Although he was quite steady on his feet, I could tell by the look in his eyes that he was drunk. We said hallo to one another and continued walking together towards the centre of the town. After a couple of hundred yards, I asked the Pole where he was going.

'*Bordel*,' he replied shortly.

I supposed it would be Jaderny's first visit to the brothel since the 15th, for I knew that he went there regularly every pay-day, and we had received our fifteen days' pay of two hundred and twenty-five francs just before lunch. As for me, I had not so much as spoken to a woman for two months.

'Me too,' I said. 'Show me the way.'

# 17

WHEN the French Government passed Marthe Richard's law making the *maison close* illegal, it applied only to metropolitan France, so that in North Africa and other French territories overseas the brothel is still just as much a part of the urban landscape as ever it was. In particular, every town which has a garrison, no matter how small, is sure to have a house—and if the garrison is a large one, a whole row of houses—sporting a red light over the door. In the case of these military towns, the brothels are usually controlled by the military, from the point of view both of price and hygiene.

Jaderny and I turned into the 'street'. A number of legionnaires in various stages of intoxication were wandering up and down it; every now and again, one who appeared to be more flagrantly out of control than his comrades would be picked up by the Military Police, bundled into a jeep, and hauled off back to the barracks and a night in prison. As we walked along the street, we saw one of our fellow competitors for the rank of corporal go through an archway into a house over which a notice, *Interdite à la troupe* (Out of Bounds), was posted. He, too, was rounded up by the MPs and taken back to barracks. Jaderny explained.

'That's an Arab brothel. The girls there'll do it for fifty francs, at a pinch, but it's too damned risky, not only because of the police but on account of the possibility of picking something up. Let's go along to the *Clair de la Lune*, like good little boys.'

The house we entered was one of the two recognized establishments in the street. It had green-painted shutters, and over the door hung a sign depicting an amorous couple bathed in the light of a silvery moon. We found ourselves in a corridor with, at the far end, a door, close against which an incredibly old and toothless Arab hag was crouching over a brazier, clutching a packet of white tickets in one hand and a packet of red in the other.

'Two,' said Jaderny, holding out twenty francs. She peeled off two white scraps of paper and handed them to him, taking the money and secreting it somewhere in the folds of her filthy robes. Then she pulled a string to release the weight which kept the door bolted from the inside; we passed through into the room beyond.

After the rigour of the training camp, the dust of the desert roads, and the smell and squalor of the Arab streets, the luxuriously appointed saloon in which we found ourselves gave me, by contrast, the impression that we had been suddenly and miraculously transported to an orgy planned by some lavish millionaire in his apartment in one of the capitals of Europe.

The room was a perfect circle some thirty feet in diameter, about one quarter of the circumference being occupied by a bar made of polished mahogany. From a point opposite the middle of the bar, a stairway, built close against the wall, led up to a balcony which ran all the way round the room at a height of about ten feet, and which gave access to the sixteen bedroom doors (painted red and green in the colours of the Legion!) equally spaced around the entire periphery. In the absence of windows, an enormous skylight, which covered almost the whole of the circle formed by the top of the circular inner wall, admitted daylight to the central hall.

On the knobs of half a dozen of the sixteen doors *képis* were hanging, in accordance with the tradition of the house, to show that the rooms thus adorned were occupied by the *képis*' owners. Two of them were blue with a red crown, while the remainder were covered with the white *couvre-képi* worn by corporals and legionnaires. It was thus possible to tell at a glance that upstairs were two *sous-officiers*.

'That's who the red tickets are for,' explained Jaderny. 'They have to pay twenty francs to come in instead of ten.'

We approached the bar, behind which a mountain of female flesh, crowned with masses of curly, red hair, was officiating, assisted by a hard-faced, black-haired woman with thin lips and flat breasts, and a small boy, whose origins might have been anything between Chinese and Maltese, and were probably both, with a lot thrown in besides.

I ordered two drinks and started looking about me. At first I pretended not to notice the dozen or so girls in various undress costumes who were soliciting my attention, and concentrated on the fresco, about eighteen inches high and divided into sixteen panels, which was painted all the way round the circular wall at five feet above ground level. It was an allegory depicting the man pursuing, capturing and seducing the woman, and then the woman, having once been seduced, binding the man to her with chains from which he tries to escape and in which he finally strangles himself. I knew enough about painting to recognize that this was work of a very high order, and I asked the fat woman behind the bar who the artist was.

She looked at me in surprise. 'I thought everybody knew that,' she said; but when I told her that it was my first visit to the house, she told me a remarkable story.

'That painting,' she said, 'was made in nineteen thirty-five by a Russian legionnaire with sixteen years' service. He had just come back from Morocco, and had been given twenty days' leave, which he was spending here in Saida. Of course, after the third day he was broke and owed me money.

' "Mama," he said one day, "how many girls you have here?"

' "Fifteen," I told him.

' "Look here," he said. "You see this damn wall, always look so bare, so damn cold, so uninviting, no damn good for whorehouse. I make you beautiful painting all round it. See, I divide him into sixteen panel. I do one panel each day. That make my sixteen days rest of leave. Okay?"

'Well, Popov—that was his name—had a very good reputation as a painter, and it was quite true that the walls were very bare; so I asked him how much he wanted for doing the job.

' "*Nichevo*," he said. "I do one panel each day for sixteen days, and you give me my food, two litre wine, and a different girl each night." I thought that was a good bargain, so I accepted.

'He started work, and the first day he suggested to me that, instead of giving him two litres of wine a day, I should give him only a quarter of a litre the first day and double the amount every forty-eight hours. I accepted, because it seemed to me that it would be cheaper; I wasn't so good at arithmetic in those days. On the eleventh and twelfth days I had to supply him with eight litres a day, and on the thirteenth and fourteenth with sixteen. For the last two days I had to order in a barrel specially for Popov. Believe me, he was so drunk those last few days, I had to get the girls to carry him down from bed and set him up on the scaffolding which he erected against the portion of the wall he was going to paint.

'But he got the work done all right,' went on the fat woman, and her eyes flashed again. 'I tell you, they were legionnaires in those days. Look!' She pointed to a part of the wall in the corner behind the bar. 'He did that on the sixteenth day, when he was so drunk he had to crawl on his hands and knees across the floor to get a brush or a tube of colour. And it's the most perfect of the lot.

'The next morning he said good-bye and left. A few hours later the police came. They told us that Popov had been found in a deserted barn on the Colomb-Béchar road. He had hanged himself.'

I drew in my breath sharply. 'Well, I'll be damned!' I said.

'And so will I,' said Jaderny. 'But tell me, Mama, if your Popov was so darned full of beans, and you say there were only fifteen girls in the house to pay for sixteen days' work, with whom did he sleep on the sixteenth night?'

The fat woman did not answer for a moment, but a tear appeared in the corner of each eye and began trickling down her plump cheeks.

'I've wasted enough time talking to you two,' she cried. 'I've got other customers to attend to. Marie, go up and knock on Lucille's door and tell her she's been there for over an hour already. What does that damned Italian corporal expect for a hundred francs, anyhow?'

She turned back to us again. 'Have a drink, you two,' she invited. 'Let's drink to the memory of that bastard Popov. *Le salopard!* He was riddled with syphilis, and in the sixteen days he was here, he put the establishment out of business for nearly two months afterwards. Damn his eyes!

'Still,' she sighed, and her bosom heaved like the swell on a troubled ocean. 'Still, he did paint some beautiful pictures, didn't he?'

The fat woman turned away and started attending to the wants of several legionnaires who were waiting to be served with drinks, leaving us to finish the two glasses of cognac she had poured out for us. Seeing that we were disengaged, two girls came across the room and planted themselves in front of us, detailing us from head to toe.

'I like you,' one of them said to me. 'My name's Odette. What's yours?'

She was a pale, frightened-looking creature, with a thin, elvish face and straight, glossy black hair parted in the middle. The hazel eyes which were set widely on either side of her narrow, straight nose gazed evenly at me with an open, frank interest. I blushed and fumbled for an answer. She put up her hand to my chin, pulled my face round and kissed me on the cheek.

'There,' she said. 'Now you won't feel so lonely. Give me a cigarette, please.'

I had no cigarettes left in my pocket, and turned to ask Jaderny for one, only to discover that the Pole had already disappeared upstairs with the other girl. Seeing my consternation, the girl produced a packet of Philip Morris from the pocket of the diminutive shorts she was wearing and handed it to me.

'I was just too lazy to get them out,' she said. 'And you still haven't told me what your name is.'

I thanked her and told her my name was John.

'How long have you been here?' I asked.

'Three years,' she replied. 'I finished my first two years' contract and then signed on for another two, because I hadn't made enough money.'

'What? Three years in this place? And what's all this about a contract? I didn't know you had to sign a contract.'

'Yes, of course. Just like a legionnaire, eh? Except that you have to sign for five, and you wear out your feet.'

'How old are you, Odette?' I asked her.

'Nineteen. I started working here when I was sixteen, and by the time I'm twenty I shall have two million francs in the bank, if my health lasts out. That should be enough to start something on, shouldn't it?'

She broke off and looked me searchingly in the eyes.

'Now, look here, Johnny,' she said angrily, 'don't for heaven's sake look at me in that pitying way, or I shall go off and find somebody else to talk to. I don't *have* to stay here with you, you know. All I have to do is ask you if you want to go upstairs with me and, if you refuse, pass on to the next one, unless you stand me a drink, and I haven't asked you to do that even, because I know you are a *bleu*. No, take your hand out of your pocket. I don't want one, thank you.'

She smiled and put her arm round my neck.

'Don't worry your head about me,' she said. 'I'm all right. Come, let me take you up to my room for a little while, and I'll show you why you don't have to trouble about me.' She dragged me by the collar of my shirt towards the staircase.

'Oh, you'll pay all the same,' she said, as we reached the balcony, and her voice was thick with sex. 'You'll pay all the same, because I don't believe in letting men have something for nothing. They never appreciate it if you do. And I want you to appreciate it, Johnny,' she purred, as she removed my *képi* and hung it on the door-knob. As she kicked off her shoes, she began singing a sweet little ditty with the refrain:

> '*Je suis une putain des légionnaires,*
> *Et j'en suis fière, que j'en suis fière!*'

When I came down the stairs again, I found Jaderny at the bar deep in conversation with Sergeant Lopez. The *chef* didn't seem to be very pleased at seeing me there for some reason or other. Perhaps it was because he wasn't very proud of being seen there himself. He offered me a drink, but continued talking to the Pole.

'Don't be a fool,' he was saying. 'Don't you realize that you can land yourself into very serious trouble for that sort of thing? The poor girl ran down here screaming that you'd been trying to strangle her. Now, for heaven's sake pull yourself together and go and apologize to the *mère maquerelle*. Tell her that you were only joking and hadn't realized the thing had gone too far.'

'But I can't,' replied Jaderny. He was very far gone in drink and was almost in tears. 'I can't do that, *chef*, because, you see, I *did* mean to strangle her, just as I want to strangle all harlots. Let 'em keep out of my sight, the bitches.'

He faced about and, with heaving breast and dilated nostrils, moved towards a bevy of the local beauties huddled together near the corner where the dance band was beginning to install itself for the evening session. Two of the girls screamed. And then things began to happen very quickly.

A legionnaire standing close by punched Jaderny on the jaw, and the Pole fell to the ground. Then, despite the restraining arm of Lopez, I moved in to the attack and knocked down the other legionnaire. Jaderny picked himself up and launched a swinging uppercut at an innocent bystander, who had merely been looking on to see fair play.

At that moment the door burst open and in came the Military Police patrol. Lopez attempted to pour oil on troubled waters, but the patrol commander was adamant.

'Orders are orders,' he said. 'I'm embarking the whole lot of them, without exception.'

So half an hour later Jaderny and I found ourselves in prison: Jaderny at the main barracks and I with Sibley, Scheer, and Kirsch. For us the feast of Camerone for the year 1949 was at an end.

We were all released at dawn the next morning, for offences committed on the day of Camerone, unless they be of a most serious nature, are never punished.

# 18

THE resumption of training after Camerone was marked, for me, by the first thoroughly unpleasant incident since my joining the Legion.

It was known that someone in the Company Office was working some sort of swindle in order to augment his meagre pay. It is not necessary to go into details except to explain that, although everybody knew it was going on, the victims of the racket also benefited from it and were at the same time themselves at fault, so that they could not be persuaded to come forward and give the evidence necessary to convict the culprit. This probably sounds rather involved, but it was like that.

One morning the officer commanding the *peloton* stopped me as I was walking across the camp. This lieutenant was not, definitely not, a legionnaire. He had been transferred for temporary service with the Legion from the regular army because of the shortage of normal Legion officers consequent upon the high rate of casualties among them in Indo-China. I shall have much more to tell later on concerning the difference between temporary and permanent Legion officers. For the moment let it suffice that the lieutenant commanding the *peloton* was of a very different type from, say, the captain at Marseilles or my old acquaintance of Sidi Bel-Abbès.

'Smith,' he said, 'I want a word with you.'

I halted, turned towards him, saluted, and stood to attention at the regulation distance of six paces.

'*A vos ordres, mon Lieutenant.*'

'Stand at ease. Look here, Smith, I want your help. You probably know that we suspect X of working a racket with the payment of advances on efficiency awards?'

'I have heard about it, *mon Lieutenant*.'

'The trouble is that we cannot get any evidence, because the men concerned have not only disobeyed orders, but have profited from the arrangement, even though we are pretty sure that they have paid the organizer a dividend.'

The lieutenant paused and waited for me to say something. There was a crafty look on his face which I didn't quite like. He could not look his man in the eye. I said nothing.

'*Voyez-vous*, Smith? This is what I want you to do. Make a list of the names of men who have dealt with X and hand it to me. You should be able to do that quite easily, simply by listening to conversation.'

He paused again. I still said nothing.

'*Voyons*, Smith,' he continued. 'I know from your record that you are an ex-officer of the British Army. We officers ought to pull together, *n'est-ce pas?*'

Had I not been so angry, I think I should have burst into laughter.

'I am afraid,' I replied, 'that I am not exactly cut out for the job of spying on my comrades. *Faire le mouchard, ce n'est pas mon métier.*'

Without waiting for his reply, I saluted, in that very smart way which turns a salute into an insult, turned on my heel and left him standing.

That same afternoon the lieutenant carried out a barrack-room inspection. My spare pair of boots, standing at the foot of the bed, was covered with dust. He awarded me eight days' *salle de police*. I do not suggest any connexion between this and my interview of that morning but—well, he ought to have looked me in the eyes when handing out the punishment. Kirsch, whose boots were also dirty, collected the same tariff.

The punishment known as *salle de police* (guardroom detention), an intermediate one between confinement to barracks and prison, was carried out in the following way. We took part in all the training and instruction and ate our meals with the section in the usual way; but, immediately after the evening meal, we had to report to the guardroom, our blankets under our arms, and spend the night in the cells.

I thoroughly enjoyed those eight days, or rather nights. As the prison was nearly full, Kirsch and I shared a cell, and we got to know each other very well. Smoking in the cells was, of course, forbidden, and we were searched before going in for the night. We always had cigarettes, however, and usually managed to while away the evening with half a pint of wine each. Smuggling things into prison is the easiest thing on earth when you know how, and Kirsch knew; he had been four years in a POW camp.

We started off the first evening by playing a game which you may, perhaps, know. It consists of supplying each in turn a letter of the alphabet, the idea being always to have a possible word in mind, but to avoid finishing a word. Example: I start with A. Kirsch supplies R. I then give T, thinking of the word 'artifice'. But, dash it, I've already lost, for I have completed the word 'art'. We played alternately in English and German to keep things even. On the whole Kirsch won, his knowledge of written English being superior to mine of written German.

The next evening we spent in composing short poems on a given subject. We would take it in turns to propose a theme and then each of us had to write a poem on it in his own language as quickly as possible. I think I had just re-read Chesterton's 'Flying Inn', so it must have been I who suggested this one. The first subject chosen was the lieutenant, but I am afraid the results were quite unprintable. I taught Hans—I was calling him by his *Vorname* by that time—how to make limericks; but for some reason or other they don't seem to come out well in German.

From time to time Hans told me, in occasional, jerky, sentimental outbursts, something of his previous life. It was a pathetic story, a story of frustration and disillusionment; everything, or nearly everything, seemed to have gone wrong for him.

He was the only son of a country doctor. The logical thing for him would have been to study medicine and take over his father's practice. But no, he wanted to be a painter; he refused to study medicine and so, of course, quarrelled with his father.

Then there was a girl whom he had loved dearly. She was, he told me, a pianist of great talent, and was studying in Dresden. She had been killed during an air-raid on the town. On our fourth evening together, Kirsch and I played the game of 'guessing tunes'. We would take it in turn to hum a classical melody and the other had to say the name of the piece and the composer. At one point I hummed the *adagio cantabile* from Beethoven's Sonata Pathétique; Hans burst into tears and told me about the girl.

He told me that, as a member of a Catholic community, he had not been particularly pro-Nazi. When war broke out, he had joined up and done his duty like everybody else. He had done six months in the ranks, and was then sent off to the military academy, being commissioned as a second-lieutenant in 1941. After a short period of garrison duty he was sent to the training camp where Rommel was forming his Afrika Korps.

As was natural, we spent hours discussing the war in the desert, comparing notes on battles in which we had both been engaged, criticizing tactics, and so on. We worked out that we must have spent a total of ten months within ten kilometres of each other.

He had been taken prisoner by a French patrol of Goumiers at Pont de Fahs just before the end of the campaign. He spent the rest of the war and two years of the peace which followed in a number of camps in Algeria and France.

But Hans' misfortunes were not yet at an end. When his turn

came for release in 1947, he suddenly remembered that he was a member of the SS, and not only a member but an official in that organization.

Like many country-bred youths in his part of North-west Germany, he had belonged to the local *Reiterverein*—a sort of riding club. He had been, in fact, a very active member of it, and spent nearly all his spare time on horseback whenever he went home on holiday. Some time in 1940 the post of honorary secretary to the club fell vacant, and Hans, because he was popular, a good horseman, and the doctor's son, was elected to it. Six months later, by a stroke of the pen, all these clubs were incorporated into the SS, and Hans was automatically designated *Oberscharführer*.

In the POW camp near Lille Hans remembered this, for some strange rumours were circulating and had been circulating for some time. It was said that in post-war Germany anyone who had held a rank in the SS, whether willingly or not, was in danger of being shot or at least imprisoned for life by the Allies. Other stories said that all their property was confiscated, and that it was impossible for them to find employment. The French Ministry of Labour was then offering employment in the mines and other local industries to prisoners who wished to stay a year or two in France. Hans stayed, as a foreman in a locomotive repair shop.

On our last evening in the cell together we began talking about art. I asked him why he had never gone back to his painting.

'I did,' he replied. 'I spent the whole of last summer as an art student in Paris. I worked in the locomotive repair shop for just over a year, saved quite a bit of money, and got myself issued with a temporary French identity card. Then I came to Paris and entered myself as a student at *La Grande Chaumière*. I remained there for six months.'

Poor fellow! It had taken him those six months to realize that he was not even second-rate. His fellow students, polite at first, soon began referring to him as the penny postcard painter or the colour photographer. They talked a language which he could not begin to understand—of concrete and abstract, of form and unform, of objectivism and egocentrification. They probably didn't understand it themselves either, but they pretended to.

Towards the end of the year a minor painter to whom he had stood a drink on the terrace of the *Deux Magots* told him that the south coast of France, and not Paris, was the true home of painters, and that many great artists who had found it impossible to produce good work in Montmartre had succeeded in doing so at Toulon or la Ciotat. Hans clutched at this information like a drowning man at a straw. He took the train to Marseilles.

He never got any farther than Marseilles. He must have reasoned the whole thing out on the way down in the train, forced himself to face the unrelenting facts, and come to the conclusion that he was going on a fool's errand.

'I spent a month or so,' he concluded, 'sitting in those little cafés along the waterfront and getting miserably drunk on cheap alcohol with what was left of my money. I would gaze unseeingly into the blue of the harbour, desperately trying to focus my thoughts on the future. From time to time I would take up my block and make a sketch of a group of boats lying at anchor. Then I would look at it in disgust, tear it up and throw it away—and order another Pernod.'

Kirsch squashed out his cigarette and turned over to go to sleep.

'And all that time,' he said, 'the gates of the Bas Fort Saint-Nicolas were just five hundred yards away, waiting for me.'

# 19

THE examinations at the end of the course were held during the second week of July and were competitive, the candidates being listed according to the marks obtained. The first forty-five on the list were promoted corporal and the remainder returned to duty as private soldiers. Among those considered unfit to hold the rank of corporal in the Legion were an ex-captain of Hungarian cavalry and an Italian flying ace who had held a rank equivalent to flight-lieutenant. The ten at the head of the list, of whom I happened to be one, were earmarked for the sergeant school which was due to begin at the end of August at Sidi Bel-Abbès.

The successful candidates received their green stripes from the hands of the *commandant* at a ceremonial parade on the fourteenth of July. The parade, of course, was to celebrate the fall of the Bastille and not the nomination of the corporals; but we all got drunk afterwards. Even those of us who didn't care tuppence for the French Revolution were not too bigoted to enjoy the wine. I got pretty drunk myself and made a speech about the 'anniversary of the greatest tragedy in French history'.

In one way it was a sad occasion for our little band, for it meant we were going to lose sight of Sibley, who had not been proposed for the sergeants' course along with Kirsch, Scheer and myself, owing to his inability to keep his mouth closed when he had drunk a drop too much. As Lopez told him, everybody drinks hard in the Legion, and whether or not you meet with disaster depends upon the effect drink has on you.

'If you confine yourself,' said Lopez, 'to insulting your best

*ve)* Ancient and mod-
... in Indo-China. The
...estic buffalo and the
...e-detector

...ionnaires with American
...pment: a Thompson
...-machine gun and a
... 300 radio set

'At the risk of losing boots and blood'

'The only thing to do: go to ground and fire back'

friend's ancestors or knocking out his front teeth, nobody worries very much about it. If you arrive at a ceremonial parade on all fours and have to be given a special escort to maintain you in an upright position while you present arms to the Colours, why, that's considered more or less normal. But if you start speaking your mind and criticizing your superiors in their hearing, then, my lad, you're for it every time.'

So the course broke up, and Kirsch and I spent six weeks as corporals instructing recruits at a place called Mascara, chiefly famous because it produces the best wine in North Africa. At the end of August we went back once more to Sidi Bel-Abbès, ready to begin the *Peloton Two*.

Of the forty candidates there assembled to compete for the rank of sergeant, about a quarter were newcomers like myself, and the rest old hands with three to ten years' service. I cannot now remember many of them. I remember that I slept next to a Corsican who was an ardent Bonapartist and with whom I got involved in some furious arguments. I am an ardent Wellingtonian myself, and he was always referring to 'an obscure British general by the name of Wesley, or something'. My reply: 'Not so obscure but that he licked the daylights out of Napoleon'; to which he would retort, 'Oh no, it was Blücher who did that.' This was so manifestly untrue, I think he must have been baiting me. I rose to it every time!

On the other side of me slept a Persian named Naza. He had twenty-five years' service and had been with the 13th Demi-Brigade in Libya. He gave out his age as forty-three, but to me he looked much nearer sixty. (There is, by the way, no age limit in the Legion. A month or two before this book went to press, the *Doyen de la Légion*, Regimental Sergeant-major Collard, died in Belgium at the age of eighty-six. He had a total of forty-eight years' service, and signed on for the last time in 1939 at the age of seventy!)

In all his twenty-five years in the Legion, it was the first time Naza had been proposed for a *Peloton Two*. He was a pleasant, garrulous old fool, but when he learnt that I also had been in Libya, he kept me supplied with cigarettes.

The *peloton* was commanded by a lieutenant who had come up through the ranks of the Legion, assisted by an *adjutant* (sergeant-major) by the name of Dupont. Dupont was of Belgian origin, fat in an agreeable way, with a flushed red face and an enormous capacity for red wine. I have known him to be blind drunk at five in the morning, then take a shower, and be on parade at half-past six, to all outward appearances perfectly sober. Of all the NCO instructors I ever met, he best knew how to temper the wind to the shorn lamb. His method was to start off the day by blasting hell out of the *peloton*. Then, half an hour later, he would relent and say, '*Cà va mieux*. That's better. *On commence à voir que vous êtes quand même des hommes*. You're beginning to show yourselves to be men after all.'

Naza, the aged Persian, was always late on parade. For a day or two at the beginning of the course the jovial sergeant-major was patient. Then, the fourth or fifth day, when Naza had once more slipped into the ranks a minute or so after everybody else, he suddenly roared, 'Naza, why are you late?'

'*J'ai été surpris, mon Adjutant.*'

'Taken by surprise?' The bull neck quivered and the fat cheeks were infused with blood. 'Taken by surprise? You haven't the right to be surprised if you're a soldier. As a civilian, when you come home and find your wife in bed with the boy friend, then you may perhaps be a little surprised, but not in the army. Eight days!'

Physically, the *peloton* was not half so strenuous as my previous instruction had been. There was a combat course, nothing like as rigorous as the one at Saida, and we only ran it once a week. Every Thursday we marched to the rifle-ranges at a place called

Khamisis, about six miles from the barracks, stayed the night there under canvas, and returned the following day. This return journey on the Friday was required to be done in less than one hour, which meant double marching, with full pack, all the way; but that was the only really exhausting thing we did during the week.

On the other hand, the mental effort demanded was much greater, for the examinations at the end of the course were designed to skim off the cream of the Legion—its corps of future *sous-officiers*.

I find that I have already used this French term extensively. I am forced to do so, for there is no exact English equivalent. *Sous-officiers* are all NCOs from the rank of sergeant up—in other words, the members of the sergeants' mess. In the Legion, there is a much wider gap between sergeants and lower ranks than there is in most other armies. *Sous-officiers* of the Legion tend to keep themselves to themselves. If they mix with anybody else it is with the officers, often drinking with them and frequently, especially under active service conditions, eating with them. I have already spoken of the enormous difference between the pay of *sous-officiers* and other ranks. There is also a considerable difference in living conditions. All ranks from sergeant upwards eat in a very well-appointed mess, sleep two or three only to a room, and are entitled to the services of a batman. Finally, *sous-officiers* of the Legion are saluted by lower ranks, and do much of the work which, in most other armies, would be done by junior officers.

As a corporate body, the *sous-officiers* of the Legion somewhat resemble an exclusive club. At the end of our course there was one candidate who, it was apparent to everybody, had qualifications which should have enabled him to pass out easily among the first five or six. Most of us were therefore very much surprised to find that he was not even promoted sergeant on nomination day. We were, I say, surprised, but we were not displeased, for he was a most unpleasant fellow, selfish, arrogant, and thoroughly ill-mannered. Later on I discovered the reason for his not being promoted. The committee of NCO instructors presided over by the lieutenant, which sat to consider the results of the examinations, had not considered the man in question a desirable member of the sergeants' mess; so his nomination had been voted down.

Scheer, Kirsch, and I sewed on our two gold stripes and donned our red and blue *képis* a month before Christmas. Together we went to pay our respects to the President of the Mess.

'*Sergent Smith, nouvellement promu, mon Adjutant-chef.*'
'*Félicitations!* Have a drink, *mon vieux.*'
'Sergeant Kirsch, newly promoted.'
'Fine! Have a drink!'
'*Sergent Scheer. Mes respects, mon Adjutant-chef.*'
'*Très bien!* What are you going to drink?'

The haughty warrant officer whom we had saluted smartly every day for the past four months seemed quite a different person perched on a high stool against the bar. Twenty-seven new sergeants presented themselves to him that morning, and it must have cost him quite a bit in drinks.

A *sous-officier* pays for his messing in full. There is no entitlement to rations. Messing at that time cost about four thousand francs a month; but, as we three were still on the small rate of pay, this was provided gratuitously until we should have completed our first year's service. We inspected the amenities of this building which, as it turned out, was going to be my home for nearly two years. On the ground floor, in addition to the bar, there was a reading-room, together with a very fine library containing about ten thousand volumes. Then there was a games-room containing a half-size billiard-table. Upstairs were the two dining-halls, one for junior and one for senior NCOs.

The junior dining-hall was arranged in tables for four. We

shared our table with another newly appointed sergeant named Vigor. He was a Frenchman of Russian extraction, and had only three interests in life: ju-jitsu, eating, and reading Shakespeare in English. He was equally enthusiastic about all three. There was a very well-appointed *salle des sports* at Sidi Bel-Abbès. Whenever its doors were open, Vigor was always there, throwing himself and other people about. When the gymnasium closed, out he would come, a volume of Shakespeare under his arm. Still full of pep and vitality he would burst into the dining-room and sit down, stretching his limbs and flexing his muscles, at the risk of sending the wine carafe flying and overturning the table.

'Decontract yourself, Vigor, for heaven's sake!' we would all shout. And Vigor would smile and help himself to the potatoes. Never have I seen a man eat as he could. When he had finished everything on our table, he would tell the waiter, whom he bribed with a thousand francs a month, to bring him the leavings from all the others. I have seen him eat twenty-five hard-boiled eggs at a sitting, and then settle down to a plate of meat and half a dozen dishes of potatoes.

He attacked Shakespeare with the same enthusiasm and energy as he attacked his ring opponents and his food. I do not think he ever read anything else. He used to start at the *Tempest*, plough straight through to the sonnets, and then begin at the *Tempest* again. He knew whole chunks by heart, including some of those very long and boring speeches in *Coriolanus* and *Timon of Athens*, which scarcely any Englishman ever reads.

At the company parade two days after our nomination, the postings were announced. Kirsch and I were detailed to remain at the *peloton* as instructors. Scheer was posted to the Transit Company, which meant that he would very soon be off to Indo-China. Those of us who were retained as instructors were told to be present at the colonel's office at two o'clock in the afternoon.

We already knew something of the colonel. He was popularly

known as 'The Terror', and everybody was afraid of him, in ascending proportion according to their rank. The men never omitted to salute smartly, very smartly, whenever he passed. The NCOs froze into a glacial immobility, and prayed inwardly that his eye would not chance to fall on them. As for the officers, they went in abject fear and trembling whenever the colonel was in the neighbourhood. In twenty-seven years, during which he had held every rank in the Legion between second-class recruit and the one he then held, he had learnt everything and knew how to do everything, generally much better than the people whose job it was to do it. I once saw him watching a recruit who was whitewashing a wall, and doing it very badly. When he could no longer restrain his impatience, he snatched the brush from the trembling legionnaire's hand, and with a 'Look, you damned imbecile, this is how you should do it,' finished off the job himself before the recruit's astonished eyes, stuffed the paintbrush into his gaping mouth, and made off, saying, 'I was doing that, and doing it well, twenty-five years ago. That's why they made me a colonel.'

Punctually, oh very punctually, at five minutes to two, five newly promoted sergeants were waiting in the corridor outside his office door. At two o'clock precisely a sergeant-major appeared and told us to go in. When we had saluted and removed our *képis*, the colonel, who was standing up, looked us all up and down for a minute or two without saying a word.

He was a tall, thin man, very erect and stiff in his bearing. Even in civilian clothes you would have known him for a soldier, but only a few intimate friends and his *ordonnance* knew what it cost him in physical torture to maintain that upright carriage of the body, and even fewer were those who had seen the huge, livid scar which swept across his torso from the right armpit to the left groin. Nobody seemed to be quite sure where he came from. Some said that, when he had signed his first five years' contract in 1922, he was a refugee from Russia. Others said that he was a Turk, who had had to flee the wrath of Mustapha Kemal. Nobody really knew, and certainly that enigmatical face, which hid the fire of its fierce grey eyes behind the steel-rimmed spectacles perched on the hawk-like nose—eyes which saw and a nose which smelt out everything—certainly that face might have come from anywhere between the Alps and the Urals.

'Stand at ease!' he ordered, and sat down behind his desk.

'Gentlemen,' he said, 'I am responsible for instruction. I need good instructors. I also need instructors who are capable of carrying out my orders. Bad training automatically results in higher casualties in Indo-China; we have already had too many. I will, therefore, not have my instructors sabotaging my methods of instruction, on the grounds that, "In my army we were taught to do such and such a thing. We always did such-and-such a thing; therefore, despite what the old man says, I will continue to do such-and-such a thing."

'I am going to take an example, so as to make what I mean perfectly clear to you: the use of the rifle in combat. I have no doubt that you have all learnt that the rifle may be fired from a prone position, from a kneeling position, or from an upright position, with the right upper arm horizontal, the left elbow well into the side, and so on. Let me tell you that in ninety per cent of modern warfare, and particularly in Indo-China, the soldier never has a chance to put himself into any of those positions. He never has a chance because he doesn't have time. He is fired upon at close quarters, from a distance of five or six yards, while he is on the march. If he can react within a split second, he has a chance of living. If he cannot, he is pretty certain to die.

'What, then, must we teach the soldier? We must teach him to shoot men in the same way the sportsman shoots a pheasant, or, better still, a woodcock. Split-second judgment and lightning reaction.'

The colonel sniffed sardonically.

'If you don't believe me, wait until you fall into your first ambush in Indo-China, and then try taking up the *position du tireur couché*, or some such nonsense. Your right knee will never touch the ground alive.'

He glinted his spectacles at each of us in turn.

'I trust you have grasped my meaning. You will receive copies of my training directives: they are to be followed implicitly. Understand that I will not have my instruction sabotaged by that deep-rooted, stubborn, traditional "I've always done it that way". Now get out!'

'Not very pleasant, the old man,' decided Kirsch, as we made our way back to the company.

I didn't think so either. I don't think so now. But I do know that had there been but fifty colonels of his ability and force of character in the French Army, there is a fair chance that the Vietminh would not now be occupying Hanoi.

# 20

I SHARED a room with Kirsch on the first floor of a building in the more important block of barracks (known as *Le Grand Quartier*), which contained the colonel's office and the administrative headquarters of the Legion. As time went on and on, as Christmas 1950 succeeded Camerone 1950, and Camerone came round again in 1951, we began to think that we were going to stay for ever as instructors at Sidi Bel-Abbès, and began settling ourselves in more and more comfortably. Kirsch bought some prints of Old Masters for the walls, I got hold of a locally handwoven carpet for the floor, and between us we bought a radio-set.

When the first course for which we were to act as instructors began, I saw two old friends of mine amongst the candidates: Jaderny and Blanc, with both of whom I had left the hospital at Marseilles nearly a year before. With that iron discipline inculcated by the Legion, they saluted me smartly and awaited my orders, as though they had never known me as a *bleu*. It was up to me to make the first move, and I did so. I invited both of them along with me for a drink at the canteen.

When the *peloton* began, I was made responsible for instruction on the 81-mm mortar and on topography, which included map-reading and orientation. The mortar drill executed in the Legion had always seemed to me to be sloppy, and nothing like up to the standard of the other instruction. I soon discovered why. There was no standard drill. Without consulting anybody, I adopted Royal Artillery twenty-five-pounder gun drill, word for word, gun crews kneeling to attention, everything, except the carrying of ammunition, done at the double. Very soon my mortar-firing practice on the ranges was worthy of a practice camp on Salisbury Plain. Since, for nearly two years, I was uniquely responsible for the entire training in mortar handling of all Legion sergeants promoted in North Africa, and since the tradition I had started was carried on after my departure by my successors, my system very soon became pretty well universal throughout the Legion. I will never forget the look of utter astonishment on the face of a British gunner captain who was doing a liaison tour in the Tongking Delta and saw a Legion mortar crew firing off a barrage. I'm quite sure he thought himself back at Larkhill!

There was another innovation I introduced, which I called the 'Topographic Marathon'. I'm afraid this is going to be rather technical, but I give the details so that those who understand may have some idea of the technical standard required of sergeants in the Legion. Non-technicians had better skip the next paragraph.

*Le Marathon Topographique* was a point-to-point march of about twenty miles divided into a number of laps, each of which was executed in a different way. First was a march of about four miles on a given compass bearing. If the candidate arrived at the destination, where the judge controlling the course was concealed from sight, he was then told to find the co-ordinates of the point on the map. He was then given the co-ordinates of his next station and was accorded thirty seconds for plotting the two points on a plane table and measuring off the bearing and distance. Next was a mile's march along a road of which he had to execute a sketch-map. The last lap was a ten-mile map march, without compass, over country which had changed considerably since the last revision of the map, so that, unless the candidate followed exclusively the physical detail as indicated by the contours, he was certain to go wrong. It will be seen that the successful completion of the entire marathon depended on the faultless execution of each lap. Candidates who failed to complete the march were not promoted sergeant at the end of the *peloton*.

The life of an instructor at the *peloton* was quite a pleasant one. We lived well, especially after we went up to the full rate of pay, and, providing we carried out the not very onerous duties imposed upon us, we did pretty well as we liked. As sergeants we were supposed to be in barracks by one o'clock each night unless we had a leave pass. I personally never applied for a night pass, although I often stayed out for the night. I was fortunate enough never to be caught. We spent our money freely, and when we hadn't any left we 'chalked up' drinks at the mess and paid at the end of the month.

Once a week we went with the candidates to the ranges at Khamisis and stayed there for the night. Those lesser mortals slept under canvas, as we had done when we were striving for the rank of sergeant. Now we, the demi-gods, slept on comfortable beds in a building and ate *en popote* with the officers in a little mess we had had constructed for ourselves. Very dangerous were those nights spent at Khamisis. A system rather similar, I believe, to the old German student beer-drinking circles was adopted, but with the fines paid in red wine instead of beer. There was a stipulated code of behaviour, and at the slightest infringement of it the offender had to pay for three litres. As there were rarely more than twelve of us at table, this often made for fairly heavy drinking. One morning Kirsch woke up to find he had spent the night in the stables, sleeping under the hooves of the long-suffering mules!

One day in the early summer of 1950 I came out of the mess with Vigor after partaking of my habitual breakfast of Camembert and red wine, when I was pulled up short by the strains of the *Marseillaise*. There was nothing unusual about that, for at the *Grand Quartier* visits by officials and dignitaries of a high enough rank to merit eight or sixteen bars of the refrain were frequent, and at least once a week some unfortunate sergeant had to command a guard of honour, the *Musique* had to parade in full dress on the square, and the appropriate flag or pennant was flown from the visitors' masthead.

What was unusual that morning was that the *Marseillaise* was followed by *God Save the King!* While remaining at the salute, I glanced at the flagpole on the visitors' side of the guardroom. Sure enough, the Union Jack was flapping away merrily, and a British general was inspecting the guard. I had a queer feeling in the pit of my stomach, and I think it was the first and last time during the whole of my five years that I felt thoroughly homesick. I pointed at the flag.

'Gosh!' I said to cover up my feelings. 'They even managed to put it the right way up without consulting me.'

Vigor, who was standing close by, looked at me quizzically. His extensive reading of Shakespeare had taught him to recognize a cheap remark when he heard one.

There were a lot of official visits to Sidi Bel-Abbès during that summer, more especially by sailors. The French Navy, the British Navy, and the United States Navy all descended upon us from time to time. So far as the latter two were concerned, I was rather vaguely designated as the chief official interpreter.

I call the visits 'official' and, indeed, they generally started off in a fairly stiff and formal way. The parties were usually about a hundred strong: a dozen or so officers, twenty warrant officers and CPOs, and the rest seamen. They mostly arrived in buses, except for the senior officers, who came by car, round about ten in the morning. They were shown round by the interpreters until midday, and then were invited to lunch in the appropriate messes. On some occasions I had to accompany the officers, but if there were an officer interpreter available, I went along with the WOs and usually acted as host. We were given a private room in the mess in which to entertain our visitors and we generally managed to scrape up an equal number of English-speaking *sous-officiers* to sit down with them. We would eat a specially prepared, magnificent meal, and the wine would flow freely, for, believe me, the Legion knows how to entertain. We made speeches and, when we were no longer capable of making them, we swapped stories and sang. Times without number the sergeants' mess at Sidi Bel-Abbès has resounded to the traditional 'folk-songs' known and loved in British messes, roared boisterously by well-oiled Naval voices.

At last, about four o'clock in the afternoon, word would be sent from the officers' mess, and we would leave the table in order to start rounding up the seamen who had been entertained by the legionnaires. Finding the seamen was easy enough; the difficulty was finding their hats, since, as a result of that extraordinary manifestation of friendship which seems to be almost universally traditional on such occasions, all the legionnaires would be wearing sailor hats and all the sailors white-covered *képis*. After about half an hour's juggling, we usually managed to get the headgear sorted out and the sailors on to the buses. Then we would wave good-bye and wait for the next arrivals.

On one occasion an incident occurred which might have had most embarrassing consequences. Certain units of the British Mediterranean Fleet had put in to Mers-el-Kebir and were due to remain there for three or four days. On the first day a visiting party came down to see us, and among the warrant officers was an old boy with twenty-eight years' service who got thoroughly pickled. He went out into the town, got even more pickled, ran out of money, sold part of his uniform to pay for more drink, and finally walked into the recruiting office in his shirt tails and volunteered to join the Legion. I knew nothing whatsoever about all this at the time. All that I, or the officer commanding the party, knew was that, when the buses left, the warrant officer in question was missing.

A couple of days later another party came down from the same ship, but this time the admiral, whose flagship it was, came down with them. There was, of course, all the usual pomp and circumstance, guard of honour to present arms, the Union Jack on the visitors' flagpole at the gate, and the band to play the French and British National Anthems when the old man arrived and was greeted by the colonel.

That day I had to act as officers' interpreter and go round with the colonel while he was showing the admiral the various points of interest. At the very moment we entered the gates of the *petit quartier*, out came a fatigue party of *bleus*, and among them, dressed in the most indescribably shabby mixture of uniforms— I have already told how recruits were dressed until they started their training—with all his hair shaved off, and looking as miserable as sin, was the warrant officer!

I could see by the startled look on his face that the admiral had spotted him (I learnt later that he was a member of the admiral's personal staff), but the old boy didn't say a word. That must have occurred at about eleven o'clock in the morning. After the tour of inspection was over, we all went along to the officers' mess, where apéritifs were served, and conversation up till lunch-time was almost exclusively about naval strategy. Still the admiral hadn't said a word about his missing warrant officer.

It was a very good lunch, copiously irrigated with burgundy followed by champagne. At about three o'clock in the afternoon, the colonel, well under way and unbending more than I had ever seen him do before, made a speech in which, among other things, he said something like this: 'And now, my dear Admiral, that I have told you how much we have enjoyed and appreciated your visit to us here at Sidi Bel-Abbès, let me put that appreciation in a more tangible form. What would you like to take away with you, when you return to your ship, as a souvenir of your visit to the Foreign Legion?'

This was the chance for which the admiral had been waiting patiently for four hours.

'My warrant officer,' he replied calmly, without even troubling to take the cigar out of his mouth.

'I beg your pardon,' said the colonel.

'My warrant officer,' repeated the admiral, and he explained the situation. 'For all I care,' he concluded, 'he could do his five years in the Legion and be damned. But he happens to be the only fellow who can keep my charts in order. I've been in a hell of a mess since he disappeared.'

The colonel, it was obvious, knew nothing at all about the business. He told me to get on the phone to the CP 3 and confirm it, which I did. The colonel was as good as his word. It appeared that the warrant officer had already signed his contract, but that was torn up; he was released, and was even lent a suit of civilian clothes to enable him to return to his ship.

The colonel issued orders that the regimental number under which the sailor had been incorporated was to be left vacant.

'I'm keeping it for the next member of the Royal Navy I catch,' he told the admiral. 'And the next time I'm not going to make any rash offers!'

# 21

'*Messieurs, à vos places!*' shouted the President of the Mess. 'To your places, please, gentlemen. The colonel's coming up the stairs.'

We moved to the table which we always occupied for these occasions and sat down. The four-piece orchestra, installed in a corner of the dining-hall, prepared for action. All along the two long rows of tables loaded with bottles, *sous-officiers* were shuffling into place.

'*Garde-à-vous!*' barked the President, and all two hundred of us sprang to a rigid attention. At the same time the orchestra broke out into the March of the Legion, the colonel came in, remained at the salute while the refrain was being played, and, followed by his retinue of officers, advanced to the place reserved for him at the top table.

'Sit down, gentlemen,' he said. 'Gérard, you little bounder, come up here and sit with me.'

Gérard was a sergeant who had been punished with fifteen days' close arrest four days before, but the annual amnesty on the occasion of Camerone had lifted the sentence and, according to tradition, Gérard had to go up and drink at the officers' table with the colonel who had punished him.

For Camerone had come round once again, my third since I joined the Legion, and my second as a sergeant-instructor at the *peloton*. The scene was the sergeants' mess at Sidi Bel-Abbès, and it was midday on April 30th, 1951. The parade and the march past the Colours had just finished, and the colonel was getting together with his officers and NCOs to drink a glass or two with us, in the best traditions of the Legion, before going on to lunch.

The silence caused by his entry was now broken by the orchestra, which struck up the song that was the overture to all sessions of this nature.

> '*Trink, trink, Bruederlein, trink.*
> *Lasse die Sorgen zu Haus. . . .*'

We all joined in the chorus, whether we knew German or not. Arm in arm, we swayed from side to side beating the measure of the song, until the last refrain had died away. Then the buzz of conversation once more took the place of the music. It was always the same sort of conversation on those occasions.

'Have you heard anything of so-and-so who was with us at Mascara?'

'Yes, I hear he's with the Fifth Regiment in Central Annam, commanding a platoon. By the way, you don't know what has happened to what's-his-name?'

'Oh, he got his last month, poor beggar. Patrol on the Cambodian frontier.'

'Pity! By the way, I hear that old thingummyjig's back again. Do you remember how he went off, saying that wild horses wouldn't drag him back to the Legion again? Well, old Moreau, who works in the *Bureau de Récrutement*, tells me he signed on in Paris for another five years two days ago.'

And at our table: 'Well, Hans,' I was saying, 'here we are again. Do you remember Camerone two years ago? All four of us in jug! That reminds me, I had a letter from Sibley this morning. He's in the third battalion of the Thirteenth D.-B., and who d'you think is his platoon commander? Yes, Lopez, now *adjutant*! But that's not the best. Sibley, as a corporal, is commanding one of the sections of the platoon—my glass is empty, by the way—another is commanded by Corporal Jaderny. . . .'

'Well, I'm damned!' Kirsch surveyed his own empty glass. 'Smith, would you mind giving me a drink out of that bottle, if it's not reserved for you personally. Just like a bloody Englishman to hog everything for himself. Thanks. Well, here's to you. And,' he continued with a change in his voice, 'here's to Scheer.'

We drank in silence. Scheer had been killed during the retreat from Langson a few months before.

'Do you realize now,' I said, when we had drained our glasses and filled them up again. 'Do you realize what a damned silly mistake we made, to come out among the first in the *sous-officier* examinations? We might have known that we'd be retained here as instructors. And The Terror's not ready to let us go yet, either. You mark my words, Hans, we'll still be here at Christmas, you especially. You're a born instructor, and the old man knows it.'

'Rot! He'll have to let us go in time for us to do a two years' tour in Indo-China, anyway.'

'Talking about the old man,' said another sergeant at our table, an instructor at the corporal school. 'Have you heard what happened at Khamisis the other day when you weren't there? Our *peloton* was at a shooting practice and Lieutenant Plon was in charge. The old man arrived, took one look at what was going on, and started hauling poor old Plon over the coals in front of his entire *peloton* there assembled.

' "*Imbécile!*" he cried, "I don't need a nitwit like you to teach these fellows how to shoot. Run away home. Wait a bit, though. How many rounds have you expended thus far? A thousand? Completely wasted! They cost twenty-five francs apiece, which makes a total of twenty-five thousand francs. I'll have that sum docked off your pay at the end of the month." And apparently he did, or at least so Plon told me.'

'Does anybody know the details of the scandal at the cookhouse in the *petit quartier*?' asked someone else.

'I do,' said Vigor. 'I was there. It was damned funny. It

reminded me of a scene out of *Henry IV*. I'd just come away from the *salle des sports* after dislocating Hammerstein's shoulder. There was still half an hour to wait for dinner-time in the mess, and I was feeling peckish, so I went along to the cookhouse over the road to see if I could pick up something to eat. As you know, things have been going badly over there, and lots of complaints have been made about the quality and quantity of the food served to the men. I arrived there just as they were going to dish out the *soupe*, and about a minute afterwards in comes the old man, making a surprise visit to find out exactly what's going on. The sergeant-cook calls everybody up to attention. The colonel walks straight up to him and says, "Show me a man's ration." So, of course, the sergeant—you know Kunzinger, the fat old bastard—he produces a plate with a bloody great slab of meat weighing two or three pounds on it, beautifully garnished with chipped potatoes and a piece of parsley or something, and hands it to the old man.

'The Terror looks at it, sneering all the way down both sides of his beak. "*Tu t'fous de ma gueule?*" he asks very quietly; and then, in a voice of thunder that must have been heard as far as the swimming-pool, "I asked to see a man's ration, not a royal banquet, you fat excrescence."

'Kunzinger trembles like a trapped football, so much so that he is quite unable to reply. "All right," says the colonel. "If you can't show me, I'll find it myself." He seizes a ladle and walks up to the pot, dips in and fishes out a piece of meat about the size of a ten-franc piece, which he pours into the hollow of his hand. He looks at it quizzically.

' "Tell me, Kunzinger," he says, "is that a man's ration?"

' "A very small one, *mon Colonel*."

' "Don't bandy words with me, you fatness. Would you or would you not serve that piece of meat as the ration of one man?"

' "*Oui, mon Colonel*."

' "Well, eat it yourself then, you fat hog," roars the old man, and he slaps the piece of meat, gravy and all, into Kunzinger's face.

'After that, he made a tour of the entire administrative services of the *petit quartier*, starting with the captain. I timed him. In exactly six minutes he dished out two hundred and eighty-five days of prison and close arrest. But they'll probably eat a little better over——'

'Ssh!' said Kirsch. 'The old man.'

The colonel had risen to his feet and the buzz of conversation slowly died down. When there was complete silence in the room, he began to speak.

'Gentlemen,' he said, 'we celebrate today the eighty-eighth anniversary of Camerone. It is a festive occasion, and rightly so. It is also a sad occasion, and rightly so. It is sad because we remember the sacrifices made by our predecessors in the name of our inflexible motto, *Honneur et Fidélité*. And it is right that we should think for a moment of our comrades fallen on many battlefields before and since Camerone, in all parts of the world where the Legion has fought and is fighting still.

'For the story of Camerone is simply this: that against overwhelming odds a handful of men tactically defeated fought on, faithful to the vow they had made, to the bitter end. Gentlemen, let me tell you, that has always been and will always be the lot of the Legion. Remember what General MacMahon said to that Legion battalion, before he sent them into the battle of Magenta. "*Légionnaire, tu es né pour mourir, et je t'envoie là où on meurt.*" That was brutal, if you like. "Legionnaires, you are born to die, so I'm sending you where men get killed." But the truth is always brutal, and MacMahon was speaking to men who were not afraid of the truth.

'Today, ninety-one years after the battle of Magenta and eighty-eight years after the battle of Camerone, the Legion's destiny remains unchanged. And, let pessimists say what they will to the contrary, the character of the legionnaire has not changed either. At the present time in Indo-China, isolated, heroic actions are being fought every day of the week. They do not make newspaper headlines, but the unknown, unsung heroes who leave their bones in the corner of some ricefield in Tongking don't really care much about newspapers.

'Now let's talk of happier things. Gérard, I don't in the least mind your filling up my glass when I'm not looking, but I very strongly object to your imagining that I didn't notice you doing it. Yes, let's talk of pleasant things. First of all, I would like to congratulate the fifteen new sergeants who have been promoted today. It is not my place to welcome you into that select circle which is the corps of *sous-officiers* of the Legion. Your President will do that, and do it extremely well, I'm sure. But I will say this.

'You, the *sous-officiers*, are the very stuff of the Legion, without whom the whole organization and discipline would collapse. When I look round me and see the sort of human material with which I am supposed to effectuate my command at the higher levels—Captain Boileau, shut your mouth: there might be a photographer in the room—when I see that, gentlemen, well, I thank God for the *sous-officiers*.'

The twenty or so officers sitting at the colonel's table looked very uneasy and sheepish. This was one of the old man's well-known *tours de force*. They had suspected that something like it was coming, and had waited for it in an agony of expectation. As everybody had noticed, the colonel had not even been looking in the direction of Captain Boileau when he had told that gallant officer to shut his mouth, and yet the captain's mouth had quite definitely been wide open. A senior major gritted his teeth. 'This time,' he seemed to be saying to himself, 'I really will lodge a complaint.' But he probably knew at the bottom of his heart that he wouldn't.

'Now, a *sous-officier* of the Legion,' continued the colonel, 'can be employed in one of two ways. I leave out of consideration the horde of stamp- and arse-lickers who work in the various *bureaux*.' He glared at a group of mild-eyed, pale-faced sergeants seated near to the orchestra. 'NCOs, real NCOs, can be employed either as chiefs of combat groups in action or as instructors. I happen here and now to be responsible for instruction, and if some of you had enough grey matter in your heads to be able to work out a simple arithmetical sum, you might be able to calculate that, with an intake of between a hundred and a hundred and fifty recruits a week, I have something like a thousand men to train in each instruction period of two months, to say nothing of the special training required for the formation of NCOs.

'And that is why, Messieurs Kirsch, Smith and company, I don't want to see any more demands for transfer to the Far East from you. You'll go to Indo-China when it pleases me to send you, and not before.'

'This is his idea of talking of pleasant things,' whispered Kirsch.

'Must be quite charming when he's unpleasant,' I replied.

'Gentlemen,' concluded the colonel, 'today is Camerone. I'm not going to tell you not to get drunk, because I know perfectly well that most of you are half-drunk already. So I'll just say, don't get too drunk. I lift my glass to the memory of Camerone, to the corps of *sous-officiers*, and—*à la Légion!*'

He spoke the last words in a rising crescendo which brought everybody to their feet, and the orchestra once more attacked the stirring rhythm of the march.

'*Tiens! Voilà du boudin, voilà du boudin!*' chimed in two hundred voices until, the refrain ended, we drained our glasses and remained standing until the colonel and his officers had left the room.

Indo-China. I had been over two years in the Legion and was still in North Africa. Men with whom I joined had already been a year and a half in the Far East. I had seen some come back already, wounded. There were many who would never come back at all. Two hundred and fifty sergeants had passed through my hands and learnt most of what they knew about mortar handling and map-reading from me. I needed a change of air. But—'you'll go to Indo-China when it pleases me . . . ,' the colonel had said.

It came at last, however. In the early autumn of that year Kirsch and I were both released from the *peloton* and were sent to the Transit Camp at a place called Nouvion, about midway between Oran and Algiers, where a draft for Indo-China was being assembled. We were to embark at Algiers at the end of September. About five or six days before we were due to join the boat, I went out for a spin on a motor-cycle. Hurtling along a country road at sixty miles an hour, I ran into a farm-cart, and landed myself in hospital for two months with a broken leg.

Kirsch came to see me the day before he sailed.

'Keep in touch,' he said. 'You'll be out of here in a month or two, and we'll meet up somewhere in Saigon or Hanoi, and have an evening together.'

Alas, we never did. Six weeks later to the day the best friend I ever had in the Legion was killed in a minor action somewhere in the Tongking Delta.

# 22

When I was fit again, I was told that I could, if I wished, remain in North Africa for the remainder of my five years' contract. If, on the other hand, I wished to do my regulation two years' tour in the Far East, I would have to renew my contract for an additional six months. I accepted the second alternative, for I was determined to see something of the Far East during my service with the Legion. There were, however, innumerable delays before I finally embarked on a very slow boat, and so I did not arrive at Saigon until March of the following year, 1952.

The voyage was as boring as a voyage on a troopship usually is, and surely of all sea voyages one accomplished on a troopship is by far the most monotonous. In the Suez Canal we passed another trooper of legionnaires returning from Indo-China.

'*Vous vous trompez de chemin!*' they shouted at us. 'You're going the wrong way!'

Two days later, in the Red Sea, we passed a British trooper on its way back to England.

'You're going the wrong way!' shouted the Tommies.

Two or three newly promoted sergeants from the *peloton* at Sidi Bel-Abbès were on the boat with me. One of them, a Dutchman by the name of Weeland, had the misfortune to disembark at Saigon as a private soldier. This was what happened.

Weeland, a somewhat reserved and taciturn fellow of about thirty-five, was detailed ship's orderly sergeant for the day of embarkation. Among the troops embarked was a detachment of

Senegalese commanded by a little, pimply-faced, French second-lieutenant. This officer told Weeland to collect a fatigue party of legionnaires and have six large packing-cases brought on board. Weeland did so, with a bad grace, for there seemed to be no earthly reason why the officer should not have used his own troops for the job, and the orderly sergeant already had his hands very full.

'The odd thing,' Weeland told me, after the ship had sailed, 'was that those packing-cases were all empty. But that was not what annoyed me. Would you believe it? That pimply little squirt addressed me as "*Tu*". I don't mind *tutoiement* from a Legion officer with a certain amount of experience, but coming from that little twerp of a colonial infantryman, it damned well annoyed me. What the hell does he want with empty packing-cases, anyhow?'

When we arrived at Djibouti we found out. The lieutenant bought thousands and thousands of packets of American cigarettes and packed the cases full. At that time a packet of Chesterfield or Lucky Strike, bought for eighty francs at Djibouti, was selling for three hundred and fifty at Saigon. Weeland and I calculated that there must have been something like twenty thousand pounds' profit in those six cases.

It was just his luck that it came round to his turn for orderly sergeant again the day we docked at Saigon. When the time came to off-load the baggage, up trotted the pimply one again.

'Sergeant,' he said, 'just send along a fatigue party of legionnaires to carry those packing-cases off the boat.'

Weeland was leaning up against the rail, talking to me.

'Go and get some of your Senegalese to do your dirty work,' he said. He spoke over his shoulder, without even troubling to turn round and look at the officer.

'Don't be insolent to me, Sergeant, or I'll put you on a charge,' snapped the lieutenant.

'*Va te faire enculer!*' replied Weeland negligently over his shoulder. That was a very rude and vulgar thing to say; and the officer, who was very annoyed, did an extremely foolish thing. He took hold of Weeland's arm and tried to pull him round to face himself. The Dutchman took one smack at him and over the side he went into the stinking waters of the harbour. Weeland fished a jack-knife out of his pocket and handed it to me.

'Cut 'em off, please,' he said, pointing to his stripes.

We spent four days at Saigon, in the Legion Transit Camp there, while waiting for the boat to Haiphong. Very few legionnaires out of our draft were retained in Cochin-China, for it was already becoming obvious that the Tongking Delta was going to be the scene of the death struggle. As we had nothing much to do during those four days, we seized the opportunity to see something of the town, the largest and most modern that many of us had seen for a long time.

In Saigon money flowed like water; not our money, for we were nearly all penniless after the voyage, except for those who had won at poker. The streets were full of large American cars. The cafés and night-clubs were full of both military and civilians. Ships could scarcely bring champagne quick enough, at two pounds a bottle, to supply the demand. Huge fortunes changed hands every night in the Chinese *bac quangs*, or gambling-dens. People paid cheerfully as much as thirty piastres—about ten shillings at the then rate of exchange—for a packet of English or American cigarettes. It all seemed very gay.

Two years later, on my way home, I again spent a couple of days in Saigon. By then I knew that all that richness, all that boundless river of gold—and money surely circulated faster in Saigon than anywhere else in the world—all those luxurious night-clubs, those gambling-dens, and those high-powered cars were bought with the blood of my dead comrades; the place made me sick.

The Indo-Chinese were sharply divided into two classes: on the one hand were the peasants and labourers who worked, and wore the national costume of loose, drab trousers and a floppy blouse. On the other, the shopkeepers and business magnates, the pimps, the panderers, and the black-marketeers, all of whom made money and wore European clothes. I am speaking, for the moment, of the men. Situated somewhere between the two classes was the whole army of pedallers of *cyclo-pousses*. These last are the national form of taxi, and consist of a sort of tricycle with a seat for the passenger in front. The driver sits behind and pedals you to the place where you want to go. These *cyclo-pousse* drivers were the minor criminals and gangsters of the whole rotten set-up.

The women were also divided into two classes: those who worked and those who whored. You think, perhaps, that I am forgetting the married women who were mothers of families. Oh no! These latter, if they were of the working-class, worked, and at the sort of work which is generally not done by women in more civilized countries: road-mending, stone-breaking, bricklaying, for example. When the time came for them to have a baby, they left off this work, had it, then came back and went on mixing mortar. And if they were not of the working kind, well, they just went out and whored, mothers of six or no, while papa sat at home and smoked his pipe of opium.

In my view the Indo-Chinese were a very primitive people, but, like many such peoples, they had that innate cunning which enabled them to absorb and profit from the worst features of the Europeans who had colonized them. I think they must have already been degenerate when the French first arrived amongst them in the last century, and, frankly, I suppose that the French have been anything but a good influence on them.

In conversation with Europeans who know nothing at all of the Far East, I have found that they tend to confuse these people with the Chinese. It should be remembered that, while they have a certain charm and a very limited culture which is all their own, they are not to be compared with their great northern neighbours. Their language, Annamite, bears no resemblance to Chinese, and, until eighty years ago, it was a purely spoken one. It was a European, a Portuguese, who taught them for the first time to write their own simple, monosyllabic language.

They are, by the way, incapable of reading silently. In order to understand what they are reading, they must read aloud. The noise made by a native schoolroom engaged in silent study is unbelievable.

Musically, they are equally undeveloped. Never give an Indo-Chinese a guitar, or any other musical instrument. He will start playing it at six o'clock in the morning and go on until midnight. During the whole of that time he will play one tune, about sixteen bars long, just as many times as he can play those sixteen bars in eighteen hours. If you tell him to change the record, he just laughs and goes on playing the same tune. He can't do anything about it, because he only knows that one. The next morning at six o'clock he will start up again. Round about midday you put your foot through the guitar, and the next morning you wake up, or rather you don't wake up, with a knife in your back.

This picture I have given you of the Indo-Chinese is perhaps superficial and probably inaccurate, but it certainly represents them as we, the vulgar soldiery, saw them and went on seeing them for two years.

The second night at Saigon I went out into town with a *sous-officier* who had come out on the boat with me. It was his second tour in the Far East, and he offered to show me round. We ate at a native restaurant: *soupe chinoise*, *nems* (a sort of rissole), salad and *ngoc man* (the native sauce made from rotten fish and smelling like a sewer). Then we went and had a few beers to get rid of the taste.

'Let's go along to the *Parc aux Bufles*,' said my companion. Not wishing to show my ignorance, I went with him.

Imagine an enormous building about the size of a royal palace, built in the form of a hollow square surrounding a central courtyard; the entire building, with the exception of a bar about thirty feet long by twenty wide, being divided into a honeycomb of five or six hundred tiny rooms.

We went in at the main entrance, where a military policeman was on duty, and found ourselves in the courtyard, where about three hundred native women were milling about, talking, smoking, laughing, winking, and trying in a variety of ways to attract the attention of the soldiery, which was also present in force. Most of the women were dressed in native costume, their diaphanous silk trousers revealing their spindly legs. A few, the ones with the better developed calf and thigh muscles, affected the European skirt.

The first thing that happened to me on entering the courtyard was to have my *képi* swept off my unsuspecting head by an unseen hand. On looking round, I saw one of the little female apes grinning all over her face and beckoning to me; but, as soon as she saw that I had located my headgear, she darted off to the bar and ordered two drinks, which I had to pay for. I then made a renewed attempt to recover my hat, but it soon became evident that this was held as a sort of hostage, only to be redeemed at the price of half an hour in bed with the holder. My companion, who apparently was a hardened habitué of the *Parc aux Bufles*, had tied on his *képi* with string.

'Yes,' he said, grinning at my astonishment. 'This is the *Parc aux Bufles*. A *bordel*, and some *bordel*! There are over four hundred permanent inmates here, all under military control. If the French achieved nothing else in Indo-China, their memory will be for ever perpetuated by the Buffalo Park, the biggest military brothel in the world.'

I was glad I had come to the place, not only because it was something of an experience, but because I met an old friend there, a man who had been a recruit with me in the same training section at Saida. He was a German by the name of Vogel, and I happened to know, quite by accident, something about him of which even the Legion authorities were ignorant. He had been a captain in the SS, and not only in the SS, but on the headquarters of that fanatically devout division, the *Leibstandarte Adolf Hitler*.

Vogel had been an undiluted product of National Socialism and, whatever else might have been said about him, I am pretty sure that he had been utterly sincere in his opinions. In the Legion he kept himself very much to himself, and seemed to spend most of his time sitting in a corner writing poetry. I read some of that poetry. It was awfully bitter, disillusioned stuff. Vogel, you see, had had the bottom kicked clean out of his little world with the defeat of Germany. Well, of course, he was a German, and not only a German, but a member of an organization which had been the cause of death and misery for millions. I know all that; I also know that not all Germans were sincere in their beliefs, and that many of them, once things started going badly, had very little faith in National Socialism.

But Vogel, I think, did believe, right up to the last, bitter, catastrophic moment. Never had he had the slightest doubt about the rightness of the cause or about its final success. For him National Socialism was not just a political doctrine but a religion. For him Adolf Hitler was not just a statesman but a god.

And there he was in the *Parc aux Bufles*, leaning up against the bar with some frightful woman and quoting Rilke to her! The funny thing was that she appeared to be hanging on to his words as though they were the last prophecy of Buddha. She didn't understand a word he was saying, of course, but I must admit she was holding his *képi* tightly clenched in her dirty little fist, so she was probably reckoning on getting fifty piastres to recompense her suffering.

Vogel was still a second-class legionnaire. I asked him why he hadn't troubled to rise in rank—he could easily have done so—but he told me that it just didn't interest him. There were a lot of fellows like that in the Legion, fellows with considerable military ability who preferred to remain private soldiers.

We had a few drinks together, and I asked him what he thought about the situation in Indo-China. He had already been there for two and a half years, whereas I was a new-comer.

'From a political point of view,' he said, 'the best thing the French could do would be to make peace with Ho Chi Minh immediately—he is the real representative of the Indo-Chinese people—push Bao Dai and his rotten administration, the most corrupt in the world even including China, into the sea, and negotiate for the retention of two or three trading concessions, such as Hanoi, Haiphong, and Saigon. If they don't do this, sooner or later the Chinese will come in either openly or by infiltration, and then the French won't be allowed to stay anywhere in Tongking. The Chinese'll want that for themselves.

'From the military point of view, well, we've just lost the only commander-in-chief who was ever any good and who's ever likely to be any good. I wouldn't like to give an opinion on General de Lattre's tactical ability, but one thing is certain—he made the officers of the expeditionary force sit up and take the war seriously, instead of treating it as a sort of money-making picnic.'

Those were Legionnaire Vogel's views as expressed one evening in April 1952 in the Buffalo Park in Saigon. I didn't see him again. His battalion was sent up to Tongking a month later, and he was killed in a minor action near Phuly.

# 23

THE distance from the port of Haiphong to Hanoi, the capital of Tongking, is exactly one hundred kilometres. The journey could be accomplished by air, road, or rail; but the only really safe way of travelling was by air. By road there was a slight risk of being ambushed, while by rail there was a considerable risk of being blown up by a mine; but the day my detachment boarded the train at Haiphong we were lucky.

The road between Haiphong and Hanoi, together with the rail-track which ran parallel to it, was, like most of the other main lines of communication in the Tongking Delta, being kept open only with great difficulty. Generally speaking, these main roads were under the control of the French Union troops by day and of the Vietminhs and their partisans by night. It was a pity that the French allowed this situation to persist. A famous writer on military tactics, whose name I have forgotten, said—and I rather think he said it in French—'He who is master of the night is master of the battlefield.' I have only forgotten the name of the writer: the French High Command appeared to have forgotten what he wrote!

I was being sent to a Transport Company, and wasn't particularly pleased about it. (I had set my mind on going to the 13th D.-B. because of old associations.) In Indo-China, although the Legion was essentially infantry, apart from a Regiment of Cavalry and the Parachute Troops, a number of legionnaires were detached to Transport, Engineer and Repair Workshop Companies, because the French regular troops lacked the necessary specialists.

The company to which I was posted occupied a disused factory in the centre of Hanoi, and was 'mixed'. That is to say, about half the NCOs and men were of the Legion, and the remainder members of the French Transport Service. Among the officers there was one who wore the *képi* of a Legion lieutenant, to make it look as though we were not quite neglected. He tried hard, but the *képi* deceived no one. It appeared that the captain commanding, who was secretly very proud of having legionnaires under his command, had decided he would bring the whole of his company up to the Legion standard of discipline. To this end he had appointed an *adjutant* of the Legion as his company sergeant-major. It was to this latter I presented myself on arrival.

'Sergeant Smith, three years' service, two years and four months in the rank, arriving from North Africa with detachment of five corporals and twenty-seven legionnaires posted to this company. *A vos ordres, mon Adjutant*.' I handed over the necessary documents. The sergeant-major gave orders to the orderly sergeant for the other ranks to be taken off my hands, and took me off to the mess for a drink.

In the shaded veranda used as a bar he ordered two cognac-sodas—the standard drink, apart from beer, during the hot season in Indo-China. I looked around. On the wall behind the bar was a photograph of General de Lattre de Tassigny, with an edging of black crêpe over one corner of the frame. I saw that picture in nearly every mess and canteen I ever entered in Indo-China. One very rarely saw the photograph of any other senior officer.

The sergeant-major's name was McAndrew. He told me, as he ordered two more cognac-sodas, that he had been posted to the company 'for a rest' two months previously after three years with infantry units up and down the Delta. Names, incidentally, are no guide to nationality in the Legion, and many recruits adopt an English-sounding name for the duration of their contract. That morning I noticed nothing remarkable about my superior, except his brilliant red nose and apparently unlimited capacity for cognac-soda.

I ordered a round of drinks, for we had been joined by two more sergeants of the Legion. The *adjutant* winked at the barman. This was a sign I was soon to learn. It was universal in Legion messes in Indo-China and signified, 'Serve the drinks, but put them down to my account. Don't let him pay for them, unless you want two extra guard duties.'

During that first day I was not allowed to pay for a single drink; but every time another *sous-officier* of the Legion came into the bar, he stood a round of which I had to partake.

'*Nom de Dieu, mon Adjutant*,' I said at midday, when we had already been standing at the bar for two hours. 'I mustn't get too drunk. When are you going to present me to the captain?'

He laughed. 'Not today, at any rate. It's your first day here and you have to get acclimatized. *Tu rentreras à quatre pattes ce soir, pour te faire piger que t'es parmi des potes.* You'll be carried to bed tonight, so you'll know you're among pals.'

He turned round, as a short, jovial-looking officer with a very red face came into the bar.

'*Mais le v'là, le 'Pitaine*,' he continued. '*Mon Capitaine*, new sergeant for you.'

The company commander, having shaken hands, slapped me on the back.

'Have a cognac-soda,' he said.

The sergeant-major had been absolutely right in his prediction. I was carried to bed that night all right. He and the captain helped with the carrying.

As Sibley had told me three years before, *sous-officiers* of the Legion tend to forget nationality among themselves. It is considered bad form to speak any other language but French in the mess, and quite unpardonable to ask a colleague what his nationality is. For ten days I never heard McAndrew speak anything but fluent French, well peppered with *argot*, or very vulgar *Wehrmacht* German. Then one day I happened to be crossing the parade-ground when he was rebuking a very callow and slovenly driver of the French Transport Service, who had just succeeded in losing a machine-gun loading apparatus and was quite incapable of giving the slightest indication as to where he had last seen it.

'*Mais, nom de Dieu! Tu dois avoir une idée, quand même, espèce de couillon!*' he shouted; and then, exasperated by the blank stare on the face of the driver, 'Hoots, mon, wull ye start to thinkin' a wee bit and take yon bletherin' daft look off yeer face?'

I stopped short. 'You wouldn't be from Scotland, by any chance?' I asked, speaking to McAndrew for the first time in English.

'Noo, I wouldna. I'm a hundred per cent American. But my oud mon was fra Inverness, and he didna care ower much for the Sassenachs.' He winked at me.

'Go and order a couple of drinks,' he said. 'I'll be there in a minute.'

'*Eh bien, enfant de malheur*,' he continued, turning once more to the unfortunate soldier. '*Veux-tu me dire où tu l'as vu pour la dernière fois?*'

'Well, you goddam, half-asleep Limey,' he roared, as he burst into the mess two minutes later. 'You're going to have to pay for champagne all round this evening, so I'll pay for these drinks now, so as you won't bust the bank. I knew who you were before you arrived, of course, on account of seeing your papers. I told the other guys that, if you discovered my nationality before the end of the first week, I'd pay for a case of fizz. As you didn't, I guess it's only right you should pay.'

We got drunk again that evening, of course, and McAndrew told me how he had come to join the Legion. At the end of the war, he had been with the American Army in France, living an extremely gay life on about three times his pay as a top-sergeant, and making up the balance by various transactions not recognized as strictly legal by the Army authorities. One day he saw real trouble coming as the result of a little deal concerning a three-ton truck complete with all its stores, disposed of to some French black-marketeers. The Military Police were on his trail, so he cleared out and hid himself in Paris, where he went on having a gay time until he had no money left.

When he had only fifty francs in his pocket he saw a poster describing the joys of being a legionnaire. He went along to the recruiting-station at the Fort de Vincennes and asked to be taken on. He was still dressed in American Army uniform. The recruiting sergeant stared at him in amazement.

'How much were you getting a month in the American Army?' he asked.

'Oh, about four hundred dollars, I guess.'

'D'you know how much you'll get here, my friend? Four hundred and fifty francs a month for the first year! That makes just about a dollar and a half!'

But McAndrew was adamant. 'I guess I'd better join, all the same,' he replied stubbornly.

'All right,' said the recruiting sergeant. 'Sign here. Now take off your uniform and put on these things. Here's a receipt for your uniform. You'll get it back in five years' time, if you're still alive. Now, listen to me. Stand to attention, damn you! You are no longer a sergeant-major in the American Army, but a second-class recruit in the French Foreign Legion. Take that mop and pail and go and scrub out the sergeants' mess; and see that you do it well.'

'The bastard,' grinned McAndrew. 'I only hope, if ever he should be posted to this company, that he's still a sergeant. He'll do orderly duty from now till Independence Day.'

After Kirsch's death I made no more close friends in the Legion.

I tried to be on friendly terms with all, but avoided being intimate with any. With McAndrew I made the exception of a purely drinking companion, both in and out of billets, and we frequently made a round of the *bistros* in Hanoi together. Mac invented a game which was utterly puerile but amused both of us. We would go into a café and have a couple of drinks. As soon as there were a few other military types in the bar, Mac would suddenly turn and shout at me in pretended fury.

'You lousy, bloody Limey!'

'You insufferable, damned Yankee!' I would shout back.

'You ugly son of a Liverpool whore,' he would scream, squaring up to me.

'You misbegotten leavings of a Kansas City bitch!' I would yell, clenching my fists.

By this time the crowd would be swarming in from the street, eagerly waiting for the fight to start. Mac and I would then pay for our drinks and walk out arm-in-arm, leaving the crowd gaping. We would turn a couple of corners, walk into another café and repeat the performance.

It never seemed to occur to us to amuse ourselves in a way more stimulating to our intellects than to our livers. There was something about that atmosphere which stultified the mind and precluded all serious, or even semi-serious, thought. Yet there was, for example, a theatre in Hanoi, and there were often quite good concerts to be heard. But no, when we went into town, drinking and whoring were the order of the day. Pity!

I cannot close this chapter without telling you about the American lady journalist. I was introduced to her one evening on the Terrace of the *Taverne Royale* by another American civilian who lived in Hanoi and with whom I had a drink from time to time. She had apparently come to Indo-China to write a series of articles for some magazine on the war in general and the Legion in particular.

'Oh, of course,' she told me, 'I know all about the Foreign Legion. About ninety per cent German, aren't they?'

I told her I thought that figure slightly exaggerated.

'Oh, you can't tell me,' she said, smiling. 'I've heard 'em talking on the sidewalks and in the cafés here. They all talk German.'

At that moment four legionnaires from my company passed in front of our table. I knew them quite well. They were a Pole, a Czech, a German, and a Hungarian. All four were jabbering away together in German.

'There you are,' said the young woman. 'There are four of them. I know by the look of them. I don't even need to hear them talking.'

That gave me an idea.

'Would you be free tomorrow evening round about six o'clock? If so I'd like to have you come along and take a cocktail at our mess.'

She agreed, and we fixed on a time and place for me to pick her up. In the meantime I arranged for all the *sous-officiers* of the Legion at the company—there were exactly ten of us—to be present at the mess at six o'clock the following evening.

When I arrived with her, all nine of them were there, drinking at the bar. I showed her to a seat a little distance from the bar, and we sat down. My comrades bowed to the lady when she came in, and then went on talking, in French, of course. The barman brought the drinks I had ordered. My fair companion seemed to be a little mystified.

'I suppose,' she said, 'that nearly all senior noncoms are Frenchmen.'

'Oh no,' I replied, 'by no means. As a matter of fact, among the ten members of this mess, including myself, whom you see assembled here, there is not a single Frenchman.' I gave a prearranged signal, and all nine of my comrades began talking in German.

'Ah, I get it,' said the journalist. 'They're all Germans, of course, though I must admit, they speak pretty good French.'

'Oh no,' I said again, 'by no means. As a matter of fact, among my nine comrades whom you see here, there is not a single German.'

'Say, what is this?' she asked, and I quickly ordered some more drinks. 'Are you trying to take a rise out of me?'

'No, please, don't think that,' I soothed. 'What I'm telling you is the absolute truth. There is not a single Frenchman and not one German amongst us here. To be frank with you, I didn't even know that until this morning, when I amused myself by finding out what the various nationalities of my messmates were. We don't normally trouble much about that sort of thing in the Legion, but, as you were coming along, I took the trouble to find out by asking the only one of us who was in a position to know. That's the big fellow there; he's company sergeant-major, and has access to the records. Let me introduce him to you.'

I beckoned Mac over.

'Miss Blank, let me introduce *Adjutant* McAndrew from Kansas City. Mac, meet Miss Blank from New York, who thought you were a German.'

They shook hands, and Mac laughed.

'That's not surprising,' he said. 'We all speak a little of the language, anyhow. Have to in this outfit. But I'd like to have you meet the rest of the lads, Miss Blank. Smith, you know already. This is Vandemeer, a Belgian; Devos, here, is a Dutchman; Schmidt, despite his name and Nordic appearance, is a Russian, and this handsome fellow is Barcsz, who comes from Poland. Czanardy comes from Hungary. Next to him is Karcev from Yugoslavia. Finally we have Mainardi from Italy and Sanchez from Spain. Last but not least, although he's not included in the number, is the barman whose name is Aldo. We don't quite know where he comes from, but I know where he's going to if he doesn't get a move on and serve those six bottles of champagne I told him to put on ice half an hour ago.'

Aldo bestirred himself. There was a rapid popping of champagne corks, and we all said, 'Here's mud in your eye', to one another. When I took Miss Blank back to her hotel an hour or so later, she was a bit mellowed by the drink, but I had the impression that she was still a little sore at me. And, of course, she wrote her damned silly articles just as she'd intended to write them all along. Ninety per cent Germans, mostly SS, and all the usual nonsense. I suppose that's what the public wants.

# 24

IF you've been thinking that, during those first few weeks with the Transport Company at Hanoi, I did very little to further the local war effort, you're quite right. None of us did, though so far as the local brewers and distillers were concerned, each and every one of us deserved a silver medal. There were hundreds, nay thousands, like us in Hanoi: officers and *sous-officiers* who sat behind desks doing nothing all day and others who didn't even put up the pretence of sitting behind desks.

And all the time combat units were screaming for cadre! In the mud and filth of the Delta ricefields, where the fighting was going on, a platoon which in theory is commanded in action by a lieutenant, was frequently commanded by a sergeant and sometimes even by a corporal. Yet the colonels and lieutenant-colonels with whom Hanoi was infested all had corporals for batmen and sergeants or even sergeant-majors as chauffeurs! At least two gold stripes were considered necessary in order to command the keys of a typewriter, and to supervise a general's kitchen staff you had to be a warrant officer.

God save old Ireland! There was even an *adjutant-chef*—a regimental sergeant-major, if you please—whose noble task it was to jump on a motor-cycle and deliver the official mail from one headquarters in the town to another, a job which any acting unpaid lance-corporal would have considered a sinecure! That *adjutant-chef* was probably earning between a hundred and twenty and a hundred and fifty thousand francs a month, for working about two hours a day as an unskilled postman.

When I left the Far East as a *sergent-chef*, or senior sergeant, I was earning one hundred and seventeen pounds a month and other ranks were paid in proportion. A lieutenant would get between a hundred and forty and a hundred and eighty according to his seniority and qualifications. All pay in the theatre of operations was free of tax. In other words, the French Army in Indo-China was the best-paid army in the world. The Americans were not in the running!

In general, I quite honestly believe that excessive pay deteriorates the fighting qualities of an army. It means that the soldier can be married, send money home, and, if he is an officer or senior NCO, build up a tidy balance in the bank; and all this tends to make him 'look over his shoulder' and watch his interests rather than concentrate on the job in hand. So it was with the French Army as a whole. That it was not so with the Legion was because ninety per cent of legionnaires spent every penny they drew as soon as they drew it.

Such was the situation in Hanoi and, after about a month of the gay life, I leapt at an opportunity of getting out of it, created by a vacancy in the Road Circulation Police at an outpost some eight miles north of the city. The post was at the Pont des Rapides, a bridge over a canal which ran parallel with the Red River. The bridge allowed only of one-way traffic and, since all convoys to and from Hanoi and the important northern and north-western zones of operation were forced to cross it, the efficient handling and control of traffic was of some importance. Although the personnel consisted of only four private soldiers who acted as policemen, it was essential that an NCO of some capacity and authority be there on the spot to enforce the orders of GHQ. It was not much of a job for a sergeant of the Legion, but it was better than sitting around in Hanoi doing nothing; so I took it.

There were many operations just to the north of the Pont des Rapides that summer. This enabled me to see something of the tactical handling of the Mobile Groups. To understand the situation it is necessary to know something of the country.

Going north from Hanoi was a single main road, just wide enough to admit of two streams of traffic. This road split into two at the northern exit of my bridge, the left-hand fork leading via Vietri to the Chinese frontier at Lao-Kay, and the right-hand one via Bac Ninh to the Chinese frontier beyond Lang Son. Each of these roads was under French control for a distance of about thirty miles north of the bridge.

On either side of each road the ricefields stretched away into the hazy distance. You cannot drive across ricefields; they are under water for most of the year, and for the remainder are very sticky swamps. You can only walk across them with difficulty and at the risk of losing your boots, sucked off by the slime, and a lot of blood, sucked out of your legs by the leeches. The ricefields are, however, divided into workable squares by raised dykes, along the top of which run narrow footpaths. The outlying villages to which the ricefields belong are connected to the main roads by cart tracks, which are rarely more than five or six feet wide.

It will easily be realized that modern military traffic was virtually confined to the main roads. It was just possible to drive along the better preserved and wider cart tracks, but impossible to pass another vehicle coming from the opposite direction, and if one truck of a convoy broke down, the whole column was halted until it was got going again.

All along the main roads under French control were 'posts'—strong-points held by anything from a platoon to a company according to size and importance, and consisting of a number of block-houses surrounded by barbed wire. The country for a distance varying from five to fifteen miles to the right and left of the roads was also controlled by posts, these latter being almost invariably established in the isolated villages. Posts were intervisible, and, as I have already explained, the system ensured that by day the enemy could not move in the French-controlled area. By night it was quite a different story. All the posts closed their barriers, no traffic was allowed on the roads, and the Vietminh and his partisans took over. Their favourite game was to mine the roads or dig huge holes in them. Sometimes they cut down trees so that they fell across the road. They very rarely cut telephone lines. They listened!

These harassing operations were carried out, not by regular Vietminh troops, but by partisans—the inhabitants of the villages, who were peasants by day and soldiers by night. Most of them were unarmed; they did not need rifles for the kind of work they did. One morning we found an enormous hole in the road about twenty kilometres north of Hanoi, which held up all traffic until well after midday. The chief of the nearest village was told to send twenty coolies to fill it in. They laughed like hell, those coolies, as they lethargically dropped clods of earth into the crater they had themselves dug during the previous night.

From time to time one of the isolated posts in the country villages would be attacked, always by night, and usually at one or two in the morning. As soon as the news reached Hanoi, the High Command would set its lumbering machine in motion. One or two of the intervention battalions stationed in and around the capital would be ordered out, mounted in columns of GMCs, and sent to recapture the fallen post. The unwieldy column of fifty or a hundred vehicles would come grinding up the main road and turn off along the dyke leading to the village where the post was situated. Usually the leading vehicles would get blown up on mines, the whole column would halt, while the troops dismounted and advanced towards the post on foot. They would retake it, usually without a shot being fired; but they wouldn't take a single Viet prisoner!

Dear me! I seem to remember, at some remote period during

the Second World War, sitting in a hall crowded with cough-subduing officers and listening to a lecture by a famous British general, of whom a few French officers have perhaps vaguely heard. It was a very simple address. He was a very simple general. He never complicated things by losing a battle, and he had a horror of massacring his own troops. He said, 'If you want to win battles, there are two things you must never do. You must never react as the enemy wants you to react, and you must never reinforce failure.'

*Eheu fugaces, O Dien Bien Phu!*

Sometimes operations on a larger scale were conducted, with the object of scouring large areas of country vaguely held by both sides. The Mobile Groups would then come into action. The *Groupement Mobile* was, I believe, more or less a copy of the American type Combat Team: three infantry battalions, complete with artillery and other supporting arms. Very handy for European warfare! But in Indo-China the vehicles merely cluttered up the very limited road system: two hundred and fifty at the very least. Then it was that the staff wallahs at Hanoi stopped drinking their cognac-sodas for five minutes and got down to a little work. They even issued Movement Tables.

One night I found two huge convoys approaching my one-way bridge from two different directions. I stopped them both, then went to each convoy commander in turn and asked to see his Movement Order. (Normally I was supposed to receive a copy of the Plan, but they often, as on this occasion, forgot to send me one.) The two convoy commanders both had orders to cross the same bridge at the same time! Too many cooks spoiling the broth? Oh no! Both orders were signed by the same captain!

As an ex-gunner the sort of thing that shook me was the kind of incident that occurred one morning on the road about ten miles north of the bridge: an entire artillery group of four batteries, a hundred or more vehicles, waiting, nose to tail, the radiator of one tractor touching the muzzle of the preceding gun, while the *commandant* and his captains conducted their reconnaissance fifty yards away. On such occasions I could have sometimes wished to be the pilot of just one solitary MIG 15. I'd have won Orders of Lenin by the basinful.

On that particular morning the traffic block caused by the halted artillery column was so intense that it stretched back as far as the bridge. I jumped on my motor-cycle and tore along to find out what the trouble was. I found a battery sergeant-major.

'What the hell's going on here?' I asked.

'Don't ask me,' he replied in a despairing way. 'Go and ask the Jules over there.' He pointed to the group of officers in the field nearby. 'If we *sous-officiers* had the job of deploying we'd do the job properly and be in action by now.'

That was a French Army sergeant-major speaking. The Legion has no artillery.

I can assure you that, in these and other observations which I have made and shall have to make on French staff work and command, there is nothing jaundiced or bitter; and I hope I am not making it appear so. The criticisms I am making would be amply endorsed by many Frenchmen who were acquainted with the situation and are prepared to be honest about it. Many of them have made the same or similar criticisms in my hearing. I have known in Indo-China and elsewhere, many French officers, Legion and other, whom I admired and respected. Unfortunately, they were in the minority. There were far too many *incapables*, who neither knew their jobs nor took the trouble to learn them, and whose only interest was to stay out of trouble by doing the minimum of work compatible with that object.

I admit that there was everything in the whole Indo-Chinese set-up to discourage professional integrity: a war which was not a war, but a so-called police action; political juggling taking precedence over military urgencies; the sordid example of the captain of the *Pasteur*; the Ministers of State, who arrived by plane from Paris and commenced their tour of inspection by a visit to the cotton factory at Nam Dinh or the cement works at Haiphong, of which they were principal shareholders. But two wrongs do not make a right, and it is, so far as I know, no excuse for being dishonest to say that one's neighbour is also dishonest.

One of the more pleasant aspects of my period of duty at the Pont des Rapides was that I met so many old friends and made so many new ones. As I have explained, all traffic from Hanoi to the north had to cross the bridge, and every day I encountered one or more of the sergeants who had suffered from my instruction at Sidi Bel-Abbès. One evening in the autumn a motor-cycle came wobbling across the bridge and drew to a jerky halt in front of the door of my office. Off it fell, rather than climbed, Jaderny and Sibley. They were both holding about as much as they could carry and each had a bottle of cognac in his pocket.

'We heard you were here,' said Jaderny. 'We're both on four days' leave in Hanoi. So we hired this old crock'—he kicked the Harley Davidson on which they had arrived—'to come up and see you. Sibley, open a bottle.'

I shook hands with both of them and congratulated Sibley, who was wearing the two gold stripes of a sergeant.

'I don't suppose I shall keep 'em more than a couple of months,' he said. 'Damn my eyes, Smith! You've got a hell of a nice, cushy job here.' He was looking round at my comfortable little combined office and sleeping quarters. 'This is a bit different from our usual accommodation, eh, Jaderny?'

'Too bloody right! A ground-sheet in a ditch is our bedroom.'

'I wouldn't mind changing with you,' I said.

'Don't be a damned fool,' said Jaderny. 'You hang on to your good luck while you've got it. Do you realize what it's like being with an infantry unit on intervention? You have a base like ours at Nam Dinh, where you leave your kit, and where you have a bed on which you sleep about one night in ten, if you're lucky. The rest of the time you're out on operations. *Tu manges des conserves et tu couches dans la merde*. It's a hell of a life.'

'I'd like to try it, all the same,' I replied. 'I'm fed-up with squatting on an office stool. I'm a legionnaire, and I want to see the Legion fighting before the end of my stay in Indo-China.'

'If you really mean that,' said Sibley, 'although I must say I agree with Jaderny, I know that our battalion commander wants a *sous-officier* for the heavy-mortar section. He knows all about you, and I'm quite sure he'd jump at you, if you applied for a transfer.'

# 25

THE next morning I arranged for a colleague to stand in for me, and went down to Hanoi, to the company, to put in my demand for transfer. I had invited Sibley and Jaderny to meet me there for lunch. When I had completed my business, I went along to the mess, and there they were waiting for me. I had just had time to order some drinks when in came Mac. He said 'Hallo' to me and shook hands with the two visitors. He looked very hard at Sibley and suddenly poked him in the chest with the forefinger of his right hand. 'Lang Son!' he said.

'Right first time,' said Sibley. 'You were commanding a platoon of the Third, if I remember.'

'Right again,' said Mac. 'I was a *sergent-chef* then. You, I think, were a corporal, and you came across to me with a message from your company commander. Your crowd were in protection on the south side of the bridge. What a *bordel* that was that day!'

'Yes,' replied Sibley. 'A friend of mine was in your platoon, by the way. I think he was killed that very morning. Name of Scheer. By God, Smith, you knew him too, of course. He was with us at Marseilles. The Alsatian with the huge scar across his face.'

I remembered him very well as the quiet, unassuming fellow who was always quarrelling with Rousseau, the pimp from Marseilles, and as a fellow prisoner on our first Camerone.

'And Rousseau?' I asked. 'What happened to him?' But nobody knew.

'Scheer,' said McAndrew, 'was my second-in-command, and a damn fine second-in-command, too. Yes, he was killed that morning, but not by the Viets. As the two of you both knew him, I'll tell you how it happened, if you like. But first of all, let's have another drink. Aldo, four cognac-sodas. *Maulen!*'

He turned to Jaderny. 'You were at Lang Son?'

'No,' said Jaderny. 'I was in hospital, getting rid of a *chancre*.'

'You were lucky,' said Mac. 'You,' he continued, turning to me, 'you weren't there, either, and you may have some pretty erroneous impressions about the situation there. You may have heard that we "retired in good order in the face of overwhelmingly superior enemy forces", or some such poppycock. We didn't. We retired in the most appalling disorder in the face of damn-all! The French High Command was all balled-up and, in attempting to hide their confusion, they got 'emselves even more balled-up. You know, when a general sits in a comfortable arm-chair in some luxuriously appointed office in Hanoi or Saigon, and tries to command a battle that's going on about five hundred or two thousand miles away, it's only natural that he does one of two things. Either he considers that the reports from the battle-front are grossly exaggerated and leaves those who are being potted at by the Viets to stew in their own juice; or he himself grossly exaggerates the importance of the reports and, sitting there, feverishly gulping his cognac-soda half a continent away from the scene of action, gets into a thorough bloody panic, and starts interfering with the job of the commander on the spot. The latter is what happened in regard to Lang Son.

'It didn't worry us too much inside our battalion, though my old pal Deweert, who was doing battalion sergeant-major—he got his later at Phu-Lang-Thuong, poor devil—told me that the *commandant* went pretty nearly off his nut, trying to execute the series of orders and counter-orders he received from three or four different sources.

'Anyhow, the orders said that we were to get out of Lang Son, though nobody quite understood why; so we did. It was in the method and timing of the evacuation that things went very badly wrong. I remember that there must have been something screwy with the transport plan. Tons of stores went up in smoke before we left and tons more fell intact into the hands of the Viets; yet, as we marched down the road, we saw whole columns of GMCs driving down the same road and in the same direction—empty!

'One of the things that has always amazed me about the Legion is that men can see that sort of thing happening and still remain disciplined. Why, in the American Army that sort of inefficiency at the higher levels would create a bloody mutiny. Yet the legionnaire sees it, understands what's going on, and understands it far better than most; and he just plods on without saying a word. Now, why is that?'

'Confidence in the immediate superior,' suggested Jaderny. 'The legionnaire sees that the *sergent-chef* or *adjutant* commanding his lot has also noticed the inefficiency, but he knows that there is nothing his superior can do about it, since he is merely obeying the damned silly orders he has received.'

'Not forgetting,' added Sibley, 'that the legionnaire fights for the Legion, as represented by those immediate superiors, and not for the French Government, as represented by the generals.'

'Not forgetting also,' I remarked, 'that the legionnaire doesn't give a damn, anyhow. It's not his war. He's just fighting it, and whether he's killed by an enemy bullet or some bloody fool's incompetence, it's all the same to him.'

'Yes,' admitted McAndrew. 'That may be so. But to get back to Lang Son. My platoon was the last but one out, and there still wasn't a Viet to be seen. As we came across the bridge, we suddenly heard a whistle and a crash, and saw a puff of smoke rising from the spot where I had left one of my machine-gunners to cover the withdrawal. Scheer turned to me with a look of incredulity in his eyes. "One-o-five!" he said. He was an ex-gunner like you, Smith. Immediately afterwards there were four or five more whistles and crashes. The salvo straddled the river, but did no damage. There was now no further doubt, for we had heard the noise made by the guns in the distance and could judge roughly where it came from. "Our own artillery!" yelled Scheer. "Don't the bloody fools know we're not out yet? Makes me damned well ashamed ever to have been a gunner."

'When the first puff of smoke had cleared away, we saw my machine-gunner writhing on the ground with a broken leg, and Scheer started off across the bridge again to bring him in. He hadn't got more than half-way, when another shell landed plumb on the bridge and got him. He didn't have a chance. The thing burst only about two yards from him and he was cut to pieces. He was still living when I got to him, but only just. He passed me his platoon pocket-book, and told me that Legionnaire Braun needed a new pair of boots and that somebody else had a pierced water-bottle. Then he asked whether anybody else had been hurt by the shell that got him. I told him that two men had been slightly wounded. "Beautiful fragmentation!" he said, and died. He was a gunner to the last, you see.

'As a matter of fact, as we discovered later, it wasn't the artillery's fault at all. They were merely acting on orders received, as also were the engineers who blew up the bridge just afterwards, before the last platoon was across. As for the Viets, they made no attempt to get into the town while we were there, but they potted at us all the way down the road, didn't they, Sibley?'

'By Christ they did,' said Sibley.

# 26

SOON after my arrival in Tongking, I had heard that Felden, *der Berliner*, as we called him, who had been with me in the barrack-room at Sidi Bel-Abbès, had been taken prisoner at Hoa Binh in February of that year; so I hardly expected to see him again.

The morning when I left the Transport Company to join the battalion at Nam Dinh I received orders to go and pick up a detachment of a dozen reinforcements at the Citadel and accompany them to my new unit, for which they were also destined, in a Dodge truck provided for the purpose. I duly reported to the Transit Company in the Citadel and the detachment was handed over to me. Among them, whom did I see, resplendent in a fancy gaberdine uniform of the most startling hue, complete with brilliant shoes of a truly revolting yellow, but Felden, the *Berliner Bauer*!

He saluted me and grinned. I shook hands with him.

'Hallo!' I said. 'Where have you sprung from, *Berliner*? I heard you'd been taken prisoner.'

'So I was, *chef*,' he replied. (I had just been promoted.) 'But I was repatriated,' he continued, and the perpetual grin spread all over his face.

'Repatriated? What on earth do you mean? Where to?'

'To Berlin,' he replied.

At that moment the truck which was to take us to Nam Dinh arrived; so I gave the order to mount, and we drove off. The vehicle and driver had been supplied by one of the newly formed Vietnamian Transport Companies. The one thing the driver could not do was drive. All he knew was how to blow the horn. In that respect he was a champion. He blew it three hundred and eighty-seven times before we were half-way through Hanoi. He seemed to think that gave him the right to drive plumb in the middle of the road, cut blind corners and mow down unsuspecting cyclists. When we arrived at the level crossing and he shot the barrier just as it was being lowered, my nerves could stand it no longer. I told him to pull up in front of the station, went into the *buvette* for a quick cognac-soda, and came out to the truck again.

'Have any of you fellows a *permis de conduire?*' I asked, poking my head into the back of the truck. Felden said he had a driving licence. I looked to see if it was in order and told him to take the wheel. As for the almond-eyed public menace, I threw him to the wolves in the back of the vehicle.

Felden was a good driver. Although he was known as the *Berliner*, he wasn't really from Berlin at all, but had worked as a tractor driver before joining the Legion, on a small farm just outside the German capital. Once, at the Bas Fort Saint Nicolas in Marseilles, he was arguing some agricultural question with another farmer from Bavaria, when he lost his temper, just as he was losing the argument, and cried, '*Ach*, you provincial peasant, you can't tell me anything. I come from Berlin.' They had called him *Der Berliner* ever since. He was a simple, kindly soul, and his mouth was always spread from ear to ear in that permanent, monstrous, fatuous grin.

In the early days he had always been wanting to desert. I remember that the other recruits persuaded him not to. I don't think he realized what he was taking on when he had enlisted. In fact, he probably didn't know exactly how he came to be in the Legion at all. There was some story of his having escaped from the Russian to the French Zone of Germany, where he had fallen in with a Legion recruiting sergeant, who had first made him drunk and then got him to sign his contract while he was too fuddled to know what he was doing. This may or may not have been true. Felden wasn't very clear about it himself.

Sitting beside me, driving that truck southwards along the Route Coloniale No. 1 at a steady, moderate forty miles an hour, he told me an amazing story. I wasn't quite sure whether to believe it at the time; but I know now that his experience was not unique, and that the same thing happened to at least twenty or thirty other German legionnaires taken prisoner in Indo-China.

He had gone into the bag during the retreat from Hoa Binh in February of that year, but it appeared that the Viets had kept him for only about three weeks and then had handed him over to the Chinese Communists who, in turn, after a delay of about a month, had handed him over to the Russians. I cannot give exact details as to time and place. Felden was extremely vague about them himself, and even vaguer in imparting them to me. I gathered, however, that some time in April or May he arrived, together with several other legionnaire prisoners whose homes were in the Russian Zone of Germany, at a sort of camp in Russia. There he had remained for about two months, and during that time he 'went to school', as he himself expressed it. The place must have been some sort of indoctrination centre, situated probably, according to his description of the country and climate, somewhere in Siberia.

Felden was possessed of that natural cunning which is the birthright of the Prussian peasant, and he must have realized that it was in his interest to reply *Jawohl!* to every question that was put to him. For two months he said nothing but *Jawohl!* with the result that, before the end of the summer, he found himself back again on the farm near Berlin—a free man.

He only stayed there for about a fortnight. He found the dull, monotonous life on the small farm a poor substitute for the gay one he had been accustomed to leading in Indo-China, whenever operations permitted. So he escaped once again into the French Zone and presented himself at a Legion recruiting station in order to finish his contract! He advanced the honouring of his contract as his chief reason for returning: I rather doubt it, but, if true, what a difference from his attitude of two and a half years before! I think the truth was that he had an urge to see his old comrades again. The fact that he had quite a packet of back-pay to draw must also have had a considerable influence. So he had come back.

He was, of course, rolling in money. Hence the frightful uniform he was wearing, which didn't last five minutes as soon as the battalion sergeant-major set eyes on it when we arrived at the rear-base.

He drove us safely down to Nam Dinh and, when he had spent the whole of his eight month's back-pay, celebrating with his cronies in the cafés and brothels of that dismal town, he volunteered, although strictly speaking he was on leave, to go out on operations with the battalion. The captain's driver was ill, and Felden offered to replace him at the wheel of the company commander's jeep.

He shouldn't have tempted Providence a second time. Just beyond Phu-Ly they went up on a mine. The captain was slightly wounded in the legs; but Felden wasn't so lucky. The gear-box took his head clean off and landed it in the road about twenty yards away. When we picked it up to bury it with his body, his poor face had that idiotic grin still spread all over it. Felden was always grinning.

As soon as I arrived at the rear-base and handed over the detachment, I was presented to the battalion commander. He confided to me the command of the 81-mm mortar platoon.

'You know something about mortars, I believe,' he said, a twinkle in his eye. 'I have heard all about your instruction at Sidi Bel-Abbès.'

I saluted, left the office, and went to take over the platoon which, as it turned out, I was to command for the remaining fifteen months of my stay in Indo-China. It was a good platoon, a damned good platoon, though I say it myself. God, and perhaps God alone, knows where they are now. I had two sergeants, a Hungarian, and a Frenchman, who each commanded a section of two mortars, and four corporals who were each responsible for one piece. The French sergeant, two of the corporals, and three or four of the legionnaires I already knew.

This continual meeting of old Legion comrades is not so coincidental as it seems at first sight. The Legion is, after all, a fairly small family. Even swollen as it was by the exigencies of the war in Indo-China, the total strength rarely exceeded twenty thousand, and it is no exaggeration to say that I knew at least a thousand of them. Many, many more knew me! Most of them moved around quite a lot and, as I had spent two years in Sidi Bel-Abbès, I had seen thousands go through there, to say nothing of the hundreds of sergeants I had helped to train. Already, after only three and a half years' service, I never walked into a sergeants' mess in Indo-China without seeing at least one or two people I knew standing against the bar ready to offer me a drink.

In fact, my French sergeant was Gérard, who at Sidi Bel-Abbès on the anniversary of Camerone in 1951 had had the honour of drinking at the colonel's table, because he had just been let off a punishment. The other section commander, whom I had not known previously, was from Budapest and his name was Nagy. Both were excellent *sous-officiers*. In the long run I came to prefer Nagy. He was slightly mad, but the men loved him. Gérard was inclined to be a bit selfish and look after his own interests rather than those of the men he commanded.

# 27

LIKE nearly all the Legion battalions, ours was engaged on 'intervention'. I should perhaps explain that troops in Indo-China, apart from the base squatters in the big towns, were employed in one of two ways: either as the permanent garrisons of the large and small posts scattered throughout the French-occupied territory, or as mobile interventionists, ready, as soon as the order was given, to move out from their base and deal with the Vietminh wherever they might be reported. For the former task Senegalese and the newly formed Vietnamian units were almost exclusively employed. The Senegalese, in particular, almost invariably spent the whole of their two years' tour in the Far East sitting in the same post.

For intervention more 'reliable' troops were required—first and foremost the Legion. It is not merely my opinion that the legionnaires were the most reliable troops in Indo-China. I have heard French, non-Legion officers admit it frequently. Next in order of reliability came the Arabs—*tirailleurs algériens et marocains*—who were also used as mobile intervention troops.

A battalion such as ours would nearly always be based on the outskirts of some big town, so that, when the main body was out on operations, the base details remained as part of the town's garrison. I had a small room which I shared with my two sergeants. There I left my kit when out on operations, which, as Sibley already had warned me, were nine days out of ten. These sorties would last anything from a day or so to a couple of months. At the end of each one, we returned to base to refit, pick up reinforcements to replace the dead and wounded, and wait for the next to begin.

The first in which I participated, the one during which Felden was killed, was not particularly exciting for my platoon. We were mounted, as usual, in two fifteen-hundredweight trucks. During the entire two days we only took the mortars out of them once, and even then we didn't fire a shot. The whole affair was a 'flop'. As so often happened, the Viets whom we had been sent to attack knew that we were coming, and disappeared from the scene the night before we left camp.

It was not always like that. One day just before Christmas we were sent out to a village near Thai Binh, about twenty-five miles to the south of Nam Dinh, which was reported to be occupied by a reduced company of Vietminh. We disembarked from the vehicles about four miles from the village and made the approach march on foot. We were not particularly worried. An hour to get there, we thought, two or three hours for scouring the village and mopping up any resistance offered by this handful of the enemy. Then we would stay the night in the village and return to camp by midday the following day in time to prepare for Christmas.

It didn't work out quite like that. We arrived in sight of the objective, quite a large group of farm buildings surrounded by tall trees. When we were about eight hundred yards away, we halted, and the battalion commander gave orders for two companies to advance and reconnoitre. I told Nagy to get the four mortars in action, behind a dyke, facing the objective, and accompanied the commander of the leading company, keeping in touch with Nagy by means of our 'walkie-talkie' radio-sets.

All this was thoroughly bad tactics, as any infantryman will recognize. The main body of the battalion should, of course, have been halted out of sight of the objective, while a mere handful of scouts were sent forward to do the reconnoitring. But, we had by then gone out on so many wild-goose chases that we had become careless.

The leading company advanced in open formation towards the village. Nothing seemed to be stirring. The men were walking stolidly over the quagmire of the half-dried ricefield, their boots squelching in the mud and their arms emitting an occasional metallic clink, as a button or a piece of metal equipment rubbed against them. Save for the squelching and the tinkling, there was complete silence. The village looked most peaceful. There wasn't a breath of smoke curling up from the houses. The place looked uninhabited. We arrived within two hundred yards of it. I noticed that, four hundred yards away on our right, there was another, much smaller, village, with a herd of buffalo grazing near by. The two had looked like one when we had started from the main dyke. About three hundred yards to my left, grouped together on one of those little raised islands which are dotted about the ricefields, was a clump of trees, mostly palms, their umbrella tops bending over under the weight of the giant leaves.

The company commander was walking along a dyke, to avoid getting his feet wet, and I was following about ten yards behind him. We were only about a hundred yards from the larger village, and I remember yawning over the futility of these operations in which nothing ever happened. Then two things did happen. What sounded like a swarm of furious bees buzzed past my ears and the captain fell over backwards into the ricefield. Of all the thoughts that raced through my head in that first fraction of a second one stands out very clearly: the back of the captain's head touched the ground before the bark of the heavy machine-gun which had fired the bullet reached my ears. The next second I was on my belly in the stubble of the ricefield, sheltering behind the dyke, and machine-guns and rifles were chattering and barking all round.

In such a situation there is no need to give orders, particularly when one is dealing with legionnaires. There is only one thing to do: go to ground and start firing back. The legionnaires did it. The first of our machine-guns opened up less than two seconds after the first enemy shot had been fired. The machine-gunner was standing bolt upright, firing from the hip. He emptied three magazines before he fell with a bullet through the heart.

It soon became evident that our situation was trickier even than it had appeared at first sight. The platoon over to my left, which had taken cover behind a dyke facing the village, was still sustaining casualties. Men were being shot in the back, and the bullets were coming from the clump of trees behind them. Over the company radio I could hear that our right flank was in a no better position, for they were being harassed by rifle and automatic fire from the small village. We had walked into a first-class ambush and were being fired upon from three points of the compass. By the calibre and intensity of the fire I judged that we were up against a battalion at the very least.

The right-hand platoon commander, a lieutenant, was repeatedly calling the company commander on the radio, and the company commander did not answer. I looked over to where he was lying and noticed for the first time that his radio operator was lying, face upwards, beside him. So I chipped in on the radio and told the lieutenant that both the captain and his radio operator had been hit, but that I could not yet be certain whether wounded or killed. The lieutenant, who was the senior, then took over command and told me to start firing on the main village. I sent through the necessary orders to Nagy and the first shells arrived as soon as I had spoken. Good old Nagy! He must have had the mortars already trained on the village, anticipating my orders, with the loaders each holding a shell in the mouth of the tube, ready to let go as soon as he ordered Fire! He very quickly got the range of the front edge of the trees surrounding the village and the fire from there slackened a little.

Meanwhile I crawled up to the side of the captain. Crawling is not my strong point, and a number of bullets whizzed too near to the seat of my pants to be comfortable, but at last I got there. When I saw the half-inch bullet hole in his forehead, I understood why he had hit the ground so quickly. The effect of a point-five bullet fired at point-blank range must have been equivalent to a five-ton lorry travelling at thirty miles an hour. The radio operator was not quite dead but was going fast, and the receiver of the set was crackling forth frantic enquiries from the battalion commander. I picked up the handset and explained to the *commandant* what had happened. He acknowledged, and I heard him give orders to the two reserve companies to attack, one the clump of trees to the left, the other the smaller village to the right. He told me to transmit orders to the lieutenant now commanding the leading company to remain in position and not attempt to move until the two attacks had gone in. We couldn't very well do anything else. We were pinned to the ground.

I looked at my watch. Two hours had passed since the first shot was fired. That is an amazing thing about this sort of action. The first five seconds are so filled with incident that you can scarcely imagine it possible for things to have happened so quickly. And then everything settles down. Men go on being killed and wounded, but at longer intervals. You still hear bullets buzzing across your nose, but you have become a fatalist. And gradually you improve your position, hide a little bit more of yourself, usually behind a tuft of grass which wouldn't stop an air-gun pellet but which gives you a feeling of not being so naked. You find a little hollow in the ground a little way to your left which will enable you to get a couple of inches lower, and bit by bit you edge your way into it. Then you look at your watch, and two hours have gone by!

Slowly but progressively, all the men of the leading company were doing the same thing; crawling a couple of feet to the right here, improving a firing position there, digging a shallow hole with trenching-tool or bayonet or jack-knife. During the whole of the action the company lost twenty-five men: twenty-one of them were accounted for in the first minute!

The artillery now began putting up quite a good show. The *commandant* had evidently asked them for support, and a battery in a fixed position five miles away began shelling the larger village. It was tricky work for them, of course, for, as I say, our leading elements were a bare hundred yards from the trees surrounding it; but they fired a bit over and landed their shells plumb in the middle of the objective among the houses. They probably didn't do a lot of damage to the defenders, since obviously the fellows who were firing at us were in the outskirts of the woods immediately in front of us. But the moral support was heartening, and I was enabled to turn my mortars on to the two secondary objectives.

The clump of trees was the first to be attacked, and it was taken fairly easily. There probably weren't more than a couple of machine-gun crews there, and the left flank of the company picked off a couple of the survivors who tried to escape to the large village. This eased the situation on our left flank considerably. My mortars had done a good job of work and had landed their shells neatly in the centre of the clump. Later, it was discovered that by a stroke of luck one projectile had landed plumb on one of the machine-guns, wrecking it and killing two of the crew.

The attack on the smaller village didn't go half so well. Nagy must have over-estimated the range for safety's sake, and I could see that the shells were bursting well behind the objective. I shortened down the range by flank observation, but, unfortunately by the time I was short enough, one or two of our men got into the outskirts and I had to cease fire. In any case, this second attack was a failure. A murderous fire was levelled at the company which had been given the task, and the main body never arrived within two hundred yards of the objective. One section pushed on to within fifty yards, and, as I say, a few of the leading men penetrated into the village, but the rest were completely written off.

Night was now falling, and hasty preparations were made for the evacuation of the wounded. I do not know of any more grisly business than this. In such a situation stretchers are not available, or at least never in sufficient quantity. The night was black as pitch and, of course, we dared not show a light. For three hours I heard badly, often very painfully, wounded men being carried or dragged along by their comrades who were floundering about in the dark, doing their very best, but often missing their step and thus involuntarily lacerating the raw wounds of those they were carrying.

I slept that night, oddly enough, from midnight till just before dawn. Gérard crawled out to me after dark and offered to relieve me, but I decided that as I was there I might as well stay there. It was safer than crawling back to the platoon, anyway! I told him to leave one man on guard at each mortar, and let the rest get as much sleep as possible. I also told him to switch off the radio till first light and to open up again only in the event of any activity starting. There was absolutely nothing I could do as regards observation in that inky darkness, so I found the driest spot in the neighbourhood and went to sleep, after I had drunk the half-bottle of cognac Gérard left with me.

I slept with the handset of the inter-battalion radio-set tied against my ear with a piece of string, and a quarter of an hour before first light I was awakened by hearing the *commandant* giving orders to the company behind us to launch a second attack on the flanking village. He told me he was going to saturate the objective for five minutes with concentrated mortar fire, while the artillery would deal with the main, frontal objective. As he was standing just by the side of my mortars, he said he would give the orders direct to Nagy. All I would have to do would be to yell 'Stop' as soon as the fire became dangerous for the attackers.

The assault was very well conceived. The village was due west of the attacking company, so that the defenders were blinded by the glare of the rising sun. It was successful, though there were a few casualties due to cross-fire from the larger village, in spite of the quite heavy artillery barrage. Four Viets were taken prisoner and twenty-two killed.

The situation, with both our flanks secure, was now much healthier. For the first time in nearly twenty-four hours we were able to move about sufficiently, behind the shelter of the dykes, to open our one-day ration tins and have a bite to eat. I poured the coffee powder and sugar into my half-full water-bottle, shook it vigorously, and sat sipping cold coffee, while I smoked a badly crumpled cigarette. I looked at the captain and noticed a bulge in his trouser pocket. I put my hand in to explore and pulled out an untouched quarter-bottle of Courvoisier. I screwed off the stopper, said '*Prosit*' in the direction of the corpse, and swigged half of it. Then I replaced the stopper and pulled the peak of the captain's *képi* down over the black hole in his forehead. His brains dropped out at the back, but he looked more peaceful that way, as though he were taking a nap on a hot summer's afternoon.

He had been a nice fellow, that captain, very well liked by his men, chiefly because he never showed the slightest fear. He always wore a *képi* in action, while everybody else wore the Australian type of bush-hat. He did so, less from a spirit of bravado than to facilitate command; but it was certain that it was going to be his undoing one day, and that day had come. He was a true legionnaire who had come up through the ranks. He was, I think, happier drinking with the *sous-officiers* in our mess than he was among his colleagues in theirs. He had always been in and out of our bar at the base, entertaining us with his stories about big-game hunting, of which he had done quite a bit during his chequered career. If you believed all the yarns he had told, during those long winter evenings at Nam Dinh, about the number of elephants which had met their deaths in prolongation of the sights of his Winchester, there couldn't have been many pairs of tusks remaining in the whole of the Far East.

During the morning a squadron of planes came along and machine-gunned the village. A couple of them also dropped incendiary bombs, and soon a pretty good fire was raging among the huts behind the trees. At midday we heard a rumbling and grinding away to the south—behind the village—which we identified as a convoy of lorries. So it appeared that it had been decided to send up reinforcements.

The rest I did not learn until the following morning. Two battalions had been brought up, and they took up positions to the south and south-west of the centre of resistance, which was thus virtually surrounded. There was some delay in the deployment of one of the battalions, so that the attack designed to reduce the defenders and scoop a Viet battalion into the bag did not go in until the next day at dawn. When it did, after a massive artillery preparation, all that was found was an empty village. No Vietminh, no civilians, not even an animal, except for a couple of diseased pigs. How or when they got out was a mystery.

Our battalion was called up just before midday to give a hand in scouring the village. All the signs of a fortified camp were there: ammunition dumps, but no ammunition; weapon-pits, but no weapons; a complicated system of underground shelters, but not a single Viet hiding in them; no wounded and no dead. There was nothing for me to do there, so, pocketing a neatly carved little wooden Buddha I had found in one of the huts, I walked back to the main dyke to rejoin my platoon.

'Joyeux Noël,' cried Gérard and Nagy. I looked at them blankly.

'Oh yes, I suppose it is,' I said. 'Happy Christmas to both of you.'

We spent the remainder of the day, all three battalions, sweeping an area of about twenty square miles, but didn't find any Viets. Back at the base we celebrated Christmas on Boxing Day. We had sustained a hundred and twenty casualties, so those of us who remained had half again as much to eat and drink as we had expected. And the Germans sang *Stille Nacht, heilige Nacht*, as only legionnaires can sing it.

# 28

NEARLY all operations in the Tongking Delta fell into one of the two categories I have just described. Either there was a wild-goose chase when one never even smelt a Viet, or else one stuck out one's neck a bit too far and had it neatly lopped off for one's pains. Of this second type was Operation 'X'. (I have my reasons for not being too explicit.)

Troops to the value of about a division and a half were engaged, but the incident I am going to describe concerns only the Mobile Group of which my battalion formed part. This group consisted of three battalions, of which two were Legion, the whole being commanded by a colonel—not of the Legion.

As I have already mentioned, many legionnaires, although of considerable military experience and ability, refused promotion and preferred to remain ordinary private soldiers. Such a one was the colonel's radio operator on Mobile Group Headquarters.

The operation had gone too far and too fast. The two Legion battalions of the group had been sent on some twelve miles ahead of the remainder of the forces engaged, had bumped up against a complete Vietminh division, and had been ordered to retire. On our way back we fell into a strong and very cleverly devised ambush, had a lot of casualties, but eventually managed to force our way back in some disorder to the strong-point which was being thinly held by the reserve battalion.

At Group Headquarters, which was established on a hill-top in the middle of the strong-point, there was full-scale panic; and the colonel, who had completely lost control of the situation, was trotting round in half-circles, quite incapable of taking any decisions or issuing any orders. And all the time the survivors of the two battalions were streaming back and just standing around waiting for somebody to tell them to do something.

Then it was that this legionnaire, the radio operator, suddenly and for a brief and glorious moment, came out of his shell. He snatched the map from the astonished colonel's shaking hands, cast a quick look round him to see how the land lay, and then, picking up the microphone, started dictating clear and precise orders for deployment to the battalion commanders. He asked the artillery for defensive fire in front of the positions, giving the co-ordinates of the objectives and full details as to method of employment. He then handed the map back to the bewildered colonel and became once more the quiet, disciplined radio operator.

He had quite certainly saved the situation and prevented disaster, but, of course, he never got any recognition for it. On the contrary, the incident was very naturally hushed up. I believe the colonel did try to use his influence to push him up a rank or two —out of sheer, unadulterated shame, I suppose—but he refused, saying he was quite happy to remain an ordinary legionnaire.

I quote this isolated incident, not only because of its intrinsic interest, but because it occurred during the last operation in the Tongking Delta in which we took part. Rumours had been circulating for some weeks that we were to be transferred to Laos, and most of us were praying that they contained some foundation of truth. I, for one, was thoroughly sick of infantry warfare in the Delta. We never seemed to be getting anywhere. It was always the same story. Either we wasted our time chasing after non-existent Vietminh, or we poked our nose in where there were too many of them and were massacred. Add to this the dreary monotony of that utterly flat, waterlogged country, and you will understand that we were all ready for a change of scenery.

The first indication that there might be some truth in the rumours came in the form of orders for the whole battalion, complete with its rear base, to move from Nam Dinh to the Hanoi area.

The move was an amazing sight. The amount of material a battalion in Indo-China managed to accumulate at its permanent headquarters was quite incredible. To begin with, everybody had at least one, if not two or three, large tin trunks in which he kept his excess kit and personal belongings, odds and ends he had bought, embroidered silks and other souvenirs. Given a battalion strength of five or six hundred, several three-ton lorries were required for the transport of these alone. Then there was all the mess and office furniture collected bit by bit ever since the formation of the unit. Packed together on the trucks, cheek by jowl with army issue plain deal chairs and tables, were the relics 'found' in the many deserted villages where the unit had operated: the typical low tables from some pagoda, tapestries, cremation urns converted to use as ash-trays, and Chinese prints and pictures.

Next came the livestock: the pigs, the ducks, and the chickens, often a cow or two, to say nothing of the pets—mainly dogs and monkeys. And lastly came the PIMs and the BMC.

PIMs (*Prisonniers Internés Militaires*) were not prisoners of war in the normal sense of the term. They were men and women, picked up in the towns and villages, who were suspected of aiding or sympathizing with the Vietminh; and there must have been several thousand of them in the internment camps all over Indo-China. There was a great deal of injustice done to many of these unfortunates, either knowingly or through sheer carelessness on the part of the authorities. Some of these PIMs honestly did not know why they had been imprisoned, and a great many who had been condemned in the first instance to six months' detention still remained in the camps after three or four years. I am quite sure that with their callous and careless policy in regard to the internment of civilians and their negligent administration of them once they had been interned, the French were firmly driving a contributory nail into their colonial coffin. There was scarcely a family in the Delta, except the very rich ones, which could not count a member or two interned in some camp or other. Ugly parallels could be and often were drawn. The comments of some of the German legionnaires on the *'französischen Konzentrationsläger'* were ironical enough.

The more 'reliable' of these PIMs were employed as coolies by military units and were often attached completely to those units. We had about sixty attached to our battalion. They formed an integral part of the battalion, and even accompanied us on operations, which was pretty odd when one came to think about it. We didn't trouble to think. We just used them. I employed about half of them to carry my ammunition.

Last, but by no means least, came the BMC. In order to explain these initials it is necessary for me to say something of the arrangements made by the French Army for the provision of an element of feminine distraction to its sex-starved soldiery. The *Bordel Militaire de Campagne* was considered a necessary adjunct to every unit of battalion strength in Indo-China. At each rear base in the Delta there could be seen in a secluded corner of the parade-ground a building around which flitted the elfin forms of the unit's prostitutes clad in their transparent white silk trousers. Into this building penetrated, when off duty, the soldiers who had fifty piastres to spare and a desire to be assuaged.

Since prostitution is considered an honourable profession among the Indo-Chinese, it can scarcely be claimed that by such practices the French were demoralizing the local inhabitants, and, since these brothels were supervised by the *Service de Santé*, it could even be claimed their use limited the spread of disease which would have resulted from the promiscuous 'picking up' of women in the streets and cafés.

It was only when one began to examine the economics of the business that one became aware of an extremely unpleasant smell.

The ostensible proprietress of the *bordel* was the *maîtresse*, who served behind the bar and was responsible for discipline among her almond-eyed *pensionnaires*. She kept a strict tally, on a printed form supplied by the battalion, of every glass of beer drunk and every half-hour spent in one of the alcoves behind the bar. Then one learnt that twenty per cent of all earnings went to the battalion, to be distributed to the various company funds. Since company funds were mainly used for ameliorating the meals on high days and holidays, this meant that the soldier ate his Christmas dinner off a woman's immoral earnings!

Were this all, it would have been bad enough; but one next learnt that the withered beauty behind the bar was not even to that extent the owner of the establishment. On a Saturday morning, she could be found plunged in a discussion of the week's accounts with a smartly dressed half-caste who had arrived from Hanoi or Haiphong in her sports car. This dusky beauty was the proprietress of the Central Military Brothel in the big city, of which the ramshackle hut with its seven or eight pitiful inmates was but a suburban branch. She took another thirty per cent, which she thrust into her voluminous handbag. Then she had a drink with the officers and went on to the next branch to collect another week's takings.

But do not delude yourself into thinking that even she was the genius whose business acumen had welded the sexual pulsations of the Expeditionary Force into one vast, money-making orgasm. If one could have paid a visit round about the end of the month to her luxurious establishment—the officers' one—in the big town, there could have been seen the rather too plump, rather too well-dressed man who arrived, in the latest American limousine stretching five yards from bumper to bumper, to collect his over-all percentage on the month's takings from the whole network. And to whom, you may well ask, did he pay toll? But no, let's leave it at that.

# 29

So we handed over to a Vietnamian Army unit our comfortable base at Nam-Dinh, with its magnificent cookhouses, its well-ordered barrack-rooms, its shaded gardens, its hot and cold showers, and its cinema, on the construction of all of which the battalion had progressively laboured for nearly two years, whenever it was not in action. It was always like that in Indo-China: the Legion constructed and then gave the results away to others.

The next day the convoy of fifty three-tonners with its assorted material, human, and animal load had wound its way north to Hanoi and dumped us in a swamp about three miles from my old home, the Pont des Rapides. When I left Indo-China six months later that swamp had turned into a fair-sized village.

The rumours were substantiated. We were to proceed to Laos in ten days' time, so I applied for four days' leave in Hanoi. At the same time we lost Gérard, who was due for repatriation; so Jaderny, who had always been interested in mortars, applied to be transferred to my platoon as a replacement. The transfer was authorized.

I met a lot of old friends in Hanoi, and the town was duly painted red. I started my leave with a fair amount of money, since, not only had it been impossible to spend one's pay during the almost uninterrupted series of operations, but I had been winning quite a lot at poker. Nevertheless, in the Tongking capital it was just as easy to spend money, if you went about the business scientifically, as in any other big town, and by the third evening I had only a few piastres left. I was thinking seriously of begging a lift back to camp and cutting my leave short, so, after strolling through the Grand Pagoda and looking at the lotus flowers in the 'Little Lake', I went across to the *Taverne Royale* to have a beer, and see if there was anybody I could touch for five hundred piastres or a lift back to base.

I hadn't been sitting there on the terrace for more than five minutes when a *cyclo-pousse* came along and deposited a *caporal-chef* in front of me. He came straight up to my table and saluted me. '*Mes respects, Chef,*' he said. I hadn't recognized him at first, but as soon as I heard his voice I remembered. It was Ambrosio, the young Italian who had sold my scarf for me at Marseilles. I asked him to have a drink and offered to pay for it, but when I saw the huge wad of five-hundred piastre notes he pulled out of his pocket, I didn't insist. I let him pay for me.

He told me that he was doing the job of NCO in charge of supplies for the two companies of his regiment which were already in Laos. His job was to order drinks and fresh vegetables in Hanoi—apparently these commodities were unobtainable in Laos—have them carted down to the airport and loaded on a plane, and then accompany them and deliver the goods to the two companies he was representing. He was making the return journey once a week, he told me, and making a very good thing out of it. He tapped his pocket and winked, and I was just going to ask him for details, when a lieutenant from the battalion came along in his jeep. I accepted his offer of a lift back to camp. I did not see Ambrosio again before I left Indo-China, so I never found out what he was up to.

When I arrived back at base, preparations for the departure were well under way. The camp was resounding to the tapping of hammers, as lids were nailed on to packing cases full of heavy armament and equipment, medical supplies, ammunition, bottles of cognac, and all the other odds and ends which go to make up a war.

The entire battalion was to be moved to Laos by aeroplane. For some time all the mountainous country along the Laotian border had been under the control of the Vietminh, so that the only means of communication between Hanoi and the Kingdom of Laos, unless one made an enormous detour via the slow journey up the Mekong river in a gunboat, was by air.

It was known that there had been a certain infiltration of Vietminh forces into Laotian territory, though the exact extent of the penetration was unknown. We were being sent there with the object of reconnoitring and ascertaining what enemy forces had been engaged and where they were located. Ostensibly our mission would be to construct a road through the forest from the Plaine des Jarres in the north to Paksane, on the Mekong, which forms the frontier between Laos and Thailand.

The plan was to send half the battalion to the north and the other half to the south; and to this end the four hundred and fifty officers and men who formed our fighting strength were to be embarked on a shuttle service of DC3 aircraft at Hanoi Airport. The movement of the personnel and stores would take three days to complete.

My platoon also had to be split in half; I sent Nagy with his section to the Plaine des Jarres in the north, keeping Jaderny, who had less experience of mortars and far less knowledge of the section, with me in the south. As things turned out, Jaderny did not accompany me immediately to Laos, for at the last minute I was told to detail a sergeant for special duties with the battalion. Since these special duties consisted in escorting the BMC on the journey, Jaderny was the obvious choice, not because he knew less about the platoon, but because he knew far more about brothels.

So we embarked at Hanoi and, after an hour and a half's flying, the DC3 which had brought me and eleven of my men circled over the Mekong and landed us without mishap on the temporary airfield. We descended from the aeroplane and marched immediately to the positions which had been allotted to us.

This was a very different country from the one to which I had been confined for the past eighteen months. To the south of us—only five hundred yards away—was the River Mekong with Thailand on the far side. To the north mountains covered by dense forest stretched away as far as the eye could see. The village itself—it had the status of an important town in that sparsely populated country—stretched for three or four hundred yards along the river, a single street of wooden houses thatched with straw. There were a few stores, which also served as cafés and were run by the inevitable and ubiquitous Chinese, the businessmen of the Far East.

All the houses were built on 'stilts', so that you had to mount a short flight of steps or a ladder in order to arrive at floor level. It appears that there are several reasons for this type of construction. Security from snakes and other dangerous animals is one, and the high floods which occur during the rainy season are another. The space underneath the house was divided into a number of pens for the livestock, the pigs, chickens, and ducks, with which that country abounds.

The Laotians themselves were also very different from the Tongkingese. Despising, like all mountain dwellers, the people of the plains, they were more primitive and less polluted by civilization. Their bodies, which were more sturdily built, looked healthier and stronger than those of the inhabitants of the Red River Delta, and their attitude was more independent. Here the sarong replaced the loose trousers as a national costume for both sexes. In the isolated mountain villages both men and women went about naked from the waist up during the hot season.

We established our first camp a mile or two north of Paksane, in a clearing about a hundred and fifty yards square. On the first night we slept under our bivouac tents. By the second night we already had houses which we had constructed during the day. Given a machette and a sufficiency of bamboo within cutting and fetching distance, it was amazing how quickly a legionnaire could build himself a little cabin.

The third day was almost entirely spent in bringing up stores from the airfield to the camp. Fortunately there was a Laotian Army transport company, equipped with GMCs, based at Vientiane, and they detached a few vehicles for our use, so that all we had to do was to load the stores on to the trucks at the airstrip and unload them at the camp. By the evening of that day all the stores were in, but there was still no sign of Jaderny.

He arrived the next morning. At about nine o'clock we saw an aeroplane circling over the ricefield which had been levelled out for an airstrip, and preparing to land; as usual, we sent off a GMC to pick up whatever had arrived. Half an hour later the truck returned. Sprawling despondently over their bundles of baggage in the back of it, many of them weeping piteously, were the eight spindly-legged sweethearts of the battalion, their yellow cheeks infused with a sickly green. Sitting with the driver in front, dishevelled, pale, and wild-eyed, was Jaderny. As soon as the truck halted, he leapt to the ground and turned towards his human load.

'*Foutez-moi le camp, bande de sales putains!*' he cried in a voice half choked with despair and anger. 'Get to hell out of my sight, you band of whores. I never want to see you again as long as I live.' And he staggered towards where we were standing, laughing our heads off, his knees trembling and his face twitching with a nervous tic.

'For God's sake, *Chef*,' he said to me, 'don't laugh. Give me a drink. I'm all in.'

As soon as we had slaked his thirst and calmed him down a little, he told us what had happened.

'I left the base at six-thirty this morning,' he explained. 'I got 'em on to the trucks easily enough, and we drove down to the airport at Gia-Lam, where a DC3 was waiting for us. There the trouble began. All that they had been told was that they were going to Laos and, as none of them had the faintest notion where Laos was, they had no idea how they were going to get there. As soon as they saw the aeroplane, the panic started. They clasped their hands together in prayer, and the air was so thick with their howls and their "*Shim, shim, Buddhas*" that you couldn't hear the noise of the motors. When I told 'em to get into the plane, they refused point-blank. My orders were to take the *boxon* to Laos, and I was damned well going to do it, so I tried to get 'em in by force; they fought like wildcats; if I hadn't given up, they'd have torn me to pieces.

'I finally succeeded in embarking them by a trick. I invited them all to come and have a drink with me at the *buvette* and talk things over. Meanwhile I whispered to the two men I had with me to load all their bundles on to the plane while they weren't looking. When we came out of the café and they saw what had happened, some of them tried to scramble into the plane and retrieve their belongings. I now played the game of refusing to let 'em pass, until at last they all made a concerted rush at me. I just stepped aside and let the whole lot of 'em dash past me, planted my boot in the backside of the last one, jumped in myself and slammed the door behind me. The pilot, seeing how things were, immediately taxied off. By the time the *kongais* had picked themselves up from the floor, we were in the air.

'God almighty! The hullabaloo they had kicked up on the ground was nothing to the din they made when they saw the ground slipping away and the Pont Doumer looking like a little toy bridge two hundred feet below. They screamed. They went down on their knees and, with tears streaming down their artificial rosy cheeks, implored Buddha to let them go back again.

'But that wasn't the worst! After about five minutes' flying *la mère maquerelle* started being sick, and very soon they were all at it, spewing up rice and *ngoc-man* all over the damned place. The smell was awful; even the pilot in his closed cabin was going green. You can have no idea what it was like.

'Well, anyhow, I got 'em here and I damned well made 'em wash the aircraft out before it took off again. But please, *Chef*, never again! Give me any sticky job you like. Send me out to certain death and I'll go cheerfully. Put me on guard for a month at a stretch. I don't mind. But never detail me for a job like that again.'

(*above*) Nails in the colonial coffin: concentration camp by the church

Captured ammunition

Dropping-ground for supplies in Laos

# 30

TWO days later work on the road started. The two elements of the battalion were about two hundred miles apart and we were to work towards one another, so that each party had, as the crow flies, about a hundred miles of road to make. But the crow does not fly in the Laotian forest. The elephant walks, and he does not always walk very straight. The result was, since we were following the elephant track, that we had nearer a hundred and fifty miles of fifteen-foot-wide road to cut. The work consisted of felling trees, clearing undergrowth, and constructing bridges and culverts over the innumerable mountain streams which crossed the track every hundred yards or so. Behind us came an engineer company—Laotians commanded by French officers and NCOs—with a bulldozer team which uprooted the tree trunks and levelled out the track, and a team of dynamiters who dealt with any rocks that impeded progress. The engineers, being specialists, were also supposed to construct the bridges, but we legionnaires, not being specialists, constructed them faster and better, with the result that, when we got into our stride, the road was soon going ahead about three times as fast as it had been planned to do, throwing everybody's schemes out of gear.

The legionnaires were thoroughly enjoying themselves, leading the carefree, open-air lives of lumberjacks. Their great delight was to bring down some giant of the forest thirty or forty feet in height, and send it crashing to its doom. As we advanced deeper into the jungle and the trees became denser, we found that it was not always so very easy to bring them down. So thick and numerous were the strands of vine and creeper that interlaced themselves among the upper branches of the close-set trees, that it became a not uncommon sight to see a huge forty-footer, measuring as much as five or six feet in diameter at the base, suspended from above, although completely severed at the bole. Then it would often be necessary to cut down eight or nine other trees in order to bring the first one down. Until the *commandant* stopped it, the younger and more active legionnaires made a practice of swarming up the suspended tree and cutting the hundreds of leathery thongs which bound it to its neighbours, descending in a swift, exhilarating rush to the ground, cradled in the tree-top, when the last tendril was severed.

Less interesting for the legionnaires, though much more so for the platoon commanders, who acted as designers and foremen, was the construction of bridges made from the tree trunks thus obtained. Usually the *sous-officier* in charge of a bridging party would name his completed masterpiece after well-known bridges in his own country. A London Bridge and a Westminster Bridge were credited to me—it may be that the notice-boards with the names printed on them are there still—and I was just about to complete Waterloo Bridge when work on the road was finally abandoned.

In order to avoid too frequent changes of position, it had been decided to move the camp by bounds of five miles each time a strip of road of that length had been completed, the stores and material being moved up in the few trucks which had been placed at our disposal. Since the track was being completed at the rate of about a mile a day, this involved a change of camp once every five days or so, and a march to work increasing in distance every day after a change of position until, on the fifth day, we had five miles to march in each direction to and from the scene of operations.

Each platoon took it in turn to send out a section on patrol to a distance of five or six miles along the elephant track beyond the roadhead, not only for the purpose of looking for the enemy, but also to reconnoitre and report on any technical difficulties which might lie ahead.

It was the evening of the first day after a change of camp. Work had then been proceeding on the road for about a month, and there was still no sign of the Viets. But on this particular evening the small patrol which had been sent northwards along the track did not return at the appointed time. Darkness fell, and there was still no sign of the sergeant and eight men who had left at seven that morning with rations for the midday meal.

Nobody was particularly worried. It was not the first time that a patrol had returned late. On one occasion a man had broken a leg while climbing over a rocky waterfall and, carrying him on an improvised stretcher, his comrades had taken two hours longer than they normally would have done to get back to the camp. On another occasion the patrol found a village where they were very well received and invited to stay for a meal with the inhabitants.

Towards midnight the sentry on guard at the point where the elephant path branched out of the northern extremity of the camp clearing heard a sound of movement. To his challenge a voice answered, 'Show a light, for God's sake. Patrol returning. Sergeant Kreschmann.'

A minute or two later the patrol commander, with five legionnaires trailing wearily behind him, stumbled into the camp. Four of the men were carrying two improvised stretchers made from bamboos and groundsheets. The fifth, though walking, was very badly wounded about the face and neck. The sergeant, in addition to his tommy-gun, was carrying a rifle. When the company commander arrived, the sergeant told him what had happened. I chanced to be at hand and heard his account.

'We completed our five miles of reconnaissance,' he said, 'and arrived at the river, which is twenty-four yards from bank to bank at that point.'

He tore a sheet of paper from his pocket-book and handed it to the captain.

'There is the detailed report of the survey,' he continued. 'I wrote it out while we were having lunch at the village by the riverside. Yes, it's not marked on the map. Quite a fair-sized place on the north bank. We had to wade across the river to get there. We wanted to buy a couple of ducks, but they didn't know the meaning of money or perhaps they didn't want it. So we traded cigarettes for them. Unfortunately, we lost the livestock on the way back.'

There was a faint groan from one of the stretchers, as a medical orderly began removing a field-dressing.

'We started back at one o'clock,' went on Kreschmann, 'which should have given us ample time to be back here by about four. You can average two miles an hour along most of the track quite easily. I was taking the usual precautions—five paces interval and arms at the ready. I had no scout ahead, because it would have been quite useless. At no point along that track can you put a man more than five yards ahead of you without losing sight of him. I myself was marching at the head of the column, because there are one or two points where it would have been possible to go wrong, and I wanted to keep my eye on the compass so as to maintain the right general direction.'

'Give me a drop of beer and a fag,' came from one of the stretchers, 'and be careful how you pull my bloody knee about.'

'We had come about a mile from the village when it happened. There was a short burst of tommy-gun fire. It sounded to me exactly like one of our MAT '49s, and I thought it must have been one of my chaps playing the fool; so I sent a message back along the column, "Who was the bloody idiot who did that?" A split second afterwards I realized that I was the only member of the patrol armed with an automatic weapon, so I immediately ordered my men to take cover.

'And that was just the thing I should not have done, and which we mustn't do in future, *mon Capitaine*. As soon as the fellows had gone to ground, there was a series of five explosions, as the grenades which had been planted on the track went off. Kaemerer had been lying almost bang on top of one and was killed instantly. Remediani here,' pointing to the man wounded in the head, 'got splinters in the neck and the base of the skull from another, while Tarquin and Peeters were both wounded in the legs from a third. And that was the end of the incident, though we didn't realize it immediately. I fired a few bursts into the forest, but I couldn't see a damned thing, so it was only wasted ammunition.

'We buried Kaemerer on the spot, not too deep, as I thought you might want to bring him in tomorrow, I have his rifle and ammunition here, and these are the contents of his pockets. When we saw that no further action was to be expected of the Viets, we set about cutting bamboos to make stretchers for the two leg cases, patched up Remediani, and pushed off back here. That was at half-past five, and it has taken us till now to get here.'

The medical officer was examining and prescribing first-aid for the wounded. The company commander was lost in thought for a moment.

'At how many,' he asked Kreschmann, 'do you estimate the strength of this ambush?'

'Impossible to tell, sir. As I say, one couldn't see a thing. You know what it's like in this forest. A man can be sitting two yards or less away from you, and you don't even suspect his presence. I think the ambush might quite possibly have been mounted by one man. We discovered that the five strings attached to the five grenades all led to one spot, about three yards from the track, where a small clearing had been made about two feet in diameter. The Viet had probably been waiting there all day without budging an inch. It's quite possible even that he saw us go out in the morning. As I see it, he waited there with his tommy-gun in one hand and the five strings held in the other. When he heard us returning, he fired his burst of four or five rounds, waited a second or two, and then pulled the strings to explode the grenades.'

'Having done which, he probably pushed off without even waiting for the results,' suggested somebody who was standing by.

'Precisely. He'll read them in tomorrow morning's bush telegraph.'

'There's one thing I don't understand,' said the captain. 'You, I see, are wearing a sergeant's *képi* and stripes. How was it he let you get away with it?'

'Because he didn't see me, sir,' replied the patrol commander irritably. This captain was not very bright. 'Don't you understand? He didn't see any of us. He didn't need to. All he needed was to hear us. Isn't it significant that not one of our four casualties was caused by a bullet? I know he couldn't have seen us because I put myself in the position where he had been squatting. Not an inch of the track could I see. Oh, by the way, Smith, here's a fragment of one of the grenades.'

He felt in his pocket and handed me a jagged splinter of rusty metal, stamped into squares on one side and covered on the other with a yellowish green paste.

'I think you'll agree with me as to what that is,' he said.

I nodded. 'Mills '36. Probably from war stocks abandoned in Burma or somewhere. Look! The explosive is only half burnt. That, of course, is why he wanted to make you go to ground. The killing range must be reduced to about five yards with material in this deteriorated condition.'

'Yes,' said Kreschmann ruefully. 'We'd probably have got away with far less damage if we'd just kept on walking.'

'Well,' he continued, turning to the doctor, who had just concluded his examination of the wounded. 'What's the verdict, please, *Monsieur le Toubib?*'

'The two legs to be evacuated. Remediani here looks a mess but is not serious. Ten days on light duties or until his wounds are healed, whichever is the sooner.'

'H'mm,' said the captain. 'That makes a total loss of one killed and two in hospital as against one Viet who probably got away unscathed. Well, in future no patrol must go out under platoon strength, that's certain. Good night to you all.' And he went off to report to the *commandant*.

I made a wry face at Kreschmann, and he sighed. The captain, of course, hadn't understood a thing. In that sort of country it made no difference whether you sent out one man or a division. As you were bound in any case to be strung out in single file, the total force you could bring to bear, whether you had five men or five thousand marching along the track behind you, was just the one or two men who happened to be at the spot where the ambush had been placed.

After that first incident, patrols were attacked almost every day and, although the NCOs on the spot did their best to minimize losses by profiting from their own and others' experience, nearly every ambush exacted its toll of killed or wounded. On one occasion, when I was out on patrol, we managed to take prisoner the Vietminh who had fired on us, but the man was mortally wounded and died before the interpreter could be brought up to interrogate him.

It was nerve-racking work, patrolling in that dense forest. To begin with, patrols were confined to the elephant track, and our opponent knew it. So thick was the forest on either side that it was quite impossible to march through it. To go a dozen yards, by dint of slashing a way through with our machettes, took anything up to three or four minutes. We tried as much as possible to avoid 'bunching' by maintaining a distance of four or five yards between men. It was no good trying to increase that interval, for you just lost sight of one another. At first I used to keep a pretty sharp lookout on either side, but after a time I gave that up as useless, for you could not see a man at a distance of three feet.

Bit by bit we worked out counter-measures for the Laotian forest type of ambush. To stay on the track, once the first shot had been fired, was obviously suicide, since we merely got cut to pieces by the exploding grenades. We decided that the best thing to do, as soon as we were fired on, was to dash away from the path into the forest, firing with everything we'd got. Then we discovered that, in the split second after the shot was fired, it was impossible to say from which side the bullets had come. Thereafter we detailed men alternately along the column to charge to the right and left respectively. Using these tactics, we managed to kill an adversary on two or three occasions and decreased our own casualties considerably.

# 31

THAT year, at least, we managed to celebrate Christmas on Christmas Day. For two or three days supplies, solid and liquid, had been pouring in from Hanoi by plane. Although in the rest of the French Army Christmas is not looked upon as a very important festival, in the Legion it is celebrated in very much the same way as in the British Army. Every man receives a handsome present bought out of Legion welfare and company funds. These presents are distributed on Christmas Eve, and then the whole company sits down together to a meal presided over by the company commander.

On the morning of Christmas Eve I went out with my platoon on patrol to a near-by village in order to buy additional supplies of meat: a few ducks, a pig or two, and, if possible, a buffalo. We arrived at the village—one which we had not yet visited—without incident. The inhabitants were very primitive. Most of them had never left the huts in which they were born. They gazed in rapt admiration and astonishment at the hundred-piastre notes with which we paid for our purchases. Apart from the chief of the village, who knew its value, none of them had ever seen money before. Under each of the raised dwellings, side by side with the pigs and chickens, was a simple hand-loom on which the women wove the sarongs that were their only covering. So far as I could ascertain, so primitive were these people that the wheel as a machine was unknown. At least, I never saw a wheel in any of those isolated villages. Its most elementary adaptation—for raising water from a well—was unnecessary, since there was no well. They took their water from the near-by river.

We acquired three ducks and two pigs, and negotiated for a buffalo. The difficulty was not buying the beast, but conducting it back to camp. For some reason best known to himself, the domestic water buffalo of Indo-China, which is about the size and shape of an ox, with very long, curved horns, cannot stand the sight or smell of Europeans and, although a little yellow child may lead him quite easily by the nose, he turns at bay, breathing fire through his nostrils, if a white man seizes the halter. (In revenge, European dogs, especially the better-bred ones, cannot stand the Indo-Chinese and take a great delight in biting them!)

By dint of much prodding and beating, we at last managed to get our champion under control and started back to camp. We hadn't gone more than a mile when we fell into one of the usual ambushes. No one was hurt by the enemy's action, but the buffalo, sensing no doubt that reinforcements were at hand, took the side of his compatriots and went berserk. He charged the legionnaire who was leading him and gored him; and to save the poor fellow's life, I had no alternative but to press the trigger of my tommy-gun and pour a stream of bullets into the beast's head and chest. Even then I was lucky to kill him with a bullet through the heart, for the first two or three bounced off his tough skull as off the armour-plating of a heavy tank.

By sheer coincidence the legionnaire whom the buffalo had tossed was the one and only Spaniard in the whole Headquarters Company: I'm sorry; he really was. In spite of three broken ribs and a ragged gash from the base of the spine to the left armpit, he found the strength to cut off the ear of the vanquished and hand it to me with a courtly, bull-ring gesture. We had to leave the carcase where it was, of course, but we cut out the tongue and a couple of joints, patched up the wounded matador, and went on back to camp.

A padre had been imported from Hanoi along with the fresh vegetables and the champagne. Before we sat down to our midnight feast, he said a Mass for three men who had been killed the day before on other patrols. Everybody attended that Mass, Catholic or not. It was very short, very simple, and very touching. The altar consisted of a packing-case covered with a blanket, on which were placed a vase of flowers, a tiny wooden crucifix, two domestic candles, and the Missal. The priest wore a simple white surplice over his khaki-drill trousers, and a black stole. At the end a German choir sang *Stille Nacht*. Then the padre took off his stole.

'Let's go and have a drink,' he said.

Tables had been arranged in the open air in the form of a square, and the whole company, with the exception of those who were on guard, sat down together. We were waited upon by the PIMs. In the middle of the square formed by the festive board an enormous camp-fire had been built, its flames rising to a height of fifteen or twenty feet. The *commandant* had decided to throw caution to the winds for that night.

'*Que diable!*' he said, as he visited us on his way round the companies. 'It's Christmas, isn't it? Let's enjoy it. If we're attacked, well, we're attacked, and we'll have a jolly good fight.'

The party continued until three in the morning, and a few hardy individuals went on till dawn. There was plenty to drink, and most of us took full advantage of the fact. I remember that Jaderny, who had already had quite enough by midnight, got up from the table at about two, to go and relieve himself. After stumbling about for several minutes in the darkness beyond the firelight, and then groping his way all round the square of tables with his arms stretched out blindly in front of him, he came back to me, weeping bitter alcoholic tears.

'I can't find the door, *Chef*,' he sobbed.

At midday the next morning, just as we were sitting down to our Christmas Day dinner, news came through on the radio that the other half of the battalion had been very heavily attacked in the Plaine des Jarres. Only about seventy-five miles of road then remained to be cut in order to effect the junction between north and south. During the afternoon the engineer company disappeared in a cloud of dust in the direction of Paksane.

There was panic in high places that night. Suddenly, where only isolated handfuls of Vietminh had been before, there now appeared to be whole battalions, or at least so the Intelligence reports said. Three or four divisions were even talked of. On the day after Christmas the High Command took fright and decided to evacuate the Plaine des Jarres. Most of the troops were evacuated by air, but the other half of our battalion, which was less than eighty miles away to the north, was ordered to continue marching southwards through the forest, while we were to march northwards to meet them. A meeting-point was arranged about midway, where there was a fairly large ricefield, which constituted a clearing in the forest about a mile square that could be used for the parachuting of supplies.

At first glance our march to the north seemed unnecessary. It was to be presumed that the other two companies were capable of finding their own way down, without our having to lead them by the hand. As events proved, however, it was just as well that we did meet them. Just before the junction was effected they were very heavily attacked, and had such a number of men wounded that they would have had difficulty in carrying them without our help. We asked for helicopters at the dropping zone, but no helicopters were forthcoming, and the wounded had to be carried all the way down the track to our roadhead. A few stretcher cases could slow down a marching column in that sort of country to such an extent that whereas we from the south took only one and a half days to do our forty miles to the north, the others took four and a half days to arrive at the rendezvous.

Among the parachuted stores were several cases of beer in just sufficient quantity to allow of the distribution of one bottle to two men. The cases, jealously guarded by armed sentries for two days, were opened as soon as the other party arrived in the late afternoon of the 31st, and I foregathered with Nagy, whom we had not seen for nearly two months, and Jaderny to toast the arrival of 1954. After a time we were joined by Sibley, who had also come down from the north. We had much to tell each other and plenty of experiences to compare. The talk continued far into the early hours of New Year's Day.

Slowly the talk veered round to the subject which was worrying all of us more and more, and was becoming a universal topic of conversation, although it was never discussed in front of the men, among Legion *sous-officiers*—the quality and standard of competence of the officers. I say that we never discussed this subject with the men; the hard core of Legion discipline would have prevented us from doing so. But in any case it would have been unnecessary. One only had to look in their eyes to see at a glance what they were thinking.

The situation had been going from bad to worse for a year or two. The officers of the permanent cadre of the Legion had always been furnished by the cream of the Saint-Cyr promotion. The highest honour to which a newly commissioned officer could aspire used to be a posting to the Legion; but, as an aftermath of the Second World War, which supplied the human material, and of the Far East theatre of operations, which made that material necessary in ever-increasing numbers, the Legion had been swollen to many times its normal strength, with the result that there were not nearly enough officers of the right type, with the right background and training, to go round; and the casualties among even those few available had been heavy.

Had the French Government left it at that, all might have been well—*sous-officiers* of the Legion were accustomed to doing the work of junior, and often of senior officers, anyhow. But it wasn't left at that. Officers from regular units, who in most cases had no particular desire to serve with the Legion, were entirely unsuited for such employment, and were often far less capable than the majority of their immediate subordinates, were transferred to the Legion for the duration of a tour in Indo-China. Many of them had only one reason for wishing to be in Indo-China at all, and that was to make money.

'*Chef,*' said Nagy, 'you don't know how glad I am to be back under your command.'

'Yes?' I replied. 'How much do you want to borrow?'

Nagy shook his head impatiently.

'Protection is what I want,' he said. 'Protection from idiotic, ill-considered orders, such as those I've been having to take from that ignorant little half-baked squirt of a second-lieutenant who was commanding our half of the Headquarters Company. If you, *Chef,* order me to execute some tomfoolery or other, I shall know that you're only transmitting orders you've received and which you yourself probably know to be ridiculous. Knowing that, I shan't be tempted to knock your block off or call you an imbecile, both of which I've been holding myself back from doing every day for the last two months, whenever that little pint-sized twerp of an officer spoke to me.'

'Oh, hell!' said another sergeant who was with us. 'He's not so bad as all that. What about the senior lieutenant in our company? He can't even read a map, and that evening when we'd been on patrol across the river he marched straight towards the setting sun and couldn't understand why he wasn't getting any farther eastwards.'

'What the hell does that matter?' put in somebody else. 'You were there to put him right, weren't you? That's what you're there for. He may be a fool, but he doesn't mind admitting his mistakes. And at least he's honest. What do you think of a company commander who receives fifteen loaves as the result of the day's parachuting, keeps five for himself, and leaves ten for distribution to the seventy men of his company?'

It was Sibley who clinched the argument.

'The best thing to do,' he said, 'is not to think. But if ever I had to write an epitaph for the Legion—and it wouldn't in the least surprise me if that were necessary before this bloody mess in Indo-China is over—I would describe it as "The best army in the world commanded by the worst officers!"'

Poor old Sibley! He grew very fond of that little epigram. He repeated it once too often. Back at Paksane, a few days later, he got very drunk and shouted it through the door of the officers' mess to all the officers assembled. A week later he came down to second-class soldier again.

# 32

A CONVOY of lorries was waiting at the roadhead ready to take us down to Paksane. How we cursed those clumsy Laotian drivers, as they slammed us into every pothole they could find on the road and stalled their engines at the bottom of each ravine. Had we known that they were the last wheeled vehicles we were to see for five hundred long, weary miles, we might have been more appreciative!

When we arrived at the village on the River Mekong, the situation was not encouraging. Savannaket, two hundred miles to the south, had fallen, and a Vietminh division was reported to be advancing on Vientiane, a hundred miles to the west. At that time, most of us were sceptical about these reported brigades and divisions; and we went on being so for the next two months, for we rarely saw the Vietminh in more than isolated twos and threes, and never in greater strength than a company. Subsequent events, however, proved that the reports were only too true; and I now know that many a time during our march through the jungle we were within only a mile or two of very large enemy forces—and within an inch of disaster.

We stayed three days in Paksane before proceeding on our first operation from that base. We refitted to the limited extent that this was possible and received reinforcements—fifty *bleus* newly arrived from North Africa. The old sweats threw up their hands in despair. They knew perfectly well what was going to happen. We were sitting exactly five hundred yards from an international frontier. A mile away, on the other side of the Mekong, was Thailand.

'Isabelle'. 'It all looked so peaceful'

The men who had nothing to lose

There were thirty deserters the first night. Eight more were absent from roll-call the second morning. In the three days a total of thirty-four men deserted. But mark this! Only one man out of the whole thirty-four had more than six months' service; and he was due for trial on a charge of cowardice in the face of the enemy!

The Thai authorities were very correct in their handling of the situation. Deserters of French origin, who were apprehended by them, were returned to us under Frontier Police escort. The others were repatriated to their country of origin, strictly according to international law. One of my fellows later received a letter from one of the deserters, dated from Hamburg exactly five days after he had deserted!

For our move from Paksane we were brigaded with a Laotian battalion, the formation being commanded by a colonel. Of the latter all I will say is that he would surely have been happier and more suitably employed sitting at home by the fireside with his feet in carpet slippers, reading history instead of attempting preposterously to create it.

The object of the operation was the seizing of an airfield, about midway between Paksane and Savannaket, before the Viets laid hands on it. We marched seventy or eighty miles through the most appallingly difficult country, living on iron rations and being supplied by parachute; but we never seized the airfield. When we were about ten miles from our objective we were potted at by a few Vietminh, and had some casualties. The colonel ordered right about turn and marched us back towards Paksane. That was the one and only time during my five and a half years' service with the Legion that I ever saw signs of breaking morale. Even then the feeling expressed on the men's faces was less one of failing resolution than of utter disgust. They would have preferred to risk heavy casualties rather than turn and run for it, as we had been ordered to do.

About thirty miles south of Paksane we took to the river, the two battalions being transported in twelve large native barges harnessed two at a time to six motor-gunboats. In this way we ascended the Mekong to a point about a hundred miles north of Paksane, waving and making rude noises to our base as we passed it.

If from now on I am a little vague as to places and dates, it is because I have forgotten them, if indeed I ever knew them. For during the two months after we disembarked somewhere to the south of Luong Pra Bang, we marched something like four hundred miles through forest and jungle, always heading towards the east. Night followed day in monotonous succession. We forgot the events of the previous day as soon as the next morning dawned. We forgot the names of the places through which we had passed. We forgot the date of the month and the day of the week. We lived only for the present, and our only realities were the loads we were carrying on our backs and the jungle path stretching out interminably before us. The only events of importance were the parachutings of supplies at the dropping zones. Our whole existence came to centre in those sacks and packing-cases dropping out of the sky at the end of their red, white, and green umbrellas.

I don't think we marched more than twenty miles in any one day, and on most of them we averaged only ten or twelve; but even ten miles in that sort of country, loaded down like packhorses as we were, was heartbreaking work. Each of us, in addition to his personal arms and ammunition, was carrying a thirty-pound pack. My men were also carrying the mortars. The 81-mm mortar is divided into three loads each weighing approximately thirty pounds—the base-plate, the tube, and the biped—and carrying any one of them was no Sunday afternoon picnic. My two hundred and forty mortar shells were distributed among six mules and six PIMs. The mortars had to be taken even through the dense jungle where they were valueless, for they could be and were used whenever we camped in one of the open ricefields used as dropping zones for supplies.

Even loaded as we were, a march of fifteen or even twenty miles in a day would have been of no great account, had we been able to step out and get the business over quickly. Two things prevented us from doing so. The jungle track along which we were travelling was, for ninety per cent of the way, a mere tunnel bored through the densely intertwining undergrowth between the trees, and this tunnel, cut by the natives to their own measure, was rarely more than five feet high. Consequently, we were forced to march bent almost double.

Secondly, we marched very slowly. When a thousand men are marching in single file, even though it be along a first-class road, there is always a constant stopping and starting towards the rear of the column; but when you are following an uneven track, dotted every two feet with the four-inch deep holes made by elephants' feet, and with obstacles such as fallen trees, rivers and boulders every two hundred yards or so, then your progress at the rear consists of a series of short moves forward of four or five yards, followed by waits of two or three minutes while the column sorts itself out ahead of you. These spasmodic halts were never long enough to allow you to drop your load and ease your aching back, so that, nine days out of ten, we would start our march at six in the morning and arrive at our destination fifteen miles away at seven or eight in the evening, without once having had a chance to remove our packs from our sweating shoulders.

For those of us who were merely carrying our loads it was bad enough; for those who were carrying stretchers containing the wounded it must have been terrible. At one time the progress of the march was impeded to such an extent by the number of stretcher cases that orders were given for all men whose legs were not broken to march. In my platoon there was one man who went on for three days with both arms smashed, and another with brush fever and a temperature which never dropped below 102°, who completed the entire march and refused to let anybody carry his pack. We had returned to the old traditional formula of the Legion, '*Marche ou crève!*' with a vengeance. 'March or die!' was the order of the day.

Our physical troubles were not the only ones. Slowly the dismal conviction forced itself into our fatigue-dimmed minds: we were no longer chasing the Viets; they were chasing us.

On the fifteenth or sixteenth day of the march, one of my mules broke a foreleg clambering down a rocky declivity with a badly adjusted load, and I had to shoot him. I distributed his load as follows: four shells to each of the five remaining mules, one to each coolie, and one to each of the six legionnaires who were carrying the smallest loads of equipment. Some fellows would have put the whole lot on the PIMs, but I didn't believe in that. They were human beings after all, even though they were prisoners, and rather under-nourished human beings at that.

The next day, or it may have been the day after, the coolie who carried the company commander's kit was killed, and he requisitioned one of my PIMs to carry his pack. I distributed the nine shells he had been carrying as one to each of the five remaining PIMs and four among the legionnaires, the mules being already dangerously overloaded.

The men were overloaded, too, and this cut down our speed considerably. That was the day when a battalion and a half of Viets was reported to be coming up in our rear, and the captain was at me all the time to get a move on.

At last I lost my temper.

'*Eh bien, mon Capitaine,*' I said. 'If you want us to go faster, just you give me back the coolie you've pinched from me and carry your pack yourself, as I'm doing.'

That suggestion didn't appeal to him an awful lot, and he asked me how many shells the PIM in question had been carrying. I told him nine.

'Throw away nine shells and get a move on,' he urged.

'What! and leave 'em to the Viets?' I said. 'Not bloody likely! I started out with two hundred and forty, and I'm going to arrive with two hundred and forty, less those that I fire.'

He didn't insist, and fortunately that afternoon we had a bit of a battle. I fired off forty rounds, thus lightening the load a little.

That same evening we came to a river crossing. I can't remember the name of the river, but it was quite a big one. There were some Viets, variously estimated from two or three men to a brigade, harassing us all the time in the rear, and some others who were reported to be bearing down on us from the northwest. It looked as though, if we managed to get safely across and destroy the boats on the other side, we might achieve a measure of temporary security. We were bringing up the rear that day, and Flouflou, as we called my company commander, was always much more jittery when we were at the head or tail of the column than when we were safely tucked away in the middle.

After he was brought down to second-class, Sibley had become Flouflou's radio operator, so he was marching with us. He told me that the orders for the river crossing were that company commanders were to remain on the west bank, until the whole of their respective companies had passed over, and then cross in the last boat. In addition, Flouflou had been assigned the task of ensuring that all boats were destroyed on the other side as soon as the movement was completed. This didn't please Flouflou very much. It meant that he was going to be the last across of the entire battalion.

As it turned out, there weren't nearly enough boats: six for the whole battalion, I believe there were; and by the time we came to cross two had been lost, so that we were reduced to four miserable dug-outs capable of carrying only two men apiece for moving an entire company across a river one hundred and fifty yards wide. In the orders he gave, the captain assigned one boat to each platoon (signals, pioneers, and miscellaneous), and the fourth to my heavy platoon and company headquarters.

It wasn't until about one o'clock in the morning that the company in front of us finished crossing. When we started, the captain told me to send the HQ men across first in the boat allotted to me. This I did. It necessitated ten journeys for the ten men left on HQ, for, after each transport, one of the two men in the boat had to bring it back again. This took quite a bit of time, and it was not until after two that I began ferrying my men across.

The captain, looking on, all dither and impatience, noticed that there was only one man in the first boat.

'What the devil are you doing there, Smith?' he asked in a hoarse whisper, as though the Viets were only five yards away, which they may have been for all I know. 'Why on earth is there only one man in that boat?'

I explained that I was ferrying my ammunition across first. Allowing fifty rounds to a boat, to be on the safe side, I had reckoned on four boat journeys to get the stuff across.

He let the first load go. It was well out into midstream before we had finished arguing about it, anyhow. When the boat returned, he told me to stop shipping ammunition and get the men across. I didn't like doing it, but I executed the order. Next I ordered five men to swim across with the mules, and we had another argument about that. He wanted me to shoot them and leave them there. Again I wouldn't play, and Flouflou was not in a very strong position for insisting on his orders being obeyed.

At last only the captain, together with Sibley and his radio set, one of my men and myself remained on the west bank. I started loading ammunition again.

'Drop that, Smith,' said the captain, very white about the gills. 'Let's get going.'

'What about the ammunition?' I asked.

'Oh, damn the ammunition,' he moaned, and there was almost a trace of tears in his voice. 'Drop the beastly stuff into the river. You've already got a few rounds on the other side. That'll be enough.'

All the rest of the company was already across. We could hear them smashing their boats on the other side. Suddenly from about a mile behind us there was a burst of machine-gun fire. I cannot imagine who it can have been. I turned to Flouflou, who was now fairly shaking. 'Why don't you take the boat and go across now?' I asked. 'I'll follow on afterwards.'

He didn't hesitate a second.

'Yes,' he said. 'I certainly ought to be getting over and organizing things over there.' He leapt into the boat and was gone. After a few minutes my legionnaire boatman came back, and I sent Sibley over, for the captain had forgotten all about his radio operator. Then we ferried the remaining ammunition and crossed ourselves, setting fire to the boat on the east side of the river.

As a matter of fact, Flouflou wasn't at all a bad fellow. I personally rather liked him. He was efficient, and I admire efficiency in a soldier. He gave clear, precise orders. He had an excellent memory, was a first-class map-reader and a very good organizer. He was even, as French officers went, fairly honest. His only failing was that he wasn't very keen on the sound of guns going off, if you see what I mean.

# 33

I AM not very proud of myself when I think of the incident I am now about to relate. It is not very pleasant to know that, because of a hastily and unthoughtfully spoken word, which one uttered vindictively, not caring where the barbed shaft fell, a man died. There is only one excuse for me. I was, as all of us were, overwrought, living on my nerves, mentally and physically worn out.

The night after the river crossing, we made camp on a dropping zone and, amongst the supplies parachuted, were several pairs of boots. As the ones I was wearing were very nearly dropping off my feet, I went to the quartermaster and drew a new pair. They seemed to be quite all right at first, but after a mile or so of marching I realized that they were slightly too short for me. As I had no desire to cripple myself, I took out my jack-knife and simply cut a hole in the toe of each boot, so as to give my toes a little more room.

Three or four days later—I say three or four days, but it may have been a fortnight, for all I know—we camped at the foot of a range of mountains which turned out to be the frontier between Laos and Tongking. That day we did not march. Having dug our trenches and weapon-pits, we were left to laze about in the sun and rest in preparation for the trek over the heights which lay before us. Sentries had been posted all around, and those who were not on duty stood about gossiping, washed their shirts, or simply lay basking. I was sitting with a group of *sous-officiers*, doing nothing very much, when Flouflou came and joined us.

He was looking very pleased with himself, for it appeared that he had just learnt his name was on the list for promotion to *commandant*. He produced a bottle of cognac, which he must have been carrying for weeks, to celebrate the occasion.

So we had a drink and chatted away about this and that. And suddenly there was one of those unaccountable breaks in the conversation when, for an uncomfortable moment or two, nobody seems to be able to think of anything to say. I was tickling my toes with a twig through the holes in the fore ends of my boots, trying to think of something witty, when the captain broke the awkward silence.

'*Sabotage*, Smith,' he said. 'Deterioration of army property! Do you know what would have happened before the war to a *sous-officier* of the French Army who did that to a pair of boots?'

I knew he was only saying it in fun, just to supply the gap in the conversation, and that he didn't mean anything by it. But I also knew that the retort was welling up inside me, and that, whether I liked it or not, it was going to burst out. As I say, our nerves were on edge, and we sometimes found ourselves saying things that would never have passed our lips in more normal circumstances.

'No,' I replied very evenly. 'What would have happened to him, *mon Capitaine*?'

'He'd have been broken,' replied Flouflou, looking at me in the half-serious, half-mocking way he had.

So then I let him have it, straight between the eyes.

'Really?' I said, negligently knocking the ash off the end of my cigarette. 'And tell me, Captain, what would have happened to an officer of the French Army who, in a fit of panic, ordered his mortar platoon commander to throw three-quarters of his ammunition into the river? What would have happened to him, *mon Capitaine?* He would, no doubt, have been decorated with the *Légion d'Honneur.*'

I don't think I shall ever forget the look on Flouflou's face. Anger was there, certainly, but not only anger. There was also the pitiful, desperate, naked look of a man whose weak point has been exposed, raw and bleeding, before witnesses. He flushed, and swallowed hard, trying to find something to say.

He never said it. Two seconds later we were all scrambling into our slit trenches, and bullets were buzzing all around. For the first time since our march began, we were being attacked in the open and in daylight. It didn't last long, but it was fierce while it lasted. We discovered later that a section of Vietminh had approached through the forest, had killed the lookout man silently with an arrow fired from one of the native crossbows, and then, seeing the whole battalion going nonchalantly about its peaceable occupations, had decided to make a kill. At the time it was evident that the attack would not last long, for we could tell that only two enemy machine-guns were firing. Meanwhile, a number of men who had been caught in the open were lying dead and wounded about the ricefield.

Among them was one man who, groaning in agony, was lying only about twelve yards in front of the trench where the captain was sheltering. We knew better than to try to get him in. The attack would be over in a minute or two. Meanwhile it would have been foolish for anyone to brave the bursts of machine-gun fire which were still pouring from the trees at the edge of the forest.

Yes, foolish even for a very brave man.

All at once we saw a figure leap from a trench and begin running across the bullet-swept open space towards the wounded man.

'Come back, *mon Capitaine*, come back!' shouted a dozen voices; but Flouflou went on. He reached the wounded man, and had started dragging him back towards the trench before the Vietminh got him. When the enemy had retired and we were able to get out and count our losses, we found that it had taken four bullets to kill him. I am pretty certain that he was hit at least once on his way out. It was a foolish, but brave act, and, in a way, I felt responsible for his death.

# 34

I THINK it took us four days to get across the mountains. I cannot be sure, for we had by then lost all sense of time; but I think it must have been about that, because we started off with three days' rations, and I know that when we arrived at our camp on the Tongking side we had had nothing to eat that day. As we staggered down the eastern foothills, we caught occasional glimpses, through the trees, of the flat, open country of the Delta.

At last the long, weary column of marching men straggled into the clearing and dispersed automatically, each company and section to its appointed defensive position. We began taking off our heavy packs and sinking lethargically to the ground. Breathing deeply, we gazed up with unseeing eyes at the sky or the leaves of the trees in the near-by forest. Some pulled out their handkerchiefs to wipe away from their eyes the sweat which was pouring down from their brows. Others, too tired to thrust their hands into their pockets, executed a similar movement with their shirt-sleeves. Grunting and swearing, the machine-gunners began placing their weapons in the positions indicated by their platoon commanders. I told Nagy and Jaderny to get their mortars into action, and assigned a firing sector to each.

'What's the name of this place, *Chef*?' asked a legionnaire. I looked at my map.

'Dien something or other,' I replied. 'I can't see properly, because my map's creased just at that spot.'

'Dien Bien Phu,' supplied Jaderny. 'But we can't be exactly there. Have a look at my map, *Chef*. See here, if this is the track we've just left, then we should be about five kilometres south of the village. Anyhow, I can't see any village.'

'And in any case, it should be bigger than a mere village,' I replied. 'Dien Bien Phu is a fairly important centre of road communications. But you're right, Jaderny, we must be here.' I indicated a point on the map with my thumb-nail.

'Not a bad position to defend, this,' said Nagy, looking about him.

'Only if you held those hill-tops,' said Jaderny, pointing to a pair of sharply rising cones, about four hundred yards away, one on each side of the path by which we had descended from the mountains.

'And you'd need much more than one battalion to hold such a position,' I asserted.

'There's a rumour going round that a couple of Legion battalions are coming up from the Delta as reinforcements,' said Nagy. 'Hallo! There's Twerp calling you for orders, *Chef.*'

'Right,' I replied, getting slowly and painfully to my feet. 'I'll go and see what's cooking.'

The lieutenant who had replaced Flouflou in command of the HQ company gave orders for the occupation of the position. He told the little group assembled round him—the battalion sergeant-major, the *adjutant* in charge of signals, the pioneer sergeant, and myself—that the plan was to stay where we were and fortify as much as possible. He confirmed the rumour that further troops were arriving, but spoke of one Legion battalion only.

'And now,' he concluded, 'there are some administrative orders. Four plane loads of reinforcements for the battalion are arriving here tomorrow morning. They will land on the airstrip at Dien Bien Phu, three miles north of here. The *commandant* has decided that all those due for repatriation up to and including the thirtieth of March will return to rear base at Hanoi by the same aeroplanes.'

'And the walking wounded?' asked the sergeant-major.

'Will be evacuated by the same planes. How many have we?'

'Six with the company and two with battalion medicals.'

'Good. Now, how many are we going to lose? Headquarters section, Sergeant-Major?'

'Repatriation? Two, sir. Corporal Blowinski and your batman.'

'Oh dear! I must see about replacing him. What about signals?'

'Four, sir,' replied the signals *adjutant*. 'We're going to be very short of radio operators.'

'H'mm! Pioneers?'

'Only one,' answered the pioneer sergeant gloomily. 'But a very important one. Garstein, the best machine-gunner in the battalion.'

'Oh, you'll replace him all right. Sergeant-Major, I hope you're making a note of all these figures?'

The *adjutant* nodded. He didn't need to make notes. The dates of repatriation of every single member of the battalion had long been recorded in his pocket-book.

'How about you, Smith?' continued the lieutenant. 'How many are you going to lose?'

'The whole platoon,' I replied absently.

'The whole platoon!' cried the officer. 'But that's ridiculous. It's just not possible. What's he talking about, Sergeant-Major?'

'*Pardon, mon Lieutenant*,' I said, coming back to earth. 'What I meant was that I'm due for repatriation myself, so that I shall, in effect, be losing the platoon. I'm due on the twenty-eighth of March. I'm the only one from my bunch.'

'I see,' said the lieutenant. 'That's a bit of a facer, that is. Sergeant-Major, we'd better ask battalion for a replacement.'

The questions of repatriation and reinforcement having been disposed of, the pioneer sergeant spoke up.

'While we're on the subject of administration, *mon Lieutenant*, would you please enlighten us as to the ration situation?'

'Why, what about the rations?'

'Merely that we were in rations till last night only, and that we have received no issue today.'

'Nonsense! I have eaten two good meals.'

'Yes, sir. But only because you ate your batman's rations for yesterday, he having taken his meals with my fellows off the remains of the pig I bought at Nam Sat.'

'Is that true, Sergeant-Major?'

'Perfectly true, *mon Lieutenant*.'

'Well, you'd better ask battalion whether rations are going to be parachuted tonight.'

'I have. They are,' answered the sergeant-major, and the orders group broke up.

'Well, there we are,' sighed Jaderny, when I told him and Nagy that I was leaving. 'Pity we couldn't have gone back together but, in any case, I ought to be following you in about a month. We'll meet up in Paris and have a drink one day. There's one thing, my pack will be lighter as from tonight, for we'll broach those two bottles of cognac I've been toting around with me ever since Paksane. After we've had some grub, we'll gather together and drink your health and a pleasant voyage. We'll try and get Sibley over, too. One of the radio ops who are leaving with you tomorrow can relieve him at the company set.'

# 35

Half a dozen of us sat round the embers of the camp-fire that evening. The battalion sergeant-major, Nagy and Jaderny, Sibley and a man from another company were there with me, and every now and then somebody would come along to shake my hand and drink a quick shot of cognac before returning to his position. It didn't take us long to get through Jaderny's two bottles, but the pioneer sergeant produced a third, and during the evening the corporal commanding number three mortar came across silently and slipped a bottle into my hand.

'A present from Number Three,' he said. 'Good luck, *Chef*.'

We were talking about the loss of memory which had affected quite a lot of us during the march, and which, indeed, was a characteristic failing of most people who had been two years or more in Indo-China.

'Don't I know it?' cried the *adjutant*. 'Unless I make a note in my pocket-book of everything I have to do, I forget half of it completely two hours afterwards.'

'Have you ever noticed,' I said, enlarging on the subject. 'Have you ever noticed that, when you look back on your life, you remember very clearly the exciting and pleasant things you have done, but very little about the ordered run of your normal, humdrum existence? That, I suppose, is why people talk about the good old days. They only remember the good parts, and all the misery, poverty, squalor, and boredom are forgotten.'

I uncorked and distributed the contents of the third bottle.

'I remember thinking only the other day,' I continued, 'what a good time I seemed to have when I was a young man earning only a few pounds a week. Of course, I probably had a miserable time, broke and bored most of it; but all I can remember now are the days at the end of the month when I went out and blew my entire salary, leaving myself with no money to buy cigarettes even until pay-day came round again.'

'Perhaps,' suggested Sibley, 'that is why people always think the cost of living as compared with earnings was lower in their youth than it is today. They think their money went farther, because they only remember the occasions when they spent it and have forgotten the times when they hadn't any.'

'When *I* look back on my early life,' said Jaderny, 'all I can remember are the bad things I did: setting a trap to make my father fall downstairs, and stealing jam from the food cupboard. Both incidents occurred before I was six years old, and I cannot remember any other things at all that happened to me at that age; certainly none of the good things I did, if I ever did any.'

'Yes,' said the sergeant-major. 'That's true enough. And I suppose, if you like to look at it that way, it's just as well to do plenty of bad things while you're young, so you'll have something to think about when you're old. Saints must have a thoroughly miserable time when they get to the age of seventy. It's a pretty good argument against the Kingdom of Heaven and eternal life. The fellows there must be bored to tears. It's the chaps down under who have a good time, swapping stories about the things they did to get sent there. But where's all this leading to, Smith?'

'I was thinking on those lines,' I replied, 'with reference to my five years in the Legion. I was wondering what I, or any of us for that matter, will think about this episode of our lives five or ten years after. Looking back now, I honestly say that I do not regret having joined. Certainly, considering the moral state I was in when I signed on, I think it was by far the best thing I could have done. The only other alternative would have been to chuck myself in the river, and it was too cold to do that.'

'My alternative would have been the cloister,' said Jaderny, 'especially as I'd had about as much as I could stand of women.'

'I thought of that, too,' said Sibley, 'and for much the same reason. I suppose, in the days when the Catholic Church was the most important international force in Europe, that would have been the solution for a good many of us. I didn't pursue the question because I felt that I wasn't spiritually up to the mark. Frankly, I don't think they'd have taken me.'

The sergeant-major yawned.

'Well, chaps,' I said, 'let's drink this up, and then I'll pour out the last one—the one for the road—and let you fellows get some sleep. You'll be needing it. The Viets are leaving us pretty well alone tonight, but who knows that they won't start up again tomorrow.'

I opened the last bottle and distributed it. Sibley was sitting smiling to himself. He lit a cigarette and smoked for a minute or two in silence. He was slightly drunk. He stood up, grasping his mug of cognac in his right hand.

'Gentlemen,' he said, 'as the most newly demoted second-class legionnaire in this assembly, it is my duty and pleasure to propose a toast to our old comrade, *Sergent-Chef* Smith, leaving tomorrow for the fleshpots of Hanoi, thence to proceed by divers means of locomotion to other and juicier fleshpots.

'*Chef* Smith was attempting just now to analyse his feelings about the five years he has spent in the Legion. Now, I always was better at that sort of thing than he. Perhaps he will remember my telling him a few home truths just about five years ago today, and I think he knows now that I was right in some of what I told him. I'll tell you why our old friend Smith, and many others like him, will always look back with a certain wistful feeling to the time they spent here. It is simply because of the *camaraderie* they have found, and I use the word in its widest sense. I am not talking of the close friendships which are often formed, and which, alas, can all too quickly be ended by the firing of a single bullet or the explosion of a single grenade. I am not even speaking of the spirit of pulling together, which certainly exists. I am referring to that far wider and deeper comradeship which binds all of us here together, and which unites the most senior *adjutant-chef* to the most newly joined *bleu*, even though they may be at opposite ends of the world and do not know of each other's existence.'

There were several bursts of machine-gun fire far away to the north-west.

'Sounds as if the Fifth are catching it,' said someone.

'What is at the root of this *camaraderie*?' continued Sibley. 'And why are the bonds uniting this brotherhood so sure? I will tell you. It is the sympathy born of a common suffering which forges the bonds, sure as those which unite twins that have travailled in a common womb. Whether it be the senior warrant officer with twenty years' service or the recruit with twenty days', they opened the same door with the same key. Both underwent the same or similar preliminary training. Before that, both had been bullied and insulted by the same sort of NCOs, after having walked through the gates of the same sort of recruiting station with nothing but the same sort of despair in their hearts.

'It was that despair, so irresistible was its force, which made you and you and all of us take the decision to walk through the gates of the Bas Fort Saint-Nicolas. The despair of those who have lost the things they held most dear and have nothing more to lose. And the shadow of that despair, my friends, has never left you. It bit so deeply into your soul that it has become part of your very being. That is what binds us together, and that is what makes the essential of the story of the Legion—not the five, ten or fifteen years you serve in its ranks, but the short, intense period of mental agony which preceded your decision to join it.'

We stirred silently but uncomfortably.

'Sorry,' concluded Sibley. 'I've made a speech. Gentlemen, here's to *Chef* Smith and—*vive la Légion!*'

I recognized a number of old friends among the reinforcements who arrived on the airstrip the next morning. Among them were *Adjutant* McAndrew, the American who had been with me in the Transport Company at Hanoi, and a legionnaire I had not seen for five years, since the day when he had strutted about in the courtyard of the Bas Fort Saint-Nicolas at Marseilles—Rousseau, the uncrowned king of the Canebière. I only had time to shake hands with both of them and wish them the traditional '*Merde!*' for the planes had orders not to remain more than ten minutes on the ground.

As the DC3 circled round and headed east towards Hanoi, I could see below me hundreds of tiny figures feverishly digging trenches all round the airstrip we had just left. Farther off to the south was another group of figures waving to us from the place which was later to be known as 'Isabelle', the southern strongpoint of the fortress of Dien Bien Phu.

It all looked very peaceful from a thousand feet up in the air, but that same night all hell was let loose there. As it turned out, we were the last *rapatriables* to come out of the place. Thereafter the few aeroplanes which succeeded in landing there and taking off again returned to Hanoi loaded with wounded, and after March 29th, even they had to stay there.

# 36

So ended the five years and a few odd months I spent with the French Foreign Legion. Hanoi, Haiphong, and a month's sea voyage, and still Dien Bien Phu and the Legion strongpoint, where I had left so many good friends, were holding out against the repeated attacks of three or four Vietminh divisions. Sidi Bel-Abbès once again and the formalities of demobilization, and still the attacks went on. I arrived in Paris just in time to celebrate April 30th at the Legion's base at Fort de Vincennes. It was a sad Camerone. At least eight battalions of the Legion were doomed, and we knew it, though we tried not to admit it. That same day the last reinforcements were dropped into the entrenched camp, mostly legionnaires and others who had never been parachuted before.

They dropped to an absolutely certain death. It was sheer military murder on the part of the High Command.

On the night of May 7th I slept in London for the first time in six years. The next morning at ten o'clock I left my hotel, and the first thing that caught my eye was a newspaper headline—DIEN BIEN PHU FALLS. ISABELLE FIGHTS ON!

I had been expecting it, of course; but it came as a very great shock, all the same. I think I wandered about London all that day in a sort of numbed daze. I bought the papers and read the accounts avidly. When I had gleaned all the information I could from the London ones, I bought *Figaro* and *Le Monde* and read them too. One thought kept running through my head. Isabelle was fighting on. In Isabelle were hundreds of men with whom I had ate and slept, fought and drunk for years. They were fighting on!

That evening I walked into a couple of friends I had not seen or corresponded with for seven years.

'Hallo, old chap, been away?' asked one of them.

'Yes. First time in London for six years.'

'Oh really? You look as if you need a drink. Let's go and have one. Must say you're looking pretty brown. Where have you sprung from?'

'Far East. Indo-China. Three doubles, please, miss.'

'Good Lord! Isn't that where the French are taking a bit of a knock? What were you doing out there, old boy?'

'I was with the French Foreign Legion.'

'You don't say so. What a lark! Here, Jack, listen. He's been with the Foreign Legion. How long were you with them, old chap?'

'Just over five years,' I said.

'Is it true,' asked the man addressed as Jack, in a rather supercilious manner. 'Is it true that this Legion thing is chock-a-block full of SS men?'

'No,' I answered, rather wearily, 'not to my knowledge.'

'Oh, come now, old fellow,' blustered Jack. 'There's no smoke without fire, you know.'

'I say, old boy,' broke in the other man, whose name was Harry. 'You weren't by any chance in this place Din Bin Poo, or whatever it's called, were you?'

'I left about the middle of March,' I replied. 'I was lucky, actually. I was due for repatriation. Had I been due to leave with the next batch ten days later, I should still be there.'

The barman switched on the radio.

'Peking radio,' crackled forth from the loudspeaker, 'said today that all French Union Forces at Dien Bien Phu had surrendered. The radio did not mention . . .'

'Judging from the reports, I should imagine you're pretty glad not to be there, eh, old man?' asked Harry.

I made an impatient gesture, and went on listening.

'... added that about two hours after the fortress itself had fallen, two thousand troops in the isolated southern outpost named "Isabelle" tried to break out. They were annihilated. ...'

Across the crunch of exploding shells and the rattle of machine-guns cut a voice.

'Guenther's had it. Send Sibley over to command set.'
'Who the hell's going to work battalion?'
'Nobody! *Fallen lassen!* Drop it. You'll have to work it yourself or do without a battalion radio. We must keep in touch with Dien at all costs.'
'Right. Off you go, Sibley!'

The Swiss jumped out of his hole and began running across the hundred and twenty yards of death which separated him from the Isabelle command post. A bullet tore a strip of burning meat from his right shoulder as he ran. He felt the warm blood running stickily over his shoulder-blade. But this was no time for worrying about trifles. He realized that he was probably the only radio operator left alive out of the three Legion battalions in the strong-point. Sibley ran on. A salvo of mortar bombs burst all around him. He was choked by the acrid smoke from the explosions, but scarcely felt the splinter which pierced his chest and lodged itself in his left lung.

He fell, rather than leapt, into the radio operator's hole and, pushing the lifeless body of Guenther away from the set, snatched the headset from his ears. One of the headphones was covered with blood and bits of brain, which he wiped away with the sleeve of his tattered shirt before adjusting the apparatus on his head.

'Isabelle calling Dien Bien Phu, Isabelle calling Dien Bien Phu. *Répondez!*'

'Dien Bien Phu calling Isabelle,' came the crackling, metallic answer. 'Dien Bien Phu calling Isabelle and Hanoi. Commanders to sets. Wait!'

Sibley made a sign to the colonel who, crouching in his own hole a couple of yards away, took up the spare headset and fitted it over his ears.

'Dien calling Isabelle and Hanoi. Situation here hopeless. I must surrender. Isabelle at the discretion of its commander. *Bonne chance*, Isabelle. I am closing down and destroying radio. *Terminé!*'

The harsh crackling caused by the emission of the Dien Bien Phu radio set, which had continued uninterrupted for nearly sixty days, suddenly ceased, and its place was taken by the faint strains of dance music from some short-wave transmitter in Japan.

The colonel stood up and hailed his three battalion commanders in turn. Cupping his hands over his mouth he shouted, 'Dien has surrendered. We are three battalions of the Legion here. We fight on.'

He turned to Sibley. 'Send something to that effect to Hanoi,' he said. The Swiss took up his microphone and began transmitting. He coughed, and a few drops of blood spattered on to the mouthpiece. He completed the message and coughed again. This time a whole torrent of blood welled up out of his mouth and flowed down the front of his shirt. He leant his forehead against the instrument panel and lost consciousness.

Two hundred yards away *Adjutant* McAndrew was trying hurriedly to regroup the two companies he was now commanding. Before him, silhouetted against the red glow of the fires which had already broken out in Dien Bien Phu, he could see the little white cross on his captain's grave. From a slit-trench fifty yards back, the lieutenant who was now commanding the battalion transmitted the colonel's orders.

'We are to fight on,' he concluded.

'What the hell!' cried McAndrew. 'I should damn well think so. Jaderny, what's the situation on your front?'

'All right, except that we can't move,' Jaderny shouted back. He was commanding all that remained of a company. 'The Viets have broken into our trenches about thirty yards in front of me and have got a whole bunch of machine-guns trained on us. Every time we poke our heads out, they let us have it. I'd like to get Nagy and four other wounded back to the first-aid post, but every time I try it the Viets let loose.'

As sometimes happens in the heat of the fiercest battle, all was suddenly silence. For a full thirty seconds no rifle barked, no machine-gun chattered, no shell exploded. From Jaderny's trenches could be heard the faint, muffled groans of the wounded and the soft, metallic clicking of a machine-gun charger being reloaded. From the enemy trenches came the gabble of a quickly whispered order, finishing with the Annamite word *maulen*— hurry up. This made the legionnaires unaccountably laugh, and somebody who was humming the Bridal March from *Lohengrin* stopped suddenly because he thought everybody was laughing at him. Then somebody fired a heavy machine-gun and everything opened up again.

At eight o'clock in the evening ammunition returns were called for, and it became obvious from the result that the stronghold could not last out much longer. The colonel gave orders for a general break-out at nine-thirty, and for the strictest economy in ammunition expenditure until zero hour.

The legionnaires settled down to a wait of fifty minutes. This, they knew, was to be the supreme hour of their lives. The hour which, if they lived, would be for ever branded in letters of fire on their memories. The hour in which, if they died, they would die as they were destined to die, as men.

The moonless sky was now lurid with the crimson glow from the fires in the main stronghold of Dien Bien Phu. Dien had fallen. The defenders had burnt their stores. They were overcome, surrounded. The enemy, from the beetling heights of the hills surrounding the pudding-bowl, had been able to observe his fire, and observe it extremely well. Dien had surrendered. Had fallen. But Isabelle remained. And in Isabelle were three battalions of the Foreign Legion. They would never surrender.

Nine o'clock. From somewhere in the entrenched camp a voice began to sing:

> '*Heute wollen wir probier'n*
> *Einen neuen Marsch marschier'n*
> *Durch den schoenen Westerwald.*
> *Ach! Es pfeift, der Wind, so kalt . . . .*'

At first a dozen, then twenty, then a hundred voices took up the chorus. An officer blew a blast on his whistle and shouted for silence; but the colonel, who was a legionnaire with twenty years' service, said, 'No! Let 'em sing. They may never be able to sing again. Let 'em sing till they burst their bloody lungs. 'T'were better thus than to let 'em burst their hearts.'

A cheer greeted these words, and when the song was finished the colonel said to a corporal who was crouching in a trench nearby, 'Come on, Rousseau, start up the old *Képis Blancs*. I want to hear it once again before I die.'

And Rousseau, a very different Rousseau from the one who had bragged in the courtyard of the Bas Fort Saint-Nicolas five years before, began singing that greatest of all songs of the Legion:

> '*La rue appartient à celui qui y descend.*
> *La rue appartient au drapeau des képis blancs.*
> *Autour gronde la haine. Autour grondent les dogmes qu'on abat.*
> *Foulant la boue sombre vont les képis blancs.*'

It is a sad song, a song which is sung softly, and there was not a legionnaire in the whole of the Isabelle strong-point capable of singing who did not hum the chorus. Even the wounded, writhing on their stretchers, forced their parched lips to murmur the last lines:

> '*Combien sont tombés au hasard d'un clair matin,*
> *De nos camarades qui souriaient au destin?*
> *Nous tomberons sans doute* . . . .'

The blast of a whistle cut across the silence which followed the last refrain. The orders were rapped out.

'Legion, prepare for the assault! Fix bayonets! You know what you have to do. Charge!'

From the three or four hundred voices still capable of shouting goes up an unearthly cry: the cry of men about to meet their death and not caring how or when they meet it. The colonel shouts a final word.

'*Vive la Légion!*' Four hundred voices reply, '*Vive la Légion!*' and the echo is submerged in the hell of machine-gun fire and exploding shells which marks the end of Isabelle and of one more episode in the history of the men who have nothing to lose.

'I said, I should imagine you're pretty glad not to be there, old boy,' repeated Harry.

I came back ten thousand miles and found myself in the bar of a London pub, talking to two men in city suits and bowler hats.

'I'm so sorry. What did you say?' I mumbled.

Harry repeated his question for the third time.

'Aren't you jolly glad not to have been there?'

'Not particularly,' I answered.